Flex on Rails

Developer's Library

ESSENTIAL REFERENCES FOR PROGRAMMING PROFESSIONALS

Developer's Library books are designed to provide practicing programmers with unique, high-quality references and tutorials on the programming languages and technologies they use in their daily work.

All books in the *Developer's Library* are written by expert technology practitioners who are especially skilled at organizing and presenting information in a way that's useful for other programmers.

Key titles include some of the best, most widely acclaimed books within their topic areas:

PHP & MySQL Web Development
Luke Welling & Laura Thomson
ISBN 978-0-672-32916-6

MySQL
Paul DuBois
ISBN-13: 978-0-672-32938-8

Linux Kernel Development
Robert Love
ISBN-13: 978-0-672-32946-3

Python Essential Reference
David Beazley
ISBN-13: 978-0-672-32862-6

Programming in Objective-C
Stephen G. Kochan
ISBN-13: 978-0-321-56615-7

PostgreSQL
Korry Douglas
ISBN-13: 978-0-672-33015-5

Developer's Library books are available at most retail and online bookstores, as well as by subscription from Safari Books Online at **safari.informit.com**

**Developer's
Library**
informit.com/devlibrary

Flex on Rails

Building Rich Internet Applications with Adobe Flex 3 and Rails 2

Tony Hillerson
Daniel Wanja

✦✦ Addison-Wesley

Upper Saddle River, NJ • Boston • Indianapolis • San Francisco
New York • Toronto • Montreal • London • Munich • Paris • Madrid
Capetown • Sydney • Tokyo • Singapore • Mexico City

Flex on Rails

ISBN-13: 978-0-321-54337-0
ISBN-10:   0-321-54337-8

Text printed in the United States on recycled paper at RR Donnelley in Crawfordsville, Indiana.

First Printing, December 2008

Trademarks

Many of the designations used by manufacturers and sellers to distinguish their products are claimed as trademarks. Where those designations appear in this book, and the publisher was aware of a trademark claim, the designations have been printed with initial capital letters or in all capitals.

Warning and Disclaimer

The authors and publisher have taken care in the preparation of this book, but make no expressed or implied warranty of any kind and assume no responsibility for errors or omissions. No liability is assumed for incidental or consequential damages in connection with or arising out of the use of the information or programs contained herein.

Bulk Sales

The publisher offers excellent discounts on this book when ordered in quantity for bulk purchases or special sales, which may include electronic versions and/or custom covers and content particular to your business, training goals, marketing focus, and branding interests. For more information, please contact:

> **U.S. Corporate and Government Sales**
> **(800) 382-3419**
> **corpsales@pearsontechgroup.com**

For sales outside the United States, please contact:

> **International Sales**
> **international@pearson.com**

Visit us on the Web: informit.com/aw

Library of Congress Cataloging-in-Publication Data

Hillerson, Tony.
  Flex on Rails : building rich internet applications with
Adobe Flex 3 and Rails 2 / Tony Hillerson, Daniel Wanja.
      p.   cm.
  Includes index.
  ISBN 978-0-321-54337-0 (pbk. : alk. paper)
1. Flex (Computer file) 2. Ruby on rails (Electronic resource)
3. Internet programming. 4. Application software—Development.
5. Web site development—Computer programs. I. Wanja, Daniel. II. Title.

QA76.625.H57 2008
006.7'6—dc22

2008044357

Editor-in-Chief
Karen Gettman

Senior Acquisitions Editor
Chuck Toporek

Senior Development Editor
Chris Zahn

Managing Editor
John Fuller

Full-Service Production Manager
Julie B. Nahil

Editorial Assistant
Romny French

Project Editor
diacriTech LLC

Book Designer
Gary Adair

Compositor
diacriTech LLC

❖

*This book is dedicated to the great
people in the Flex and Rails
communities. You've taught us a lot in the
last few years, and here's hoping that both
communities gain a little more overlap
because of this book. Cheers!*

—Daniel and Tony

❖

Contents at a Glance

Contents

Foreword

This is the decade of the web application: business logic and data storage provided on a centralized server or servers while end users interact with the user interface on their own machines. In 2004, Macromedia (now Adobe) took the world of web applications further with the introduction of Flex. Flex is a set of languages, frameworks, and tools for building Rich Internet Applications (RIAs)—the evolution of the web application. By using the ubiquitous Flash Player, installed on over 98 percent of Internet-connected PCs, application developers can deliver a top-notch user experience while still leveraging the compelling distribution and update model of the web application.

The latest version of Flex, Adobe Flex 3, was released in early 2008 to great fanfare. This version added more capabilities to the IDE used by most Flex developers, Adobe Flex Builder, including a profiler, enhanced design view, and refactoring support. We also greatly enhanced the data visualization capabilities of Flex by improving our charting controls and adding hierarchical data grids and simple OLAP components. This release has been our most successful to date, with the number of developers adopting Flex growing by over 130 percent year over year.

One thing that encouraged this kind of adoption is that Flex 3 was released as open source under the Mozilla Public License. As developers investigate the technologies they'll use for future software development, a criterion has come to the forefront to have visibility into future plans and potentially influence them. Adobe has acknowledged this and has been embracing open source and standards heavily over the last few years, including the standardization of PDF, opening of the SWF file format, and, most importantly, the open source release of Flex as well as the data connectivity solution, BlazeDS.

Flex is at its best when displaying and allowing the modification of data, and BlazeDS provides a number of ways for moving that data from server to client and back again. BlazeDS includes the specification to the Action Message Format (AMF), which allows for more efficient data transfer than any other standard technique on the web today. While most of the runtime code for BlazeDS is written in Java, the available specifications allow any back-end technology to leverage AMF for data transfer. And Ruby on Rails is one of the back-ends that supports AMF through a number of solutions, including RubyAMF and WebORB.

At the same time that Flex has been establishing itself as the best way to produce RIAs, Ruby on Rails has been growing quickly as a top choice for building web applications. With the ability to rapidly create databases, value objects, and business logic, Ruby on Rails is a great back-end choice for a Flex front end. The ease of wiring data together with Rails, combined with the compelling visualizations and user interface elements of Flex, make the two a perfect pair.

Flex on Rails is a great resource for those of you looking to use these two great technologies. Tony Hillerson and Daniel Wanja walk through all of the elements you'll need to know to build an application using Flex and Rails. While this book should not generally serve as a pure introduction to either technology, you do not need extensive experience to benefit from it. The approach is straightforward: get up and running with the two sides talking to each other, then learn the techniques for leveraging the best of both systems. The first section provides broader introductions to areas like data transfer, testing, and using features of the Flex framework and related projects to your advantage. The second section includes examples of some of the more advanced things you'll need to know as you build a robust application. There's no question you're going to be a better Flex and Rails developer when you're done reading this book.

There may be no better time in software development than now. With constant improvements in the tools and technologies for building applications, you've chosen two that are at the forefront of the revolution. I think I speak for all of us at Adobe when I say that we're excited to see what you can do with them.

Matt Chotin
Senior Product Manager
Adobe Systems, Inc.

Preface

In 2004 yet another framework for making websites appeared. It was called Ruby on Rails, and when web and enterprise developers who had never heard of Ruby before started to work with it, they discovered that it wasn't like all the others. Why?

Rails offers the promise of fewer configuration files, less boilerplate code, less red tape, and, most of all, the promise of having fun again while programming. Rails was designed to make development more about getting common development tasks done by following conventions, not offering endless flexibility for the remote possibility of connecting up with any number of hypothetical legacy back-ends sometime in the future. By taking away unnecessary choices and offering simple solutions for common problems, Rails lets developers focus on writing applications, and developers have paid Rails back in accolades and adoption.

Around the same time as Rails was emerging, Macromedia (later bought by Adobe) was bringing a product codenamed "Royale" to market as Flex—a server-side Flash compiler. Flash had been experiencing a groundswell of developers wanting to build rich interfaces for web applications, not just animations or "Punch the Monkey" ads. Flash developers loved that they could build interfaces that would be extremely hard, if not impossible, to produce in HTML and JavaScript, but the Flash IDE was more suited to timeline animations. Flex changed all that by offering an easy-to-understand XML language for developing Flash interfaces, as well as a component set that made it dead simple to build applications. Flex 2 made things even better by taking the Flex compiler off the server so that there was no requirement of building and deploying Flash movies (SWFs) using the Flex framework and compiler. Flex 3 is one step better by being open source!

The Flex language has come a long way too. Bruce Eckel, the author of such books as *Thinking in C++, Second Edition* (Prentice Hall, 2000) and *Thinking in Java, Fourth Edition* (Prentice Hall, 2006), said it best when he said, "Flex is a DSL for graphics, multimedia, and UIs" (www.artima.com/weblogs/viewpost.jsp?thread=193593). DSL, or Domain Specific Language, is a language with terms that match up well with a certain problem domain, and the term DSL should resonate with Rails developers. Flex, more than HTML with JavaScript, is a language for building rich interfaces quickly and easily.

Flex and Rails developers haven't crossed paths that often, but more and more as the word gets out about each technology, developers want to know what these two are about. Having worked for years with both Flex and Rails, we believe that both have something powerful to offer developers who want to build desktop-like functionality into web apps quickly, in a team environment, with the ability to be agile and react to the ever-changing requirements of building and delivering an application to the web.

Audience for This Book

Chances are you're reading this introduction to figure out if this book is for you. Have a look at these "stories" and see if any of them sound familiar.

Rick—Rails Guy

Background	Worked with Java for years: Struts, EJB, Spring, all that. Then discovered the joy of working with Rails and hasn't looked back.
Overheard	"Edge Rails? Is there any other kind?"
Goal	"HTML/CSS/JavaScript is fine for simple interfaces, and I don't mind how crufty it is as long as I don't have to deal with it. I'd be interested in finding out how to build richer interfaces, though—interfaces that don't just look better but also give users better tools and an overall better experience."

Jill—Java to Flex Convert

Background	Worked with Swing and understands desktop applications. Got into "The Web" and did lots of J2EE. Loves Flex for the ability to build desktop-like functionality on the web, usually in front of J2EE back-ends.
Overheard	"GridBagLayout? What were they thinking?"
Goal	"I love working with Flex, but I'm getting a little tired of all the work it takes to set up the back-end with Java. Enterprise software is great when I need the flexibility of all that configuration, but what about when I have a straightforward model and I just want it to work? There's got to be an easier way."

Pete—Flash/PHP guy

Background	Has done lots of design work and building of interfaces with Flash. Has built websites with PHP and also integrated PHP back-ends with Flash.
Overheard	"I don't [skip intro], I [make intro]"
Goal	"I know what I can do in Flash, and I know how to feed Flash UIs with data from PHP. I'd really like to see what this Flex thing is all about though, since I'm not always building timeline animations. I've also heard a lot about Rails and how easy it is to get a back-end up and running."

If any of these stories sound a bit like you, then this book is for you. Rails and Flex have both revolutionized the way we develop web applications on both the front- and the back-ends.

Developers who have found Rails and left the world of enterprise framework stacks behind would very rarely willingly go back to the slow development cycles and bloated boilerplate code they had to endure. Flex developers have found the declarative XML language much cleaner and less crufty than HTML and able to do things like 3D and video that would be impossible without Flex.

Of course, there are the normal disclaimers. Rails isn't for every project and neither is Flex. David Heinemeier Hansson wrote about PHP in a blog post (www.loudthinking.com/posts/23-the-immediacy-of-php):

> I've been writing a little bit of PHP again today. That platform has really received an unfair reputation. For the small things I've been using it for lately, it's absolutely perfect. . . .

> For the small chores, being quick and effective matters far more than long-term maintenance concerns. Or how pretty the code is. PHP scales down like no other package for the web and it deserves more credit for tackling that scope.

And the same goes for Flex. HTML doesn't need to be compiled and needs no special tools besides the ubiquitous browser to view it, whereas Flex needs a compiler and the Flash Player. However, when you find yourself with a medium to large web project with a database back-end, working with a team on a set of complex forms, rich visual interactions, video integration, 3D features, or a very large set of views, then Flex and Rails make a great choice.

The Flex and Rails story has a lot to do with discovering the integration capabilities and learning the ins and outs of making them talk to each other. We've gone a bit beyond that, though, and tried to assemble enough information about the next steps, common tasks, and how-to's that developers will want to know about sooner or later.

We thought that, for the most part, Flex developers who have never used Rails will want to learn some of the features that they'll run into during integration, but also during daily work. Likewise, developers who are already familiar with Rails will want to know a bit more about how Flex works than just consuming Rails' XML services.

> **Note**
>
> This book is not an introduction to Rails nor to Flex. If you haven't used at least one of these technologies before, you may find yourself a little lost. If you've used or are pretty familiar with one technology and haven't been exposed to the other, then this book is a great companion to reading a primer about the other, either first or at the same time.

What's in This Book?

The book is designed to take you through the process of learning about integrating and beginning to explore Flex and Rails. In Part I, Flex and Rails Essentials, we cover the core topics that you need to be familiar with in order to get you Flex and Rails projects going.

In Chapter 1, Developing with Flex and Rails, we talk about how to set up your environment. Then in Chapter 2, Passing Data with XML, and Chapter 3, Flex with RESTful Services, we'll show you how to integrate Flex and Rails using XML, both with a regular and with a RESTful Rails service.

Chapter 4, Using Fluint to Test a Flex with Rails Application, addresses testing. Chapter 5, Passing Data with AMF, discusses how to integrate Flex with RubyAMF, which uses the Flash-native AMF protocol.

Sooner or later you're going to want to learn how to debug your applications on the front- and back-ends to learn about what's going on or going wrong with them, so Chapter 6, Debugging, discusses debugging in both environments.

One of the great features of Flex is that it's easy to start making very powerful data visualization features available in your application, so Chapter 7, Data Visualization, introduces several pieces of that topic.

Chapter 8, Flex MVC Frameworks, talks a bit about a common topic in the Flex community—which frameworks to choose—and discusses two popular ones.

Chapter 9, Performance and Optimization, finishes the main section of the book with a discussion of how to get to the bottom of performance problems in both Flex and Rails and some tips about optimizing your applications.

Part II, Cookbook Recipes, was a lot of fun to bring to you. It's in the form of a cookbook, which contains many "recipes" or short discussions and how-to's about topics that you'll have questions about at some point. In Chapters 10 through 22, we cover everything from working with common source control systems and authenticating to pushing data and deploying Flex and Rails applications.

- Chapter 10: Source Control Flex and Rails Projects
- Chapter 11: Building Flex with Rake
- Chapter 12: Deploying Flex and Rails Applications
- Chapter 13: Read the Source!
- Chapter 14: Using Observers to Clean up Code
- Chapter 15: Authenticating
- Chapter 16: Reusing Commands with Prana Sequences
- Chapter 17: Hierarchical Data with RubyAMF
- Chapter 18: Advanced Data Grid and Awesome Nested Set
- Chapter 19: Runtime Flex Configuration with Prana
- Chapter 20: Server Push with Juggernaut
- Chapter 21: Communicating between Flex and JavaScript
- Chapter 22: File Upload

Let's Get Started

Now that you've decided to take the first steps to putting Flex on Rails, let's take a look at what you'll need to get your development environment in shape. Start with Chapter 1, Developing with Flex and Rails, to make sure you have all the pieces in place.

Acknowledgments from Tony Hillerson

I remember a job interview for a company called Taliant in December 2004. One of the interviewers had a weird accent, and I couldn't give my full attention to the interview because I was trying to place it. I thought I heard some French, but I was picking up German as well. "Is it Swiss?" I wondered. I wasn't brave enough to ask, but it turns out I was right. That was my coauthor, Daniel. I mumbled some stuff about design patterns or something, not too impressive, I'm sure, but something was enough to get me the job. That job introduced me to a lot of people who were excited about using Flash as the front end to an "enterprise" application, which was my main motivation for getting the job because I was excited, too. Daniel, Tom Wilcoxen, Sean Voisen, Rajesh Karup, Dustin Burkhardt, John Blanco, and many others taught me a lot about Flash, as well as a lot about programming. Daniel got another technology called Flex into a small piece of the application that we were building. Once I got a chance to check that out, it was painfully obvious how much we could have used that on the main project! Even in its 1.0 and 1.5 incarnations as a server-side application, it was exactly what we needed to build user interfaces in Flash.

Lee Marlow, another coworker, turned me on to a language called Ruby, and when Daniel, Tom, and Lee all started talking about how great Rails was, I jumped on the bandwagon, too. I never would have thought that it would have taken me here: to cowriting a book that hopefully helps people learn how to use these great technologies together.

A big change happened for me when another, younger, spikier-haired coworker left to join a fledgling band of Flash and Flex geeks. Sean Christmann left and joined a company called EffectiveUI in 2006, and I followed soon after. I left because I didn't like the drive to work anymore and the new office was closer, but also because I was very interested in working with Flex full time. Of course, I brought the Rails bug with me, and luckily, I've been able to use both technologies on project work with EffectiveUI. A rare opportunity, and one I'm very grateful for.

Thanks to:

- Daniel, for all your mentoring over the years, and all your help writing this book and our RailsConf 2008 talk.

- Aaron Smith for "giving" me RubyAMF to maintain. Derek Wichusen for approaching me to write this book. Chuck Toporek for patience while we got this thing going.

- The rest of the team at Addison-Wesley: Romny French, Chris Zahn, Julie Nahil, and Chuti Prasertsith, and the folks at diacriTech. Everyone at EffectiveUI for letting me geek out with the technologies I love and work with the greatest group of people I've ever worked with.

- Matt Chotin and Deepa Subramaniam from the Flex Team for your hard work and fun times at conferences.

- And, of course, Lori and Titus, my wife and son, for letting me spend so much of their time writing this book. It's been a huge effort for me, but I'm proud of it. I love you guys.

Acknowledgments from Daniel Wanja

Writing this book all started when Tony sent me the following email:

Tue, Jul 10, 2007 at 5:11 PM

Daniel,

Derek contacted me today about co-authoring a book on Flex and Rails. Details are below. I'm going to take him up on it. His idea, since he's at least as busy as I am, is to have a set of authors with responsibilities of around 4-5 chapters, mostly around building functionality in a sample application and describing it (correct me if I'm wrong, Derek).

Are you interested? Don't worry, I think we can edit your crazy Swiss-talk:) Tony.

Here's what I answered:

Tue, Jul 10, 2007 at 9:37 PM

Hi Tony,

Being part of a team to write a book is an appealing idea. Can we write it in French? No just kidding, I feel more comfortable writing in English. This would give me a chance to improve my writing and find my voice (like Dave Thomas says). Just for a background to Derek, I was always attracted to having a Flex UI on top of a Rails application...even way back (early 2005) when it didn't made sense (Flex being an expensive enterprise framework and Rails being opensource). You can find that work under http://flexon-rails.com/. I don't think any of that code works anymore, but was fun playing with it. Also on my blog, http://onrails.org, there are several articles relating my "experiments" integrating Flex and Rails.

Daniel.

This email exchange is basically when I decided to jump on board writing this book, and I am glad I did, but little did I know about how involved this process is. This book wouldn't have been possible without all the people I worked with and interacted with over the last twenty years of my career. The list is long, so thanks to all. If I limit myself to those directly related to Flex and Rails and this book, I can keep the "Thanks list" shorter . . . here we go:

So first, thanks to Derek Wischusen for starting the process of writing this book and involving Tony, who then involved me. Derek quickly realized this wasn't the time for him to write this book and moved on to other things, but he helped get the ball rolling, and without him, this book wouldn't have seen the light of day. Writing this book was a very challenging and surprisingly pleasant experience; I learned so much about myself, my limits, and more importantly, about how to express and transfer my thoughts into words. Tony Hillerson, the coauthor of this book, being an experienced writer and knowledgeable teacher, was a great mentor during this process. Thank you for that and all the heavy lifting you did.

I wouldn't have come to Rails so early if it weren't for Lee Marlow, who kept telling me how cool ActiveRecord was and how Rails had huge potential at a time when it just wasn't on anybody's radar. Of course, I had to try Rails and it wasn't long after, together with Lee, that we created a framework to have Flex and Rails communicate. Lee was also a reviewer on this book, and as with any project I work on with him, his eye for detail was invaluable. Special thoughts to Lee and Marla's son, Jay, who brightened our lives with his incredible smiles during the time we wrote the book. We love you, Jay.

Thanks to Solomon White for hiring me on my first Rails project: I learned so much from you, and not just from a Rails perspective. To Lee, Lomax, and Solomon, thanks for putting a hold on our startup, MySpyder.net, while I completed this book. On the Flex side, it all started with Sean Voisen, who first got me into the beta of Flex, then Royale, and for bringing me on board on these different, cool projects. Oh yeah, and thanks for reviewing this book. There isn't anyone I have spent more time coding Flex with than Rajesh Kurup over the last couple of years; thanks for being so patient with me. I just joined an exceptional team at Pinnacol that is creating all their new apps with Flex and Ruby on Rails, and it's fun to be on board with so many smart people. Thanks to DeLynn Berry for getting me in there. And thanks to the entire team at Addison-Wesley.

Writing a book without a supportive family is impossible. So I cannot express how much of this book was possible thanks to the love of my life, my wife, Kathy, who is an incredible supporter of all the crazy things I do and who managed to deliver our lovely girl, Nina, on the exact original due date of the book. And, of course, to my kids who make all this worthwhile. Nina, Joshua, and Noah, I love you.

About the Authors

Tony Hillerson is a software architect for EffectiveUI. He graduated from Ambassador University with a BA in MIS. On any given day, he may be working with Flex, Java, Rails, Maven, Ant, Ruby, Rake, Capistrano, or shell scripts. Tony maintains RubyAMF, a Rails plug-in that allows Flex applications to pass AMF messages to and from Rails. Tony has been a speaker at 360Flex, Adobe MAX, and RailsConf, as well as at local user groups. In his nonexistent free time, Tony enjoys playing the bass, playing *World of Warcraft,* making electronic music, brewing beer, learning Latin, and studying philosophy. Tony lives outside Denver, Colorado, with his wife, Lori, and son, Titus.

Daniel Wanja, a native of Switzerland, has lived in Denver, Colorado, for more than six years with his wife and three children. Daniel is a dynamic, skilled enterprise software architect and developer with more than twenty years' experience. He has worked in the banking, insurance, and high-tech industries around the world, delivering mission-critical software. Daniel is president and part owner of two Flex and Ruby on Rails consulting agencies, Nouvelles Solutions, Inc., in Denver (http://n-so.com), and ProDesign Sarl in Geneva, Switzerland (http://prodesign.ch). Daniel started the http://onrails.org blog on Ruby on Rails and related matters in 2005.

Flex and Rails Essentials

Developing with Flex and Rails

There's no better way to learn new technology than to see it run, make changes, and see what happens as a result. As we walk through examples in the book, you'll be running the sample code as we go, so set up your environment to build and run Flex and Rails applications. You're encouraged to change the examples in any way you'd like.

What's great about the Flex and Rails ecosystem is that all the software you need to build production-ready applications is freely available, as long as you don't mind using your favorite text editor. For the best experience working with Flex, though, you'll probably want to use Flex Builder.

Installation: What You Need to Get Running

Here's a list of the software you should install to run the basic examples. You may need other software to run more advanced examples, and if so, we'll tell you how to get the software when we cover those topics.

SQLite 3

SQLite is a free and simple database server that requires no configuration to get running. All the Rails examples use SQLite to quickly get up and running.

Installation: Go to www.sqlite.org/ and follow the instructions for your platform. SQLite is already installed on MacOS Leopard.

Ruby

Ruby is an open source, interpreted, object-oriented language. Rails is written in Ruby: thus, Ruby on Rails. You can find out more here: www.ruby-lang.org/en/. All the sample code was written using Ruby 1.8.

Mac Installation: Ruby comes preinstalled on Leopard and Tiger. You can test this by typing `ruby -v` at a command prompt. If you get a "command not found" error, go to www.ruby-lang.org/en/ and download the latest version for your Mac.

Windows Installation: Go to http://rubyforge.org/projects/rubyinstaller/ and download the latest version. The One-Click Ruby installer comes with Ruby, a lot of popular gems, and a syntax-highlighting editor.

Linux Installation: If Ruby isn't already installed, use your system's package manager to install Ruby. Test to see if Ruby is installed by typing `ruby -v` at a terminal. If you get a "command not found" error, you'll need to install it.

Ruby Gems

Ruby Gems is a package manager system for Ruby. A gem is something like a plug-in for Ruby. What's great about gems, though, is that Ruby Gems knows how to install them from the web when you simply type a gem's name at the command line of your browser. Ruby Gems can handle updating, uninstalling, and managing different versions of the gem. Ruby Gems 1.2 was used during the writing of this book.

Installation: Go to http://rubyforge.org/projects/rubygems/ download, and follow the instructions for your operating system.

Rails

Installation: Rails can be installed as a gem by typing `gem install rails` at a command line. Rails comes preinstalled with Mac OSX 10.5 (Leopard). Unless otherwise noted, examples for the book should work with Rails 2.1.

Mac and Linux users: You'll probably need to run the `gem` command through sudo: `sudo gem install rails`.

Flex SDK

If you decide to use Flex Builder, you'll already have SDK. Otherwise, install Flex SDK. All examples of the book should work with any version of the Flex 3 SDK.

Installation: Go to www.adobe.com/products/flex/downloads/ and download the latest SDK; follow the instructions. Make sure that mxmlc is in your path; if you type `mxmlc` from your command line and get an error, consult the documentation on how to make sure mxmlc is in the path for your system.

Mongrel

Mongrel is an HTTP server that knows how to run Rails applications. Most Rails applications in production run on Mongrel, so it makes sense to run Mongrel locally to help keep your development environment as much like your production environment as possible. Learn more about Mongrel here: http://mongrel.rubyforge.org/. Mongrel is optional, since Rails ships with a web server called WEBrick. However, most people use Mongrel, so it doesn't hurt to get used to it.

Installation: Mongrel can be installed as a gem by typing `gem install mongrel` at a command prompt.

SQLite Gem

Install the SQLite gem to help Ruby best work with SQLite.

Installation: Install as a gem with `gem install sqlite3-ruby`.

Editors

All these editors are optional. Use any text editor you'd like to edit Flex or Ruby files. If you don't want to get Flex Builder, you can instead install the free Flex SDK and use the command line tools to compile your Flex project. See the instructions above to install the Flex SDK.

Eclipse

Eclipse is an IDE Framework. It's most famous for its Java IDE, but it supports other languages with other plug-ins. If you want to run a Rails editor alongside your Flex Editor, install Eclipse first, and then install RadRails and the Flex Builder plug-in. If you plan to use a different text editor for Rails, skip Eclipse and just install Flex Builder.

Installation: Go to www.eclipse.org/downloads/ and get the distribution you'd like. Download the program, and follow the instructions.

Aptana/RadRails

Aptana with RadRails is an IDE plug-in for Eclipse for HTML and Rails projects. Download and install the Studio, and follow the instructions for installing the Rad Rails plug-in.

Installation: Go to www.aptana.com/ and get the Aptana studio, download and install.

ruby-debug, ruby-debug-ide

Aptana requires these gems to debug ruby code. If you'd like to debug from the command line instead, as discussed in Chapter 6, Debugging, you'll at least need ruby-debug.

Installation: Install as a gem by typing `gem install ruby-debug` and `gem install ruby-debug-ide` at a console.

Flex Builder

Working with Flex projects is a lot easier with Flex Builder. Flex Builder not only provides code-coloring and code-hinting, but also provide tools that really help as your project starts to grow. Tools include an easy way to find files, methods across the project, and powerful refactoring tools. It also has a great design mode view that helps when laying out your Flex UI.

Installation: Go to www.adobe.com/go/tryflex to get the free trial and download. Install Flex Builder either as a standalone application or as an Eclipse plug-in. The benefit to working with the Eclipse plug-in is that you can work with other plug-ins, such as RadRails, in the same IDE. Experiment with a few different methods until you hit on the one you like.

TextMate

You can't mention Rails and editors without mentioning TextMate. Unfortunately, TextMate is only for the Mac, but Rails developers swear by it. It has some great Ruby- and Rails-specific features, such as the capability to run Ruby code right from the editor with Command-R (great for editing and running tests), but it is still easy to use and lightweight.

Installation: Purchase TextMate from http://macromates.com/ and follow the instructions for installation.

Once everything is installed, we can start to look at how a Flex and Rails application is structured.

The Structure of a Flex and Rails Application

Flex and Rails have something of a long-distance relationship. Flex runs in the browser using Adobe's Flash plug-in. It's possible to run Flex alongside HTML applications in the browser, as you'll see in the cookbook recipe in Chapter 21, Communicating between Flex and Javascript, but most Flex applications run by themselves, taking up the whole browser window. When that's the case, you use none of the view part of Rails, only the controllers.

In fact, Flex generally knows nothing special about Rails except that some kind of service exists at a certain URL. Since Rails excels at providing services for different types of clients, serving HTML, XML, and, as you'll see, AMF-formatted data from the same controllers with little extra code, Rails doesn't need to know anything special about the Flex side of the application.

We recommend keeping the source code for the Flex and the Rails sides of the application separate from each other and not putting the Flex code inside the Rails project, as might be your first impulse. Another reason for keeping things separate is that the Rails code is deployed to a server as-is, since it's interpreted and not compiled. Flex is compiled into a SWF file, which is all you need to deploy. The Flex source code doesn't go on the server with the Rails code.

The way we like to organize our projects is to put the Flex and Rails code side by side in a directory, in directories named flex and rails, just like in Figure 1.1. Any other code that may have to do with both parts of the project can go here too.

Figure 1.1   The flex and rails directories.

Rails has a standard directory layout, and it makes it easy to create a project by typing `rails <project name>` from your command line. That command creates a ready-to-run Rails application in a directory named after the project. If you're already in the directory, you could type `rails .` to create a project in place. Look at Figure 1.2, and we'll go over the contents of a Rails application directory.

Figure 1.2   Rails directory structure.

The **app** directory contains the **models**, **views**, and **controllers**, along with view **helpers** in appropriately named directories. Those files contain all of the application logic. The **config** directory contains configuration for the application and plug-ins you install. The **db** directory contains information, called migrations, on how to set up the database. **Doc** contains generated documentation for your application. **Lib** is where you put any sort of code, such as helper scripts and extra rake tasks, that doesn't fit into another place. Log files go in the **log** directory. The **public** directory is the root of the public-facing web application—static HTML, Javascript, and CSS files go here, and this is also where your Flex-generated SWF files go. See the cookbook recipe in Chapter 12, Deploying Flex and Rails Applications, for more information. The **script** directory contains some standard script files for doing things like starting the server or generating code. **Test** is almost as important as **app**—it's where your unit, functional, and integrations tests go, the test models, controllers, and the full rails application, respectively. The **tmp** directory is where a lot of temporary files go. You'll probably never use this directory. Lastly, the **vendor** directory is where, among some other things, plug-ins are installed by running ./script/plugin install.

Cross-Domain Policy Files

One thing you may need to know more about as you get further into developing with Flex is a **cross-domain policy file.** Flash won't load data from a server that is not in the domain from which the SWF file originated unless there is a crossdomain.xml in the server's root. More information can be found at this link: http://kb.adobe.com/selfservice/viewContent.do?externalId=tn_14213. If you want to allow Flash to access data, such as XML data served from Rails, a crossdomain.xml that looks like Listing 1.1 can be placed in the Rails public directory.

Listing 1.1 **A basic crossdomain.xml**

```
<?xml version="1.0"?>
<cross-domain-policy>
    <allow-access-from domain="*" />
</cross-domain-policy>
```

This is a very quick overview of the Rails directory structure. The Flex directory structure is a lot simpler at the root, as shown in Figure 1.3.

Figure 1.3   The flex directory structure.

This is the standard new project structure created by Flex Builder. You can choose the same structure if you just use the SDK. The bin-debug directory is where Flex Builder compiles the SWF built from the MXML files. It's called "debug" because Flex Builder can also compile a non-debug version for publishing. The non-debug version is what the Flex SDK compiler compiles by default. The **html-template** directory is created by Flex Builder to contain template HTML files that are useful for building the HTML container for a Flex Application. The **lib** directory is where you put SWC files, or Flash libraries, that get compiled into your application. **Src** is where the source files go. Usually one root MXML application file goes in this directory, and included MXML and ActionScript files go in subdirectories following a package structure similar to Java's.

Now you know how to get around the example source code.

The Example Code

The source code that comes with this book corresponds to chapters, and most chapters have some source code. When parts of each file are discussed, we'll call out where that file is located within the code for that chapter and often which lines we're discussing.

Compiling MXML

If you've made sure that mxmlc is in your path (following the directions from above), then it's relatively easy to compile your MXML source files, with the .mxml extension and a root MXML tag of Application, into SWF files that are viewable in the Flash Player in the browser.

If you have an MXML application named Main.mxml in the src directory, you'd go to that source directory and type:

```
$ mxmlc Main.mxml
```

That would create a SWF file in that directory. For more information about the compiler, go to: http://livedocs.adobe.com/flex/3/html/compilers_13.html. For more information about how to create the HTML wrappers, look here: http://livedocs.adobe.com/flex/3/html/wrapper_01.html.

If you'd like to learn about automating the compilation and common tasks associated with building the Flex project, look at the cookbook recipe in Chapter 11, Building Flex with Rake.

Running the Rails Server

Finally, to run the Rails examples in the source, all you have to do is go to the Rails directory in your console and type `script/server`.

The web server that ships with Rails, Webrick, will run, or if you installed Mongrel, then that should run. The Rails application will be available at http://localhost:3000.

Summary

Now you should have the groundwork in place to start running the examples we'll be covering. Let's get started with running Flex on Rails.

2

Passing Data with XML

Stunning Flex applications can be built on top of Ruby on Rails using XML as data transport. As this book shows, XML is not the only mechanism available for building a Flex application that interfaces with Rails, but XML will be the first choice for many who pass data between Flex and Rails because both environments provide incredible facilities to generate and consume XML. Since Rails embraced the RESTful approach, it has never been easier to get XML data in and out of a Rails application. Since ActionScript 3.0 embraced XML as a native data type with powerful binding and manipulation functions, it has never been easier to consume and generate XML with Flex. Flex can also easily connect to a Rails application via standard `HTTPService`. In this chapter, I will show you how straightforward it is to integrate a Flex front end with a Rails application, enabling you to quickly create awesome applications.

XML in Rails

In this section, we will create a Rails application that manages a list of people you know. The following five command lines create an initial RESTful rails application with a data model and controller ready to run.

```
$ rails rails
$ cd rails
$ rake db:create:all
$ ./script/generate scaffold person first_name:string last_name:string\
 address:text
$ rake db:migrate
```

This is a standard way to begin creation of a Rails application. Just in case you are not familiar with these commands, let's review each one. The `rails` command generates the whole folder structure for a Rails application, with the root folder being the name you passed to the command. In our case, the root folder is called "rails." The `rails` command also creates the different configuration files required, such as the database configuration file, which defines three databases, one for each runtime environment: development, test, and production. In our case, the three databases are named "development.sqlite3," "test.sqlite3," and "production.sqlite3." At that stage, the databases are not yet created; therefore, we use the `rake db:create:all` command to create all three databases. You can, of course, use any tool to create the databases as long as the database configuration file points to the appropriate database.

Now we have an empty database and no application files. The `generate scaffold` command comes into play here. It's a quick way to create the basic elements for a working application by generating an `ActiveRecord` class, a database migration file, a RESTful controller, and the HTML views based on the attributes you pass to the command.

Finally, we run the generated database migration file to create the people table in the development environment. Notice that Rails creates tables based on the plural form of the model name, and the plural of person is people. Now we are ready to create some data.

I will now use the script console to create a person with the Person active record and transform it to XML.

1. Start the console:

   ```
   $ ./script/console
   ```

2. Create a person:

   ```
   >> daniel = Person.create(:first_name => 'daniel', :last_name => 'wanja',
   :address => 'denver')
   ```

3. Now, to generate XML from that active record, just use the `to_xml` method:

   ```
   >> daniel.to_xml
   ```

4. The method outputs the following XML:

   ```
   <?xml version="1.0" encoding="UTF-8"?>
   <person>
     <address>denver</address>
     <created-at type="datetime">2007-12-07T09:29:48-07:00</created-at>
     <first-name>daniel</first-name>
     <id type="integer">1</id>
     <last-name>wanja</last-name>
     <updated-at type="datetime">2007-12-07T09:29:48-07:00</updated-at>
   </person>
   ```

Notice that the XML elements now are dasherized: `<first-name>`. To read that element from Flex, assuming you have a variable named `person` containing that XML, you would use the following syntax:

```
person['first-name']
```

This is because the dash is not a valid character for a Flex identifier, which prevents you from using dot notation (person.first-name). Resolve that issue by passing the `:dasherize => false` option to the `to_xml` method in Rails, as follows:

```
>> daniel.to_xml(:dasherize => false)
```

Passing the `false` option returns the following XML:

```
<?xml version="1.0" encoding="UTF-8"?>
<person>
  <address>denver</address>
  <created_at type="datetime">2007-12-07T09:29:48-07:00</created_at>
  <first_name>daniel</first_name>
  <id type="integer">1</id>
  <last_name>wanja</last_name>
  <updated_at type="datetime">2007-12-07T09:29:48-07:00</updated_at>
</person>
```

This technique enables you, from Flex, to refer to the first name in a more natural way where `person.first_name` would be used to access the first name. This form of XML also can be used to create active records from XML, as shown below.

Creating an active record from XML is nearly as easy as creating the person with the Person active record.

First, create a string containing some XML definition of a person:

```
person = "<person><first_name>tony</first_name>\
<last_name>hillerson</last_name><address>denver</address></person>"
```

The easiest way to create a Person active record from this XML string is as follows:

```
>> Person.new.from_xml(person).save
```

The `Person.new` statement returns an empty instance of an active record. The `from_xml` method call loads this empty active record instance from the XML string. The root element of the XML string, `<person>` in this case, doesn't matter. We could have used any element name. As you know, `Person.new` creates an instance in memory that is not saved until the `save` method is called.

If we want to use `Person.create` to automatically save to the database, we can write the following code:

```
>> Person.create(Hash.from_xml(person)['person'])
```

`Person.create` requires a hash containing all the attributes of the person and doesn't take an XML string as parameter. Fortunately, the `Hash` class in Rails adds the `from_xml` method. Now let's rewrite the `Person.create` statement in three lines of code, so I can highlight some of the hash usage.

```
>> person_hash = Hash.from_xml(person)
>> person_attributes_hash = person_hash['person']
>> Person.create(person_attributes_hash)
```

`Hash.from_xml(person)` returns the following hash with one key, `'person'`, having as its value another hash containing all the attributes of the person:

```
{"person"=>{"first_name"=>"tony", "address"=>"denver",
"last_name"=>"hillerson"}}.
```

Passing this hash directly to the `Person.create` method would create an exception, as there is no `'person'` attribute on that active record. So, we retrieve all these attributes by accessing the `'person'` key, found one level down in the hash `from_xml` returned. This returns the following hash that can be passed to the create method:

```
{"first_name"=>"tony", "address"=>"denver", "last_name"=>"hillerson"}
```

We use the `'person'` string as the key and not the symbol `:person` that you may be used to seeing. When sending XML to a controller, as we will do later in this chapter, Rails transforms the XML string into `HashWithIndifferentAccess`, which allows us to refer to keys of a hash using a string or a symbol. The good news is that we can do the same in the console by using the `with_indifferent_access` method provided by the hash. Let's create a person from the XML string, and then we can analyze the different steps:

```
>> Person.create(Hash.from_xml(person).with_indifferent_access[:person])
```

As you can see, generating XML from an active record couldn't be easier, and creating an active record from XML is also as easy.

XML in Flex

Flex implements the ECMAScript for XML specification known as E4X, which provides native support for the XML data type and functions to manipulate and query XML. ActionScript 3.0 includes the following E4X classes: XML, XMLList, QName, and Namespace. Additionally, Flex provides the `XMLListCollection` class to facilitate sorting and filtering of XML. In other words, Flex rocks when it comes to displaying, creating, and manipulating XML. Let's dive right into it.

The following application creates a variable named `list` that contains some XML. Notice that the XML is not a string and contains no single or double quotes; it's just plain XML directly in the source code.

```
 <?xml version="1.0" encoding="utf-8"?>
<mx:Application xmlns:mx="http://www.adobe.com/2006/mxml"
layout="absolute"
    applicationComplete="main()">
<mx:Script>
   <![CDATA[
  private var list:XML =
     <people>
       <person>
           <first_name>tony</first_name>
           <last_name>hillerson</last_name>
           <address>denver</address>
        </person>
       <person>
           <first_name>daniel</first_name>
```

```
            <last_name>wanja</last_name>
            <address>denver</address>
          </person>
      </people>;
    private function main():void {
        trace(list);
    }
    ]]>
</mx:Script>
</mx:Application>
```

Running this code in debug mode outputs the following in the console:

```
<people>
  <person>
    <first_name>tony</first_name>
    <last_name>hillerson</last_name>
    <address>denver</address>
  </person>
  <person>
    <first_name>daniel</first_name>
    <last_name>wanja</last_name>
    <address>denver</address>
  </person>
</people>
```

E4X allows you to query this list. We will now investigate a few tests highlighting several of the possibilities offered.

```
assertTrue(list.person is XMLList);
assertEquals(2, list.person.length());
assertTrue(list.person[1] is XML);
assertEquals("daniel", list.person[1].first_name);
assertTrue(list.person[1].first_name is XMLList);
assertEquals("daniel", list.person[1].first_name.toString());
assertEquals("<first_name>daniel</first_name>",
list.person[1].first_name.toXMLString());
assertEquals("tony", list.person.(last_name=='hillerson').first_name)
assertEquals(2, list.person.(last_name=='hillerson' ||
last_name=='wanja').length())
assertEquals("tony", list..first_name[0]);
```

I am not using any test framework here, just the following two methods to verify the code:

```
private function assertTrue(condition:Boolean, message:String=""):void
{
    if (!condition) trace("expected true but was false"+message)
}
```

```
private function assertEquals(expected:Object, actual:Object,
                             message:String=""):void {
  if (expected != actual)
    errorTrace("expected:<" + expected + "> " +
               "but was:<" + actual + ">" + message);

}
```

Let's look at these tests one by one.

1. `assertTrue(list.person is XMLList);`

   `list.person` is an E4X expression that requests all `<person/>` nodes from the
   XML and returns the result as an XMLList. An XMLList can contain one or more
   XML elements and doesn't need to have a root element. The ability to extract
   parts of an XML document often is convenient. For instance,
   `list.person.first_name` returns the following XMLList:

   `<first_name>tony</first_name>`

   `<first_name>daniel</first_name>`.

   The result doesn't have a root element.

2. `assertEquals(2, list.person.length());`

   Let's make sure that our list contains two people. `list.person` is an instance of the
   XMLList class, which provides methods to work with one or more XML elements.

3. `assertTrue(list.person[1] is XML);`

   This example is interesting because it shows that the XMLList can be accessed
   similarly to the way an array is accessed. When accessing an individual element of a
   list, you get an XML object back.

4. `assertEquals("daniel", list.person[1].first_name);`

   In this test, I access the XML returned by accessing the second element of the
   XMLList and reading the `first_name` attribute.

5. `assertTrue(list.person[1].first_name is XMLList);`

   Querying the XML returned in test 4 returns again an XMLList that is
   `<first_name>daniel</first_name>`.

6. `assertEquals("daniel", list.person[1].first_name.toString());`

   To get the value of `first_name`, use the `toString()` method of the element.

7. `assertEquals("<first_name>daniel</first_name>",`
   `list.person[1].first_name.toXMLString());`

   The `toXMLString()` method returns the name of the element and the value in it
   as an XML-formatted string.

8. `assertEquals("tony", list.person.`
   `(last_name=='hillerson').first_name)`

E4X is powerful and supports filtering. In this example, we are limiting the list to people with a last name equal to "hillerson." We then are only interested in the first name of each person. In this case, only one element is returned and we get the `first_name` attribute of that element. This technique is useful if you have unique identifiers like the ID element that Rails returns.

9. `assertEquals(2, list.person.(last_name=='hillerson' ||`
   `last_name=='wanja').length())`

The `.(expression)` is E4X syntax to enable filtering of a list. The expression enables you to filter on multiple attributes and elements using || (Logical Or) and && (Logical And). For example, the following expression would find one person:

`list.person.(last_name=='hillerson' && first_name=='tony')`

10. `assertEquals("tony", list..first_name[0]);`

The E4X expressions are not limited to a specific depth. You can query for any element at any depth using the descendant operator "..". This operator will return elements named `first_name` regardless of the element's depth. With our people list, it doesn't make a difference, but let's consider the following XML:

```
var list:XML = <root>
                   <item>one</item>
                   <item>two</item>
                   <parent>
                       <item>tree</item>
                   </parent>
               </root>
assertEquals(2, list.item.length());
assertEquals(3, list..item.length());
```

`list.item` returns only items at the first level, while `list..item` returns items at any level in the XML.

These few tests demonstrate how powerful Flex is for creating and consuming XML.

Getting XML to Flex

The key to getting XML from Rails to Flex is `mx:HTTPService`. First, let's start the server for the application we created in the XML in Rails section.

```
$ ./script/server
```

We can now create a Flex application that shows all the people in a data grid.

```
<?xml version="1.0" encoding="utf-8"?>
<mx:Application xmlns:mx="http://www.adobe.com/2006/mxml"
layout="vertical"
    applicationComplete="index.send()">
<mx:HTTPService id="index"
  url="http://localhost:3000/people.xml" resultFormat="e4x" />
```

```
<mx:DataGrid dataProvider="{index.lastResult.person}"
  width="100%" height="100%">

    <mx:columns>
        <mx:DataGridColumn headerText="First Name" dataField="first-name"/>
        <mx:DataGridColumn headerText="Last Name" dataField="last-name"/>
    </mx:columns>
</mx:DataGrid>
</mx:Application>
```

The code in this listing is the complete working application. Let's look at the detail.

1. `<mx:HTTPService id="index"`
   `url="http://localhost:3000/people.xml" resultFormat="e4x" />`

   The `HTTPService` tag specifies that the expected result format is e4x. This format is important and ensures that the XML string returned by the request is transformed into an ActionScript XML object.

   As we create a RESTful Rails application, we specify the URL that will invoke the `index` action of `PeopleController`. By specifying the `.xml` at the end of the URL, we make sure that the XML format handler is invoked. When looking at the Rails controller, the `@people` variable is returned; this is an array of `Person`. The `to_xml` is invoked implicitly by the `render` method, if required.

   ```
   class PeopleController < ApplicationController
     def index
       @people = Person.find(:all)
       respond_to do |format|
         format.html # index.html.erb
         format.xml  { render :xml => @people }
       end
     end
   end
   ```

2. `<mx:Application xmlns:mx="http://www.adobe.com/2006/mxml"`
   `layout="vertical"`

   `applicationComplete="index.send()">`

   When the application is started and ready, the `HTTPService.send` method is invoked, or if `HTTPService` is named index so `index.send()`, the `HTTPRequest` is triggered to the specified URL.

3. `<mx:DataGrid dataProvider="{index.lastResult.person}"`
   `width="100%" height="100%" >`

   We don't specify any result handler. We use the Flex built-in binding mechanism to let the grid update itself when `HTTPService` `lastResult` changes. Note that `lastResult` is an XML object because we specified a `resultFormat` of e4x and we filter it to extract all the people from that list. Earlier in the chapter, we learned that `index.lastResult.person` is an XMLList object.

4. `<mx:DataGridColumn headerText="First Name" dataField="first-name"/>`

As we used the default-generated controller, which implicitly calls to_xml on the array of Person instance, we get the dasherized version of the elements, in this case, "first-name" and not first_name.

Sending XML to Rails

The PeopleController Rails controller we generated above provides the methods outlined in Table 2.1.

Table 2.1   **Methods Provided by PeopleController**

Controller Method	URL to invoke
index	# GET /people.xml
show	# GET /people/1.xml
new	# GET /people/new.xml
edit	# GET /people/1/edit
create	# POST /people.xml
update	# PUT /people/1.xml
destroy	# DELETE /people/1.xml

The new and edit methods are not relevant to our Flex application; they are just used for HTML-based applications to render an HTML form. The right column dictates how we need to configure HTTPService to invoke the specific controller method from Flex. Let's focus one moment on the update method. In our example, we have the PeopleController controller class, which accepts updates in the XML format via PUT requests. From Flex, we can send that XML to the update method of this controller by using the following HTTPService tags.

```
<mx:HTTPService id="update"
url="http://localhost:3000/people/{grid.selectedItem.id}.xml?_method=put"
  contentType="application/xml"
  resultFormat="e4x"
  method="POST"
  result="index.send()" />
```

Let's look at this service declaration in detail.

1. ?_method=put and method="POST"

The current Flex HTTPService implementation is limited to the GET and POST methods due to a limitation on how the Flash Player is integrated with the browser. Thankfully, Rails knows how to work around this Flex limitation and verifies the _method parameter of the request to override the real method of the request. So, by appending ?_method=put" on the URL and specifying method="POST" for HTTPService, the proper routing occurs and the update

method of `PeopleController` will be invoked. We could have used the default
`GET` method. However, the length of data passed to the server may be limited
when using `GET`, so adding `POST` can avoid some issues when sending larger XML
structures.

2. `contentType="application/xml"`

   This command tells Rails that the data send is effectively in the XML format, and
   Rails will automatically transform it into a hash. `PeopleController` can then
   access the hash by referring to `params[:person]` as follows:

   ```
   @person.update_attributes(params[:person])
   ```

3. `resultFormat="e4x"`

   In this case, this result is not important because the server doesn't return the
   updated person. It just returns a status of: ok.

Now let's look at the source code of the full application:

```xml
<?xml version="1.0" encoding="utf-8"?>
<mx:Application xmlns:mx="http://www.adobe.com/2006/mxml" layout="vertical"
    applicationComplete="index.send()">
<mx:Script>
    <![CDATA[
        private function updatePerson():void {
            var person:XML = <person/>
            person['first-name'] = firstNameField.text;
            person['last-name'] = lastNameField.text;
            update.send(person);
        }
    ]]>
</mx:Script>
<mx:HTTPService id="index"
  url="http://localhost:3000/people.xml" resultFormat="e4x" />
<mx:HTTPService id="update"
  url="http://localhost:3000/people/{grid.selectedItem.id}.xml?_method=put"
  contentType="application/xml"
  resultFormat="e4x"
  method="POST"
  result="index.send()" />
<mx:DataGrid id="grid"
  dataProvider="{index.lastResult.person}" width="100%" height="50%" >
        <mx:columns>
            <mx:DataGridColumn headerText="Id" dataField="id"/>
            <mx:DataGridColumn headerText="First Name" dataField="first-name"/>
            <mx:DataGridColumn headerText="Last Name" dataField="last-name"/>
        </mx:columns>
</mx:DataGrid>
```

```
    <mx:Form>
        <mx:FormItem label="First Name">
            <mx:TextInput id="firstNameField"
text="{XML(grid.selectedItem)['first-name']}" />
        </mx:FormItem>
        <mx:FormItem label="Last Name">
            <mx:TextInput id="lastNameField"
text="{XML(grid.selectedItem)['last-name']}" />
        </mx:FormItem>
    </mx:Form>
    <mx:Button label="Save" click="updatePerson();" />
</mx:Application>
```

The `updatePerson` method assembles the XML with the first-name and last-name values to be set on the person. The XML is then sent using the `send` method of the `update` `HTTPService`. The `url` of this service is automatically updated with the ID (`id`) of the selected grid item, thus updating the attributes on the correct active record.

Mapping Data Types

When passing data with XML, we need to define how Rails and Flex handle different data types. In Rails, most of the active record attributes are one of the following data types:

:string	:text	:integer	:float
:decimal	:datetime	:timestamp	:time
:date	:binary	:boolean	

Before diving into the details of data type mapping, let's first extend the `people` database table with the following migration:

```
class AddAttributesToPerson < ActiveRecord::Migration
  def self.up
    add_column :people, :bio, :text
    add_column :people, :net_worth, :float
    add_column :people, :number_of_ipods, :integer
    add_column :people, :birthday, :date
    add_column :people, :birthday_and_time, :datetime
    add_column :people, :rails_programmer, :boolean
    add_column :people, :flex_programmer, :boolean
  end

  def self.down
    remove_column :people, :flex_programmer
    remove_column :people, :rails_programmer
    remove_column :people, :birthday_and_time
    remove_column :people, :birthday
    remove_column :people, :number_of_ipods
    remove_column :people, :net_worth
```

```
        remove_column :people, :bio
    end
end
```

Then let's run `$ rake db:migrate` and load some additional data:

```
>> daniel = Person.find_by_first_name('daniel')
>> daniel.update_attributes(:net_worth => 0.02, :number_of_ipods => 6, \
:birthday => Date.parse("1965/06/21"), \
:birthday_and_time => DateTime.parse('Mon Jun 21 06:45:35 GMT 1965'), \
:rails_programmer => true, :flex_programmer => true)
```

Now `daniel.to_xml(:dasherize=>false)` returns the following XML:

```
<?xml version="1.0" encoding="UTF-8"?>
<person>
  <address>denver</address>
  <bio nil="true"></bio>
  <birthday type="date">1965-06-21</birthday>
  <birthday_and_time type="datetime">1965-06-21T06:45:35Z</birthday_and_time>
  <created_at type="datetime">2007-12-07T09:29:48-07:00</created_at>
  <first_name>daniel</first_name>
  <flex_programmer type="boolean">true</flex_programmer>
  <id type="integer">1</id>
  <last_name>Wanja</last_name>
  <net_worth type="float">0.02</net_worth>
  <number_of_ipods type="integer">6</number_of_ipods>
  <rails_programmer type="boolean">true</rails_programmer>
  <updated_at type="datetime">2007-12-14T11:28:32-07:00</updated_at>
</person>
```

Notice that Rails annotates each element with the `type` attribute.

The way Rails handles these data types dictates how we need to handle them in Flex. As we have seen, the `Hash` class has been extended in Rails and provides the basis for the XML conversion. Having a better understanding of what happens under the hood of that class will tell us how to map data types. For the curious, I recommend looking at the following file from the Rails source code: activesupport/lib/active_support/core_ext/hash/conversions.rb.

It defines the module `ActiveSupport::CoreExtensions::Hash::Conversions`. The `Conversions` module defines `XML_TYPE_NAMES`, mapping Ruby class names to the type attributes that the `to_xml` and `from_xml` methods use (see Table 2.2). The `Conversions` module additionally defines `XML_FORMATTING` and `XML_PARSING`, which are the procedures used to format and parse the XML (see Tables 2.3 and 2.4, respectively).

Table 2.2   **XML_TYPE_NAMES Mapping of Ruby Class Names to the Type Attributes Used by to_xml and from_xml**

Ruby Class	XML Type Attributes
Symbol	symbol
Fixnum	integer
Bignum	integer
BigDecimal	decimal
Float	float
Date	date
DateTime	datetime
Time	datetime
TrueClass	boolean
FalseClass	boolean

Table 2.3   **XML_FORMATTING by Rails of XML Type Attributes**

XML Type Attributes	Rails Formatting Implementation
Symbol	Proc.new { |symbol| symbol.to_s }
Integer	value.to_s
Decimal	value.to_s
Float	value.to_s
Date	Proc.new { |date| date.to_s(:db) }
Datetime	Proc.new { |time| time.xmlschema }
Boolean	value.to_s

Table 2.4   **XML_PARSING by Rails of XML Type Attributes**

XML Type Attributes	Rails Parsing Implementation
Symbol	Proc.new { |symbol| symbol.to_sym }
Date	Proc.new { |date| ::Date.parse(date) }
Datetime	Proc.new { |time| ::Time.parse(time).utc }
Integer	Proc.new { |integer| integer.to_i }
Float	Proc.new { |float| float.to_f }
Boolean	Proc.new { |boolean| %w(1 true).include?(boolean.strip) }
String	Proc.new { |string| string.to_s }
Double	same as float

Rails extends the `DateTime` class with an `xmlschema` method that formats the represented time in an appropriate format for use with XML:

```
def xmlschema
   strftime("%Y-%m-%dT%H:%M:%S#{offset == 0 ? 'Z' : '%Z'}")
end
```

For more information, see www.w3.org/TR/xmlschema-2/#dateTime.

Now, armed with this knowledge, let's see how Rails handles different scenarios from the Flex application perspective.

Flex to Rails

When sending data to Rails, you don't need to add the `type` attribute. Just ensure that the value can be parsed by the Rails parsing implementation described above. For the `String`, `Text`, `Boolean`, and `Numbers` data types, ensuring this is a fairly straightforward process. For `Date`, you must use the YYYY-MM-DD format, and for `DateTime`, you can use the W3C date format as returned by the `xmlschema` method shown above (e.g., 1965-06-21T06:45:35Z) or any format that `Time.parse` can handle (e.g., Mon Jun 21 06:45:35 –0600 1965).

Rails to Flex

When receiving data from Rails, the XML is annotated with the `type` attribute. Consider the type when using dates, boolean data, and numbers in case you need to manipulate them as native ActionScript types, for example, testing whether a Boolean is true, mapping a datetime or date field to a `DateSelector`, or adding numbers. Having the type attribute doesn't help, because you usually know in what context to use a given attribute.

```
       assertTrue(person.rails_programmer == true);
       assertEquals(0.02, Number(person.net_worth));
       assertEquals(6, Number(person.number_of_ipods));
       assertEquals("1965/06/21", person.birthday.toString().replace(/\-/g, '/'));
       assertEquals("Mon Jun 21 06:00:00 1965 UTC", new
Date(person.birthday.toString().replace(/\-/g, '/')).toUTCString());
       assertEquals("Mon Jun 21 06:45:35 1965 UTC",
DateUtil.parseW3CDTF(person.birthday_and_time.toString()).toUTCString());
```

Out of the box, the Flex SDK doesn't provide a facility to parse the `DateTime` data returned by Rails. One approach is to include "as3corelib." Download it from http://code.google.com/p/as3corelib and copy corelib.swc to the FLEX_HOME/libs folder. This library provides DateUtil.parseW3CDT, which knows how to convert the `datetime` returned by Rails.

For the Date format, Flex supports the following strings when using `Date.parse`:

- Day Mon DD HH:MM:SS TZD YYYY

- MM/DD/YYYY HH:MM:SS TZD

- HH:MM:SS TZD Day Mon/DD/YYYY

- Mon DD YYYY HH:MM:SS TZD

- Day Mon DD HH:MM:SS TZD YYYY
- Day DD Mon HH:MM:SS TZD YYYY
- Mon/DD/YYYY HH:MM:SS TZD
- YYYY/MM/DD HH:MM:SS TZD

Therefore, we need to convert the YYYY-MM-DD string to YYYY/MM/DD.

Error Handling

One important aspect of working in Flex and Rails is to understand how to deal with HTTP errors in your Flex application. The Flash Player imposes a restriction on the status code that is passed to your application, and not every error that Rails will return to you can be handled by your Flex code unless we add some specific error handling code to your Rails application. Before we show you one way to deal with this restriction, let's first look at how the PeopleController Rails controller deals with errors. Table 2.5 presents a summary of the code that is invoked for the different RESTful HTTP requests with the error handling code highlighted in bold.

Table 2.5   **Code Invoked for Different RESTful HTTP Requests**

Method	HTTP Request	HTTP Response (from Rails)
Index	GET /people.xml	`@people = Person.find(:all)` `render :xml => @people`
Show	GET /people/1.xml	`@person = Person.find(params[:id])` `render :xml => @person`

Create	POST /people.xml	`@person = Person.new(params[:person])`
		`if @person.save`
		   `render :xml => @person, :status => :created`
		`else`
		   `render :xml => @person.errors, :status =>`
		`:unprocessable_entity`

Update	PUT /people/1.xml	`@person = Person.find(params[:id])`
		`if @person.update_attributes(params[:person])`
		   `head :ok`
		`else`
		   `render :xml => @person.errors, :status =>`
		`:unprocessable_entity`

Delete	DELETE /people/1.xml	`@person = Person.find(params[:id])`
		`@person.destroy`
		`head :ok`

When Things Go Right (200s)

Most likely, your HTTP request will succeed and an HTTP status of 200 will be returned to your Flex application indicating successful completion of the request. When the controller invokes "head :ok," this will return a status of 200 with no content.

When the controller returns data and does not specify a status, in other words renders `:xml => @people` in the show method, the default successful HTTP status of 200 is used. When the `create` method succeeds, the status is set to `:created`, which corresponds to the HTTP status of 201.

Active Record Validation (400s)

One standard scenario is when using active record validations. For example, the user asks to create a new Person or update an existing Person if any validation fails, the record is not saved, or the specific error is returned and the status code is set to `:unprocessable_entity` (422).

When Things Go Wrong (500s)

Another scenario is when an internal server error occurs and a status of 500 is returned. An internal error is basically an unhandled exception that can occur in the above controller code if an invalid `params[:id]` is passed as the `Person.find` throws an `ActiveRecord::RecordNotFound` exception. Of course, unhandled exceptions also occur if you have a programming error.

HTTP Error Codes

See http://www.iana.org/assignments/http-status-codes for a list of all HTTP status codes. Rails maps these codes to symbols (such as `:created` = 201 and `:unprocessable_entity` = 422). Check out the Rails source code: actionpack/lib/action_controller/status_codes.rb.

Flash Player Restriction

The Flash Player doesn't pass all the errors code to your Flex application when an error occurs. The main reason for this restriction is that the Flash Player uses the browser to handle HTTP requests and some browsers limit what information is passed back to the Flash Player. Adobe wants to be consistent across all browsers, so your Flex application will only get cryptic errors messages rather than informative XML errors it deserves.

So, let's add a validation to our Person active record:

```
class Person < ActiveRecord::Base
  validates_presence_of :first_name
  validates_presence_of :last_name
end
```

And, let's add some error handling code to our Flex application:

```
<mx:HTTPService id="update"
url="http://localhost:3000/people/{grid.selectedItem.id}.xml?_method=put"
    contentType="application/xml"
    resultFormat="e4x"
```

```
  method="POST"
  fault="mx.controls.Alert.show(event.toString())"
  result="index.send()"
  />
```

When trying to update a person without specifying a first or last name, the Rails application returns an error message in XML format, but Flex just displays the following:

```
[FaultEvent fault=[RPC Fault faultString="HTTP request error"
faultCode="Server.Error.Request" faultDetail="Error: [IOErrorEvent
type="ioError" bubbles=false cancelable=false eventPhase=2 text="Error
#2032: Stream Error. URL: http://localhost:3000/people/8.xml?_method=put"].
URL: http://localhost:3000/people/8.xml?_method=put"]
messageId="65EBBA92-5911-68D2-1710-18A687C28455" type="fault" bubbles=false
cancelable=true eventPhase=2]
```

This is not a useful error message.

Until the HTTP status handling of Flash Player is improved, we can simply change all our controllers and return the error in XML format, forcing the status to be 200. That way, Flex can find out if an error occurs just by checking whether the response is an XML response starting with the <errors> tag. Rather than changing all the methods of each controller, we can modify the ApplicationController as shown in Listing 2.1.

Listing 2.1   **app/controllers/application.rb**

```ruby
class ApplicationController < ActionController::Base

  after_filter :flex_error_handling
  def flex_error_handling
    response.headers['Status'] = interpret_status(200) if
response.headers['Status'] == interpret_status(422)
  end

  def rescue_action_in_public(exception)
    render_exception(exception)
  end
  def rescue_action_locally(exception)
    render_exception(exception)
  end
  rescue_from ActiveRecord::RecordNotFound, :with => :render_exception
  def render_exception(exception)
    render :text => "<errors><error>#{exception}</error></errors>", :status => 200
  end

end
```

So to handle the :unprocessable_entity (422) status that can occur due to an
active record validation error during the create or update method, we are adding an
after_filter that is simply going to reset the status to 200 if the status is 422.
The response body is already the XML that contains the error, and we will write a
common function in our Flex application to trap this occurrence. In Flex, we add a
handleResult function, which will verify whether the returned XML starts with the
<errors> tag:

```
private function handleResult(result:XML):void {
    if (result && result.name()=="errors") {
        mx.controls.Alert.show(result.toXMLString());
    } else {
        index.send();
    }
}
```

We then change the HTTPService result handler to pass the result to the method we
just created:

```
<mx:HTTPService id="update"
  url="http://localhost:3000/people/{grid.selectedItem.id}.xml?_method=put"
  contentType="application/xml"
  resultFormat="e4x"
  method="POST"
  fault="mx.controls.Alert.show(event.toString())"
  result="handleResult(event.result as XML)" />
```

Now if a validation error occurs, let's say we forgot to specify a last name, the Rails
validation error message is returned to our Flex application as follows:

```
<errors>
  <error>Last name can't be blank</error>
</errors>
```

When an internal server error occurs, the after_filter is never reached. Rails
comes to the rescue by enabling us to provide a specific rescue handler that can deal
with this type of error. There are the catchall internal error methods for public and local
requests: rescue_action_in_public and rescue_action_locally. In addition, we
can specify a particular rescue method for specific exceptions, if those specifications are
needed. In our application, we register the ActiveRecord::RecordNotFound
exception just to show you the syntax. Which approach to handling the 500 errors is
more appropriate depends on the requirements of your application.

Summary

Passing XML data between Rails and Flex is a fairly straightforward process, enabling
you to create applications that display and maintain complex data structures. The rest of
this book covers advanced topics highlighting many of the aspects of passing XML data
we just visited.

3

Flex with RESTful Services

More frequently than not, Rails applications are written using a RESTful approach, which provides a coherent way of organizing your controller actions for applications that serve HTML pages. It also has the added benefit of exposing your application as a service that can be accessed via an API. This capability is important because it enables our Flex application to communicate with the Rails application by passing XML data using the Flex `HTTPService` components. In Chapter 2, Passing Data with XML, we looked at the underlying mechanisms of using the `HTTPService` component and the implications of using XML. In this chapter, we will look at the larger picture of how to access a RESTful Rails application and how to consume nested resources with custom verbs, which are common in RESTful applications. You should still be able to follow this chapter, even if you are not familiar with RESTs. This chapter will guide you through building the "Stock Portfolio" application, which will introduce REST concepts, such as CRUD verbs and nested resources, and use custom REST actions. You will see how to code this application from both a Rails and a Flex perspective.

Let's jump right into it.

Creating the Stock Portfolio Rails Application

The Stock Portfolio application is an online trading application that allows you to buy and sell stock. Of course, this sample application will walk you through what a RESTful Rails application is, even though it doesn't include many aspects that a real-world trading application needs. The data we want to manage is the following: An account holds positions in stock, for example, 50 shares of Google and 20 shares of Adobe. Each position has many movements created when the stock is bought or sold. To get started, let's create a new Rails application:

```
$ rails rails
$ cd rails
```

Now you can create the Account, Position, and Movements "resources" as follows:

```
$ ./script/generate scaffold Account name:string
$ ./script/generate scaffold Position account_id:integer quantity:integer\
 ticker:string name:string
$ ./script/generate scaffold Movement price:float date:datetime\
 quantity:integer position_id:integer operation:string
```

In Rails terms, a resource is data exposed by your Rails application following a convention to access and manipulate the data via HTTP requests. From a code point of view, this translates to a controller that can be invoked to create, read, update, and delete the data, and the controller will access the active record of concern to perform the requested action. To access the controller methods, define in the routes configuration file the exposed resources; this definition will dictate which URL can be used to access these resources. We will do this step by step hereafter. Again, when we mention a resource, think of it as combination of the URLs to manipulate the data, the controller that exposes the data, and the active record used to store the data.

The `script/generate` command is a facility to create the files we need as a starting point. We need to apply several changes to the generated code to get a fully functional application. If you look at the `script/generate` commands above, we specified the Account, Position, and Movement resources, their attributes, and how the resources are linked to each other. The Movement resource has a `position_id` column that links the movements to the positions, and the Position resource has an `account_id` column that links the positions to the accounts. The `script/generate` command does not add the code either to associate the active records or to constrain the controllers. Let's do that now. You can add it to the Account, Position, and Movement active records and add the `has_many` and `belongs_to` associations as follows:

```
class Account < ActiveRecord::Base
  has_many :positions, :dependent => :destroy
end

class Position < ActiveRecord::Base
  belongs_to :account
  has_many :movements, :dependent => :destroy
end

class Movement < ActiveRecord::Base
  belongs_to :position
end
```

This code will give you fully associated active records. Assuming you have some data in your database, you could, for example, find all the movements of the first position of the first account using the following Rails statement:

```
Account.first.positions.first.movements
```

Changing the active records was the easy part. The controllers will require more work because to respect and constrain the resource nesting, we want to ensure that the positions controller only returns positions for the specified account, and the movements controller only returns movements for the specified position. In other words, we want to have movements nested in positions and positions nested in accounts. Change the config/routes.rb file to the following:

```
ActionController::Routing::Routes.draw do |map|
  map.resources :accounts do |account|
    account.resources :positions do |position|
      position.resources :movements
    end
  end
end
```

Routes tells our application what URL to accept and how to route the incoming requests to the appropriate controller actions. By replacing three independent routes with nested routes, we indicate that, for example, the positions cannot be accessed outside the scope of an account. What URLs does the route file define now? From the command line, type the following rake command to find out:

```
$ rake routes | grep -v -E "(format|new|edit)"
```

The rake routes command gives you the list of all URLs as defined by your routes configuration file. We just pipe it into the grep command to remove from the list any extra URLs we don't want at this stage. For the account resource, we now have the URLs shown in Table 3.1.

Table 3.1   **URLs for the Account Resource**

HTTP Verb	URL	Controller
GET	/accounts	{:action=>"index", :controller=>"accounts"}
POST	/accounts	{:action=>"create", :controller=>"accounts"}
GET	/accounts/:id	{:action=>"show", :controller=>"accounts"}
PUT	/accounts/:id	{:action=>"update", :controller=>"accounts"}
DELETE	/accounts/:id	{:action=>"destroy", :controller=>"accounts"}

To access the positions, we need to prefix the URL with the account ID that nests the positions (see Table 3.2).

Table 3.2   **Account IDs Added as Prefixes to the URLs**

HTTP Verb	URL	Controller
GET	/accounts/:account_id/ positions	{:action=>"index", :controller=>"positions"}
POST	/accounts/:account_id/ positions	{:action=>"create", :controller=>"positions"}
GET	/accounts/:account_id/ positions/:id	{:action=>"show", :controller=>"positions"}
PUT	/accounts/:account_id/ positions/:id	{:action=>"update", :controller=>"positions"}
DELETE	/accounts/:account_id/ positions/:id	{:action=>"destroy", :controller=>"positions"}

Finally, we need to prefix the URL with the account and position that nests the movements (see Table 3.3).

Table 3.3   **URL Prefixes to Nest the Movements**

HTTP Verb	URL	Controller
GET	/accounts/:account_id/ positions/:position_id/movements	{:action=>"index", :controller=>"movements"}
POST	/accounts/:account_id/ positions/:position_id/movements	{:action=>"create", :controller=>"movements"}
GET	/accounts/:account_id/ positions/:position_id/movements/:id	{:action=>"show", :controller=>"movements"}
PUT	/accounts/:account_id/ positions/:position_id/movements/:id	{:action=>"update", :controller=>"movements"}
DELETE	/accounts/:account_id/ positions/:position_id/movements/:id	{:action=>"destroy", :controller=>"movements"}

List all the movements of the first position of the first account, for example, by using the following URL: http://localhost:3000/accounts/1/positions/1/movements.

Defining the routes makes sure the application supports the nested URLs. However, we now need to modify the controllers to enforce implementation of this nesting, so we'll add such constraints to all the controllers. But first, let's remove the HTML support from our controllers because, in our case, we want the Rails application to only serve XML, and we don't need to worry about supporting an HTML user interface. Let's simply remove the respond_to block from our controllers and keep the code used in the format.xml block. For example, we change the index method from the following:

```
class AccountsController < ApplicationController
  def index
    @accounts = Account.find(:all)

    respond_to do |format|
```

```
      format.html # index.html.erb
      format.xml  { render :xml => @accounts }
    end
  end
end
```

to the following:

```
class AccountsController < ApplicationController
  def index
    @accounts = Account.find(:all)
    render :xml => @accounts
  end
end
```

You can effectively consider the `respond_to` as a big switch in all your controller methods that provide support for the different types of invocations, such as rendering either HTML or XML. To constrain the positions controller, we will add `before_filter`, which will find the account from the request parameters and only query the positions of that account. Change the index method from the following implementation:

```
class PositionsController < ApplicationController
  def index
    @positions = Position.find(:all)

    respond_to do |format|
      format.html # index.html.erb
      format.xml  { render :xml => @positions }
    end
  end
end
```

to this one:

```
class PositionsController < ApplicationController
  before_filter :get_account
  def index
    @positions = @account.positions.find(:all)
    render :xml => @positions.to_xml(:dasherize=>false)
  end
  protected
  def get_account
    @account = Account.find(params[:account_id])
  end
end
```

The `Position.find(:all)` was changed to `@account.positions.find(:all)`. This change ensures that only the positions for the specific account instance are returned.

The `before filter` loads that account for each method. We also are modifying the format of the returned XML to use underscores instead of dashes in the XML element names to better accommodate Flex, as explained in Chapter 2. When requesting the http://localhost:3000/accounts/1/positions URL, the controller now returns an XML list of all the positions with an ID of 1 that belong to the account. Now we do the same with the movements controller and scope the movements to a specific account and position, as follows:

```
class MovementsController < ApplicationController
  before_filter :get_account_and_position
  def index
    @movements = @position.movements.find(:all)
    render :xml => @movements.to_xml(:dasherize => false)
  end
  protected
  def get_account_and_position
    @account = Account.find(params[:account_id])
    @position = @account.positions.find(params[:position_id])
  end
end
```

So when requesting the http://localhost:3000/accounts/1/positions/1/movements URL, the controller returns an XML list of all the movements of the given position from the given account. First the account is retrieved, and then the positions from that account are queried, enforcing the scope of both the account and the position. Don't directly query the positions by using `Position.find(params[:position_id])` or a similar statement because the users could tamper with the URL and query the positions of a different account.

Before changing the rest of the methods, let's do some planning and see how we will use all the different controllers. Table 3.4 gives an overview of all the actions for our three controllers.

Table 3.4   Overview of Actions of the Three Controllers

Controller Method	Accounts Controller	Positions Controller	Movements Controller
Index	All accounts	All positions for account	All movements for position in account
Show	Not used	Not used	Not used
New	Not used	Not used	Not used
Edit	Not used	Not used	Not used
Create	Creates an account	Buy existing stock	Not used
Update	Updates an account	Not used	Not used
Destroy	Deletes the account	Sell stock	Not used
Customer verbs	None	Buy	None

For our application, several nonrelevant methods don't apply when rendering XML that would apply when supporting an HTML user interface. For example, the controller doesn't need to generate an edit form because the Flex application maps the XML to a form. In the same way, we don't need the new action, which returns an empty HTML entry form. Additionally, as in our case, since the index method returns all the attributes of each node, we don't really need the show method because the client application would already have that data. We don't use the show, new, and edit methods for all three controllers, so we can delete them.

For the positions controller, we won't update a position; we will simply buy new stock and sell existing stock, meaning we are not using the update method. We also differentiate buying new stock and buying existing stock, because for existing stock, we know the ID of the position and find the object using an active record search. But, for a new stock position, we pass the stock ticker and we create the new position, which may not save and validate if the ticker is invalid. Therefore, to support these two different usage patterns, we decided to use two different actions: we use the create action for existing stock, and we add the custom buy verb to the positions controller to buy new stock.

The movements controller doesn't enable any updates since movements are generated when buying and selling positions, so only the index method is significant. Providing such a mapping table of the verbs serves as a good overview of the work you will do next. First, you can remove all unused methods. As you already implemented the index methods earlier in the chapter, we are left with seven methods, three for the accounts controller and four for the positions controller. Let's dive into it. For the accounts controller, in the create, update, and destroy methods, we simply remove the respond_to blocks and keep only the XML rendering.

```ruby
class AccountsController < ApplicationController
    def create
      @account = Account.new(params[:account])
      if @account.save
        render :xml => @account, :status => :created, :location => @account
      else
        render :xml => @account.errors, :status => :unprocessable_entity
      end
    end

    def update
      @account = Account.find(params[:id])
      if @account.update_attributes(params[:account])
        head :ok
      else
        render :xml => @account.errors, :status => :unprocessable_entity
      end
    end
```

```
    def destroy
      @account = Account.find(params[:id])
      @account.destroy
      head :ok
    end
end
```

We saw earlier that the positions controller `index` method was relying on the
`@account` variable set by the `get_account` `before_filter` to only access positions for
the specified account. To enforce the scoping to a given account, the remaining methods
of the positions controller will also use the `@account` active record to issue the find
instead of directly using the `Position.find` method. Let's go ahead and update the
`create` and `destroy` methods and add a `buy` method, as follows:

```
class PositionsController < ApplicationController
  def create
    @position = @account.positions.find(params[:position][:id])
    if @position.buy(params[:position][:quantity].to_i)
      render :xml => @position, :status => :created,
             :location => [@account, @position]
    else
      render :xml => @position.errors, :status => :unprocessable_entity
    end
  end

  def destroy
    @position = @account.positions.find(params[:position][:id])
    if @position.sell(params[:position][:quantity].to_i)
      render :xml => @position, :status => :created,
             :location => [@account, @position]
    else
      render :xml => @position.errors, :status => :unprocessable_entity
    end
  end

  def buy
    @position = @account.buy(params[:position][:ticker],
                             params[:position][:quantity].to_i)
    if @position.errors.empty?
      head :ok
    else
      render :xml => @position.errors, :status => :unprocessable_entity
    end
  end
```

For the `buy` method, we simply use the ticker and invoke the `buy` method from the account active record:

```
class Account < ActiveRecord::Base
  has_many :positions, :dependent => :destroy
  def buy(ticker, quantity)
    ticker.upcase!
    position = positions.find_or_initialize_by_ticker(ticker)
    position.buy(quantity)
    position.save
    position
  end
end
```

The `Account#buy` method in turn calls the position `buy` method, which in turn creates a movement for the `buy` operation.

```
class Position < ActiveRecord::Base
  belongs_to :account
  has_many :movements, :dependent => :destroy

  def buy(quantity)
    self.quantity ||= 0
    self.quantity = self.quantity + quantity;
    movements.build(:quantity => quantity, :price => quote.lastTrade,
                    :operation => 'buy')
    save
  end
end
```

Now let's extend the position active record to add a validation that will be triggered when saving the position. The first validation we add is the following:

```
validates_uniqueness_of :ticker, :scope => :account_id
```

This check simply ensures that one account cannot have more than one position with the same name. We verify that the ticker really exists by using the yahoofinance gem. Install it first:

```
$ sudo gem install yahoofinance
```

To make this gem available to our application we can create the following Rails initializer under config/initializers/yahoofinance.rb that requires the gem:

```
require 'yahoofinance'
```

That's it. Now we can write a `before_validation_on_create` handler that will load the given stock information from Yahoo Finance, and then we add a validation for the name of the stock, which is set by the handler only if the stock exists.

```
class Position < ActiveRecord::Base
  validates_uniqueness_of :ticker, :scope => :account_id
  validates_presence_of :name,
                          :message => "Stock not found on Yahoo Finance."
  before_validation_on_create :update_stock_information

    protected

    def quote
      @quote ||= YahooFinance::get_standard_quotes(ticker)[ticker]
    end

    def update_stock_information
        self.name = @quote.name if quote.valid?
      end
    end
end
```

When referring to the `quote` method, the instance variable `@quote` is returned if it
exists, or if it doesn't exist, the stock information is retrieved from Yahoo Finance using
the class provided by this gem:

```
YahooFinance::get_standard_quotes(ticker)
```

The `get_standard_quotes` method can take one or several comma-separated stock symbols as a parameter, and it returns a hash, with the keys being the ticker and the values being
a StandardQuote, a class from the YahooFinance module that contains financial information
related to the ticker, such as the name, the last trading price, and so on. If the ticker doesn't
exist, then the name of the stock is not set and the save of the position doesn't validate.

The `sell` method of the positions controller is similar to the `buy` method, but less
complex. Let's take a look:

```
 class Position < ActiveRecord::Base
  def sell(quantity)
    self.quantity = self.quantity - quantity
    movements.build(:quantity => quantity, :price => quote.lastTrade,
                    :operation => 'sell')
    save
  end
end
```

Similar to the `buy` method, the `sell` method updates the quantity and creates a `sell`
movement, recording the price of the stock when the operation occurs. There is one
last thing: we need to add the custom `buy` verb to our routes. Do this by adding the
`:collection` parameter to the positions resource.

```
ActionController::Routing::Routes.draw do |map|

  map.resources :accounts do |account|
    account.resources :positions, :collection => {:buy => :post} do |position|
```

```
      position.resources :movements
   end
end
```

This indicates that no ID for the position is specified when creating the URL, thus invoking the buy verb on the positions collection. The URL would look something like this:

```
/accounts/1/positions/buy
```

If you wanted to add a custom verb that applies not only to the collection of the positions, but also to a specific position, thus requiring the position ID in the URL, you could have used the :member parameter to the positions resource.

Our application starts to be functional. By now, you certainly did a migration and started playing with your active records from the console. If not, play around a little, then keep reading because we are about to start the Flex part of our application.

Accessing Our RESTful Application with Flex

In this section, you will build a simple Flex application that will enable a user to create and maintain accounts, to buy and sell stock for those accounts, and to view the movements of a given stock. The application will look like what is shown in Figure 3.1.

The application has three grids. The ones for Accounts and Positions are editable, so they can be used to directly update the name of an account or to enter the stock ticker and quantity to buy. Let's create the application in three steps: first the accounts part, then the positions, and finally, the movements.

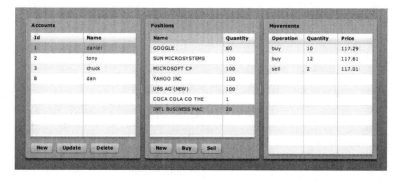

Figure 3.1   The application interface.

Accounts

Accessing a RESTful Rails resource from Flex consists of creating one HTTPService component for each of the actions the resource supports. For the account resource, the Rails application exposes the four URLs shown in Table 3.5.

Table 3.5   **The Four URLs Exposed by the Rails App for the Account Resource**

Action	Verb	Url
index	GET	/accounts
create	POST	/accounts
update	PUT	/accounts/:id
delete	DELETE	/accounts/:id

Before we create the service components, let's declare a bindable variable to hold the data the server returns.

```
[Bindable] private var accounts:XML;
```

And let's declare the data grid that will display this list of accounts.

```
<mx:DataGrid  id="accountsGrid"
    dataProvider="{accounts.account}"
    editable="true">
  <mx:columns>
    <mx:DataGridColumn headerText="Id" dataField="id" editable="false"/>
    <mx:DataGridColumn headerText="Name" dataField="name" />
  </mx:columns>
</mx:DataGrid>
```

We make the grid editable except for the first `id` column. We will use this later when adding the create and update functionality. Note also that we set the `dataProvider` to `accounts.account`. The `accounts` variable will contain the following XML, as returned by the Rails accounts controller index action:

```
<?xml version="1.0" encoding="UTF-8"?>
<accounts type="array">
  <account>
    <created-at type="datetime">2008-06-13T13:56:04Z</created-at>
    <id type="integer">1</id>
    <name>daniel</name>
    <updated-at type="datetime">2008-06-13T13:56:04Z</updated-at>
  </account>
  <account>
    <created-at type="datetime">2008-06-13T14:01:41Z</created-at>
    <id type="integer">2</id>
    <name>tony</name>
    <updated-at type="datetime">2008-06-14T02:19:46Z</updated-at>
  </account>
</accounts>
```

And specifying `accounts.account` as the data provider of the grid returns an XMLList containing all the specific accounts that can be loaded directly in the data grid and referred to directly in the data grid columns. The first column will display the IDs of the accounts and the second column the names.

Before declaring all our services we can define the following constant in ActionScript to be used as the root context for all the URLs.

```
private const CONTEXT_URL:String = "http://localhost:3000";
```

To retrieve the account list, we need to declare the following index service:

```
<mx:HTTPService id="accountsIndex" url="{CONTEXT_URL}/accounts"
    resultFormat="e4x"
    result="accounts=event.result as XML"/>
```

In the result handler, we assign the result to the accounts variable we declared above. Again, we need to specify the resultFormat on the HTTPService instance, which in the case of "e4x" ensures that the returned XML string is transformed to an XML object.

Next we can declare the create service, as follows.

```
<mx:HTTPService id="accountsCreate"  url="{CONTEXT_URL}/accounts"
    method="POST" resultFormat="e4x" contentType="application/xml"
    result="accountsIndex.send()"  />
```

We set the HTTP verb using the method attribute of the HTTPService component to match the verb Rails expects for this operation. We also need to set the contentType to "application/xml" to enable us to pass XML data to the send method and to let Rails know that this is an XML-formatted request. Also notice that we issue an index request in the result handler. This request enables a reload of the account list with the latest account information upon a successful create, and thus, by reloading the data in the grid, we would now have the ID of the account that was just created.

For the update service, we need to include in the URL which account ID to update. We use the grid-selected item to get that ID. Since the name column is editable, you can click in the grid, change the name, and press the update button (which we will code shortly). Also note that, in this case, we don't reload the index list because we already have the ID and the new name in the list.

```
<mx:HTTPService id="accountsUpdate"
 url="{CONTEXT_URL}/accounts/{accountsGrid.selectedItem.id}?_method=put"
    method="POST" resultFormat="e4x"  contentType="application/xml"  />
```

As explained in the previous chapter, the Flash Player doesn't support either the delete or put verbs, but Rails can instead take an additional request parameter named _method. Also note that we reload the account list after a successful delete request, which provides the effect of removing the account from the list. We could have simply removed the account from the account list without doing a server round trip.

```
<mx:HTTPService id="accountsDelete"
    url="{CONTEXT_URL}/accounts/{accountsGrid.selectedItem.id}"
    method="POST" resultFormat="e4x" contentType="application/xml"
    result="accountsIndex.send()" >
  <mx:request>
    <_method>delete</_method>
  </mx:request>
</mx:HTTPService>
```

When the Flex application starts, we want to automatically load the account list. Implement this by adding the `applicationComplete` handler to the application declaration, and issue the send request to the account `index` service.

```
<mx:Application xmlns:mx="http://www.adobe.com/2006/mxml" layout="vertical"
  applicationComplete="accountsIndex.send()">
```

Now when your application starts, the account index request is made to the server, and the result is assigned to the `accounts` variable, which is bindable, meaning the grid reloads automatically when the assignment occurs. Next we'll add the create, update, and delete functionality for the account list.

What we don't show in these examples is the overall layout of the application. But, in short, we have a horizontal divide box that contains three panels, one for each resource:

```
<mx:HDividedBox>
  <mx:Panel title="Accounts" />
  <mx:Panel title="Positions" />
  <mx:Panel title="Movements" />
</mx:HDividedBox>
```

Each panel contains the grid and a control bar that has several buttons for the accounts and positions panels:

```
<mx:Panel>
  <mx:DataGrid />
  <mx:ControlBar>
      <mx:Button />
      <mx:Button />
  </mx:ControlBar>
</mx:Panel>
```

More frequently than using an editable data grid, your application may have data entry forms that show the detail of the selected record or a new entry form when adding data. This is also how a typical Rails application generates HTML. In our example, we are using the editable grid to achieve the same functionality, but in the end, which approach you use will depend on your application requirements.

To add a new account, we need the New button.

```
<mx:Button label="New"
  click="addNewAccount()"
  enabled="{accountsGrid.dataProvider!=null}" />
```

This button invokes the `addNewAccount` method, which simply adds a new XML node to the XML accounts list. There is no server call happening yet.

```
private function addNewAccount():void {
  accounts.appendChild(<account><id></id><name>new name</name></account>);
}
```

The user can then change the name of the account directly in the grid and use the following `Create` button to send the new account information to the Rails application:

```
<mx:Button
  label="{accountsGrid.selectedItem.id==''?'Create':'Update'}"
  click="accountsGrid.selectedItem.id=='' ?
         accountsCreate.send(accountsGrid.selectedItem) :
         accountsUpdate.send(accountsGrid.selectedItem)" />
```

If the selected item has no ID, it's a new record and the label of the button is set to `Create`, and the click action triggers the `accountsCreate` service. If an ID exists, the button transforms into an `Update` button, which uses the `accountsUpdate` service. Now we just need to add the delete functionality. If the selected item has an ID, in other words, if it exists on the server, the click handler invokes the `accountsDelete` service, which deletes the current record. We also support the scenario where you click the new button but want to cancel the creation, and the account list is then just reloaded from the server in this case.

```
<mx:Button label="Delete"
  click="accountsGrid.selectedItem.id=='' ?
      accountsIndex.send() : accountsDelete.send()"
  enabled="{accountsGrid.selectedItem!=null}" />
```

In the end, very little code supports the create, update, and delete functionality. In a real application, you may want to move some of the logic we added directly to the button's click handlers to a controller class, but the underlying principles and calls are the same.

Positions

Implementing the positions functionality is very similar to implementing an account grid and services, with just a few differences. For instance, the position resource is a nested resource, so make sure the URL is set to retrieve the positions for the selected account. Another difference is that the positions resource has the custom `buy` action. And, finally, when a new account is selected in the accounts grid, we want to automatically retrieve the positions. Let's get started.

As for the accounts, we declare a variable to hold the list of positions retrieved from the server:

```
[Bindable] private var positions:XML;
```

Next let's create the grid and bind it to the positions. Again, we use an E4X instruction to get an XMLList containing each position. We also make the grid editable, although the `name` column is only editable when the position has not yet been saved to the server. This can be verified by the fact that no ID is assigned, which enables us to use the name column to specify the ticker to buy.

```
<mx:DataGrid id="positionsGrid" width="100%" height="100%"
      dataProvider="{positions.position}"
      editable="true">
  <mx:columns>
    <mx:DataGridColumn headerText="Name" dataField="name"
      editable="{positionsGrid.selectedItem.id==''}"/>
    <mx:DataGridColumn headerText="Quantity" dataField="quantity"/>
  </mx:columns>
</mx:DataGrid>
```

Now you can add the following buttons to a control bar below the data grid.

```
<mx:Button label="New"
  click="addNewPosition()"
  enabled="{positionsGrid.dataProvider!=null}" />

<mx:Button label="{XML(positionsGrid.selectedItem).id==''?'Buy New':'Buy'}"
  click="buyPosition()" />

<mx:Button label="Sell"
  click="sellPosition()"
  enabled="{XML(positionsGrid.selectedItem).id!=''}" />
```

Each of the New, Buy, and Sell buttons will invoke a corresponding function that we will implement just after creating the services. Now, as we explained earlier, you must build the create service to buy an existing stock, the delete service to sell stock, the buy service to buy a new stock, and, of course, the index service to retrieve all the positions. These services will be mapped to the URLs shown in Table 3.6.

Table 3.6   **Service URL Mappings**

Action	Verb	Url
index	GET	/accounts/:account_id/positions
create	POST	/accounts/:account_id/positions
delete	DELETE	/accounts/:account_id/positions/:id
buy	POST	/accounts/:account_id/positions/buy

Also notice that for the nested resource, the prefix is always the same. So let's assume we have selected the account number 2. The prefix for the positions would be `/accounts/2`, and the complete URL to list all the positions for that account would be `/accounts/2/positions`. Another example for the same account, but this time to sell the position with an ID of 3, would go like this: the URL will be `/accounts/2/positions/3`. Flex provides several approaches to assembling the URL with the proper account ID, and here we simply create a string in MXML using the `mx:String` tag and bind that string to the selected item of the accounts data grid.

```
<mx:String
id="positionsPrefix">accounts/{accountsGrid.selectedItem.id}</mx:String>
```

We named this string `positionsPrefix` and will use it in all the URLs for the positions resource. Now each time we issue the `send` command for a service, the selected account ID is automatically part of the URL. Create the `index` service as follows:

```
<mx:HTTPService id="positionsIndex"
    url="{CONTEXT_URL}/{positionsPrefix}/positions"
    resultFormat="e4x"
    result="positions=event.result as XML"/>
```

Note the binding to the `positionsPrefix` string in the URL. The result of this service sets the `positions` variable we declared earlier, and as this variable is bound to `positionsGrid`, the grid reloads automatically.

The create and the buy services are declared with the same parameters, with only the URLs being different. Both are used to buy stock, but in the first situation, you need to pass the ID of the position, and in the second, the ticker of the stock you want to buy. Now this could have been implemented differently, and we could have used only one action and passed different parameters to differentiate the two situations, or we could even have checked whether the ID is a string and assumed you wanted to buy new stock.

```
<mx:HTTPService id="positionsCreate"
    url="{CONTEXT_URL}/{positionsPrefix}/positions"
    method="POST" resultFormat="e4x" contentType="application/xml"
    result="positionsIndex.send()"  />
```

```
<mx:HTTPService id="positionsBuy"
    url="{CONTEXT_URL}/{positionsPrefix}/positions/buy"
    method="POST" resultFormat="e4x" contentType="application/xml"
    result="positionsIndex.send()"  />
```

Now the `delete` service is used to sell stock, so it differs from the accounts delete service in the way that we will need to pass additional information parameters to the send call. So you cannot just define the required _method request parameter using the `mx:request` attribute of the service declaration, as it would be ignored when issuing the `send` call with parameters. We can, however, stick the _method parameter at the end of URL.

```
<mx:HTTPService id="positionsDelete"
  url="{CONTEXT_URL}/{positionsPrefix}/positions/
    {positionsGrid.selectedItem.id}?_method=delete"
  method="POST" resultFormat="e4x" contentType="application/xml"
  result="positionsIndex.send()">
```

You created the New, Buy, and Sell buttons to invoke respectively the
`addNewPosition`, `buyPosition`, and `sellPosition` functions when clicked. Now
that we have the services declared, let's code these functions. The `addNewPosition`
function simply adds a `<position />` XML node to the `positions` variable which, via
data binding, adds a row to the positions grid where you now can enter the ticker name
of the stock you desire to buy and specify the quantity.

```
private function addNewPosition():void {
  positions.appendChild(<position><id/><name>enter ticker</name></position>);
}
```

The `buyPosition` function determines if you are buying new or existing stock by
checking the ID of the currently selected position. In the case of a new stock, we used
the name column to accept the ticker, but the Rails controller expects a `:ticker`
parameter; therefore, we copy the XML and add a `ticker` element to it. For existing
stock, we send the information entered in the grid.

```
private function buyPosition():void {
  if (positionsGrid.selectedItem.id=='') {
    var newStock:XML = (positionsGrid.selectedItem as XML).copy();
    newStock.ticker = <ticker>{newStock.name.toString()}</ticker>;
    positionsBuy.send(newStock)
  } else {
    positionsCreate.send(positionsGrid.selectedItem)
  }
}
```

To sell a position, we pass the `id` and `ticker` to the `send` call.

```
private function sellPosition():void {
  var position:XML =
  <position>
    <id>{positionsGrid.selectedItem.id.toString()}</id>
    <ticker>{positionsGrid.selectedItem.ticker.toString()}</ticker>
    <quantity>{positionsGrid.selectedItem.quantity.toString()}</quantity>
  </position>
  positionsDelete.send(position);
}
```

Next, we want the positions grid to reload when the account is changed. We can do
this by adding a change handler to the accounts data grid. Here you may just want to
clear out the `positions` and `movements` variables before performing the call to avoid

showing for the duration of the remote call the positions of the previously selected account. Then, if it's not a new account, you can invoke `send` on the `positionsIndex`.

```
<mx:DataGrid  id="accountsGrid" width="100%" height="100%"
    dataProvider="{accounts.account}"
    change="positions=movements=null;
        if (event.target.selectedItem.id!='') positionsIndex.send()"
    editable="true">
```

Movements

The movements are much simpler than accounts and positions, since we just want to display the list of movements for the selected position of the selected account. So, for the `index` service, you can simply bind the selected account and selected position to the URL as follows:

```
<mx:HTTPService id="movementsIndex"
    url="{CONTEXT_URL}/accounts/
        {accountsGrid.selectedItem.id}/positions/
        {positionsGrid.selectedItem.id}/movements"
    resultFormat="e4x"
    result="movements=event.result as XML"/>
```

You also need to declare the following variable to keep the results

```
[Bindable] private var movements:XML;
```

Then you just need to declare the following grid, which is bound to the `movements` variable. This time, we don't specify that the grid is editable because the movements are read only.

```
<mx:DataGrid id="movementsGrid" width="100%" height="100%"
        dataProvider="{movements.movement}">
  <mx:columns>
    <mx:DataGridColumn headerText="Operation" dataField="operation"/>
    <mx:DataGridColumn headerText="Quantity" dataField="quantity"/>
    <mx:DataGridColumn headerText="Price" dataField="price"/>
  </mx:columns>
</mx:DataGrid>
```

When selecting a new account, we simply want to clear out the movements grid. So we need to add this to the accounts grid change handler:

```
<mx:DataGrid  id="accountsGrid" width="100%" height="100%"
    dataProvider="{accounts.account}"
    change="positions=movements=null; if (event.target.selectedItem.id!='')
positionsIndex.send()"
    editable="true">
```

And, finally, when selecting a new position, we want to request the movements for that position. We can achieve this with the following change handler on the positions grid. Again, we clear the movements before issuing the call:

```
<mx:DataGrid id="positionsGrid" width="100%" height="100%"
     dataProvider="{positions.position}"
     change="movements=null;
          if (accountsGrid.selectedItem.id!='' &amp;&amp;
              positionsGrid.selectedItem.id!='') movementsIndex.send()"
     editable="true">
```

Note that when placing code directly in the MXML declarations, you cannot use the ampersand character directly due to the parsing rules of XML on which MXML is based; otherwise, you get a compiler error. So, in the above code, we need to replace the logical AND expression `&&` with its XML-friendly equivalent: `&amp;&amp;`. This issue is avoided when writing code inside an `mx:Script` tag due to the use of the XML CDATA construct, which indicates to the XML parser that anything between the CDATA start indicator and end indicator is not XML, therefore allowing the use of the ampersand character.

Et voila! You can now create and maintain accounts, buy and sell stock, and see the movements for these positions. In this Flex application, we directly linked the services to the data grid and directly added logic in the different event handlers, and this makes explaining the code easier as you have everything in one file. This is definitely not a best practice, and for a real application, you may want to consider using an MVC framework to decouple the code and make the application more modular.

Summary

We covered lots of ground in this chapter. You created a RESTful Rails application with three nested resources and you created a Flex application enabling you to maintain these resources. In the end, all this functionality doesn't require much code. Hopefully, this guidance will provide a good starting point for creating your own RESTful Flex with Rails applications.

4

Using Fluint to Test a Flex
with Rails Application

As you know, Rails has a very effective built-in testing framework. Rails lets you write tests at several levels, so you can test different parts and aspects of your application. Write unit tests to test the model, functional tests to test one controller, and integration tests to test the flow between several controllers. Now, what about testing a Flex application that runs on Ruby on Rails? How do you ensure that a change in Rails doesn't break your Flex application? How do you ensure that a change in Flex doesn't break your Rails application? How do you take advantage of Rails fixtures from you Flex unit tests? Is Flex considered the "View" of the Rails application? Furthermore, isn't a Flex application itself an MVC application? Hold on! This chapter will answer all those questions.

In this chapter, we walk you step by step through the process of testing a Flex with Rails application. You will learn how to test the relevant aspects of your Flex with Rails application, quickly iterate and improve the Flex and the Rails parts of your application, and ensure that the resulting application works as expected. And, yes, the Flex part of your application will be the "View" of the Rails application, and the Flex part itself is built using an MVC approach. We will write tests for your Flex application at the model, controller, and view levels. The examples in this chapter use Cairngorm, but the principles are the same if you use another MVC framework, such as PureMVC, or even if you just use Flex without an external MVC framework. We'll write tests in Flex that call the Rails server, and we'll ensure that the integration between the Flex UI and the Rails server operates as expected. Does that mean you don't need to write Rails tests but just Flex tests, because the Flex tests trigger Rails code? Because the Flex tests pass, Rails will work? Wrong! You need to write Rails unit tests and Rails functional tests to ensure that your Rails models and controllers operate as expected and to quickly pinpoint any issues that are specific to the Rails part of your code. If you do not render HTML from Rails, your controller tests will be very straightforward. This book does not cover how to write Rails tests in Ruby. We will only show the Flex unit tests we are writing in ActionScript.

Using Fluint to Write Your Flex Unit Tests

Flex has several good unit test frameworks, such as FlexUnit, ASUnit, and the recent Fluint, formerly named dpUint. The first unit test framework that appeared for Flex and many Flex developers use is FlexUnit. All these frameworks are very similar and follow closely the widely known JUnit framework, a testing framework for Java written by Kent Beck and Eric Gamma. All these frameworks use a similar structure and provide a TestCase class to group related test methods, a TestSuite class to group related test cases, and a TestRunner to run tests. FlexUnit provides some extensions to the TestCase class to support the asynchronous nature of Flex development. These extensions are still limited and proved too cumbersome when testing remote calls for a Flex with Rails application. They are not well suited to test a user interface that mostly relies on asynchronous events. Fluint jumps in here. Fluint provides a nice way of testing remote calls and user interface events, and even supports asynchronous setup methods for your test case. Everything that can be done with Fluint can be done with FlexUnit, but just not as elegantly. That's why I selected Fluint for this chapter—and several of my client projects.

By now you are thinking, "Hey you've got the name wrong . . . shouldn't it be flUnit . . . to follow the same naming as all the other frameworks?" Fluint is effectively the correct name and stands for **Fl**ex **U**nit and **Int**egration, and is pronounced as "Fluent." Digital Primate is the company that developed and open sourced the framework, and formerly named this test framework dpUint, but with the 1.0 release aligned the name with Flex. The "uint" in the name refers to "Unit and Integration," which better describes the level at which we can test a Flex application. Similar to the way in which Rails organizes its tests at three levels (unit, functional, and integration), we will write Flex unit tests to test at three distinct levels, too:

- Delegates—We will test the delegate, which will assert that the remote calls operate correctly.
- Events/Commands—We will test the events and commands and assert that the model is changed appropriately.
- Views—We will test the interaction with the UI components.

If you are not familiar with unit testing, make sure you understand what a TestCase, TestSuite, and TestRunner are at a high level and how they are used. You will be better prepared to follow our examples in this chapter. In brief, a TestCase is a collection of test methods that share a common test environment; a TestSuite is a collection of TestCases; and a TestRunner runs all yours tests. You create classes that extend these classes to create and organize your tests. Start by creating a TestCase that will let you write test methods, the names of which start with "test" followed by a description of what the method is testing. Examples might include `testTotalIsZero, testNoteIsCreated`, and so on. Each test method is used to assert one specific aspect of your application and should not impact or depend on another test method. In the test methods, you will use assertions to verify that the outcome of an action produces the expected result. In our example application, we will create the `NoteResource` class, which is used to make all the remote calls, and we will test it with the `TestNoteResource` class. The `TestNoteResource` class will have several test methods, such as `testCreate` and `testUpdate`, to verify several aspects of your class. In our first example, the TestRunner will run the `TestNoteResource` tests directly and ensure that all your tests pass. As development moves on and the functionality of your application grows, you will add new test cases to test different aspects of your application. These test cases will be grouped in test suites, which the runner will "run." Got it? If not, just keep reading. It will make more sense as we move through the code.

In the next section of this chapter, The Basics of Testing a Flex Application, we will set up the Rails application and implement some initial HTTP services to invoke the server and introduce you to the basics of testing a Flex on Rails application. In the following section, Testing a Cairngorm-based Application, we will create a real user interface and use the Cairngorm MVC framework to organize our code. We will also guide you through the various aspects of testing the different layers of your MVC application. We end the chapter by showing you some ways to use Rails fixtures for your test harness.

The Basics of Testing a Flex Application

To guide you through the testing process, we will build NoteTaker, an online note-taking application enabling you to quickly jot down notes wherever you are. This application is a RESTful Rails application with a Flex user interface enabling the user to add, update, delete, and read notes. We will use Fluint to ensure that the application behaves as expected. Let's create this project in the following small increments.

1. Create the structure of the Flex project.
2. Set up the Flex test environment, and create the files required to write a small sample test.
3. Create the `NotesResources` class with an instance of `mx:HTTPService` enabling access to the Rails application
4. Write a test to query the Rails server. Oops, it fails! We need the server side of our application.
5. Create the structure of the Rails project.
6. Create a small Rails application.
7. Run the tests. Now it passes!
8. Hold, on! I said small increments.

Enough said . . . let's code.

Create the Structure of the Flex Project

With FlexBuilder, create a new project. Call it NoteTaker. Here's the directory structure:

```
bin-debug
html-template
libs
   src
```

Download Fluint from http://code.google.com/p/fluint/ and copy fluint_v1.swc to the libs folder of your Flex application.

Set Up the Flex Test Environment

With Fluint, we need to create an application that will run all our tests. Let's name it TestRunner.mxml and create a small sample test TestCase to ensure that we can run tests. Name it `tests.TestNotesResource.as`. It should extend the `net.digitalprimates.fluint.tests.TestCase` class.

TestRunner.mxml (see Listing 4.1) is a Flex application that includes `fluint:TestResultDisplay` and `fluint:TestRunner`. `fluint:TestRunner` defines which tests should run and runs them. `fluint:TestResultDisplay` shows if the tests pass or not using either a green or a red bar.

Listing 4.1   **TestRunner.mxml**

```
<?xml version="1.0" encoding="utf-8"?>
<mx:Application xmlns:mx=http://www.adobe.com/2006/mxml

xmlns:fluint="http://www.digitalprimates.net/2008/fluint"
               layout="absolute"
               creationComplete="startTestProcess(event)"
               width="100%" height="100%">
    <mx:Script>
        <![CDATA[
            import tests.TestNotesResource;

            protected function startTestProcess( event:Event ):void {
                testRunner.startTests( new TestNotesResource() );
            }
        ]]>
    </mx:Script>
    <fluint:TestResultDisplay width="100%" height="100%"/>
    <fluint:TestRunner id="testRunner"/>
</mx:Application>
```

As you saw, we need to create the TestNotesResource test case. We will just add on a "dummy" test method at this stage to ensure that we can compile and run the tests (see Listing 4.2).

Listing 4.2   **tests/TestNotesResource.as [v1]**

```
package tests
{
    import net.digitalprimates.fluint.tests.TestCase;
    public class TestNotesResource extends TestCase
    {
        public function testTruth():void{
            assertTrue(true);
        }
    }
}
```

When running the test, the output looks like that shown in Figure 4.1. The green bar indicates that all our tests passed. This test is not useful right now, but we have all the infrastructure in place, so let's go add real tests.

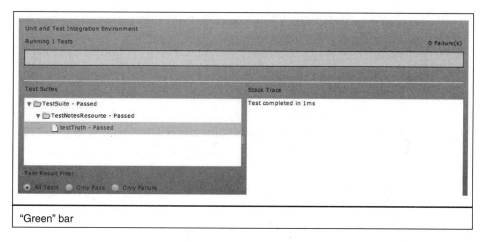

Figure 4.1   Test output.

Create NotesResource.mxml to Call the Rails Server

Knowing that the next test we want to write will call the Rails server, we are creating a nonvisual MXML component we will use to perform the HTTP requests to invoke the Rails application. NotesResource is also the class where we will add the different create, update, and delete methods (later in this chapter). Right now, it's a non-visual component and is based on the EventDispatcher class (see Listing 4.3). Later in this chapter, we will refactor it to be cairngorm:ServiceLocator.

Listing 4.3   **NotesResource.mxml [v1]**

```
<?xml version="1.0" encoding="utf-8"?>
<EventDispatcher xmlns:mx="http://www.adobe.com/2006/mxml"
xmlns="flash.events.*" >
    <mx:HTTPService id="notes"  url=http://localhost:3000/notes.xml
resultFormat="e4x" />
</EventDispatcher>
```

With this class in hand, let's write a test that will invoke it.

Write a Test to Query the Rails Server

Let's add some meaningful tests to our `TestNotesResource` test case class. To invoke this service, the test will declare the `notesResource` variable, which has the notes `HTTPService` we can then use to "send" the request to the server. The main code we want to test is the following:

```
var notesResource:NotesResource = new NotesResource();
notesResource.notes.send();
```

When the "send" is called, the Flex application will issue the HTTP request to the `http://localhost:3000/notes.xml` URL, and three things can happen:

- The call works, and the server responds. When this happens, we just need to test if we receive the expected result.
- The server doesn't like our request and returns an HTTP error (500, 404, ...).
- We don't have a server, or the server doesn't respond and we have a timeout situation.

Of course, we haven't yet creates the Rails application, so we can expect a timeout. But, just in case, we can go ahead and write the test supporting all three scenarios. Read the test code in Listing 4.4. I will explain the details next.

Listing 4.4   **tests/TestNotesResource.as [v2]**

```
package tests
{
  import net.digitalprimates.fluint.tests.TestCase;
  import net.digitalprimates.fluint.async.TestResponder;

  import flash.events.Event;
  import mx.rpc.AsyncToken;
  import mx.rpc.IResponder;
  import mx.rpc.events.ResultEvent;
  import mx.rpc.events.FaultEvent;

  public class TestNotesResource extends TestCase
```

Listing 4.4 *Continued*

```
{
  private var notesResource:NotesResource = new NotesResource();

  public function testList():void{
    var call:AsyncToken = notesResource.notes.send();
    var responder:IResponder = asyncResponder(
        new TestResponder( assertTestList, handleFault ),
                          1000, null, handleTimeOut );
    call.addResponder(responder);
  }
  public function assertTestList(result:ResultEvent,
                                 passThroughData:Object):void {
    assertEquals(2, result.result.note.length());
    assertEquals("MyString", result.result.note[0].title);
  }
  protected function handleFault(fault:FaultEvent,
                                 passThroughData:Object):void {
    fail("Failed to invoke notesResource."+fault.fault.faultString);
  }
  protected function handleTimeOut(event:Event):void {
    fail("Failed to invoke notesResource. Timeout.");
  }
 }
}
```

Let's walk through this test case step by step to highlight different aspect of using Fluint to test asynchronous remote calls.

```
var call:AsyncToken = notesResource.notes.send();
```

As you learned earlier in this book, calling a Rails application with `HTTPService` is asynchronous. So, from the `testList` method, we call the server, but the `testList` method is completed before the call returns from the server. Therefore, we cannot test the result from the remote call from within the `testList` method. As you know, to handle an asynchronous call, we can use a responder to indicate which method to invoke for either success or failure. In fact, invoking an HTTP method from `HTTPService` returns an `AsyncToken` on which we can set the responder. The following line sets the responder for the *send* call:

```
call.addResponder(responder);
```

How does the test framework know when the response arrived? The magic is in a method that the `TestCase` class provides, the `asyncResponder` method, which enables you to break up one test method in one or more chained asynchronous methods. The `asyncResponder` returns a responder, which you need to set as the responder to your call. Then, when making a call that expects an asynchronous response, the test method is only completed when the response arrives. In addition, the `asyncResponder` enables you to specify a timeout method in case the server doesn't respond. In our `testList` method, we want to deal with the three scenarios:

- The call worked (HTTP Success STATUS 2XX).
- The call failed (HTTP Error STATUS 4XX, 5XX).
- The call timed out.

Let's look at the different parts of this line of code:

```
var responder:IResponder = asyncResponder(
     new TestResponder( assertTestList, handleFault ),
                        1000, null, handleTimeOut );
```

In case of a successful remote call, the `assertTestList` method is invoked. If the call fails, the `handleFault` method is called, and if the call times out after one second (1,000 milliseconds), the `handleTimeOut` method is invoked. The `assertTestList` method name follows a naming convention that quickly indicates that this method asserts the results of a call issued from the `testList` method. You can really name these callback methods the way you wish.

Let's run the test. The results are shown in Figure 4.2. Oh, no, the test failed!

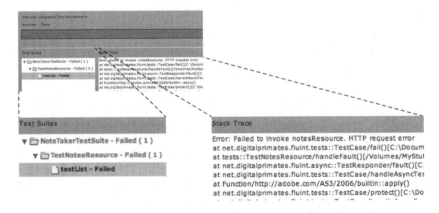

Figure 4.2   This test output indicates failure.

If we look at the error, it indicates that the request failed to invoke `notesResource` due to an HTTP request error. This result was expected, since we don't have a server. Remember: when we configured the responder to the call, we specified the `handleFault` method to be called in case of a fault.

```
var responder:IResponder = asyncResponder( new TestResponder(
assertTestList, handleFault ) , 1000, null, handleTimeOut );
```

handleFault then invokes the TestCase `fail` method to indicate the issue:

```
fail("Failed to invoke notesResource."+fault.fault.faultString);
```

Maybe it's time to create the server side of the application.

Creating the Rails Application

By now, you may be used to the sequence we follow to create a new Rails project.

```
$ rails rails; cd rails
$ ./script/generate scaffold note title:string body:text
$ rake db:create:all
$ rake db:migrate
```

You now have a fully functioning RESTful Rails application with the following routes:

```
    notes GET  /notes          {:controller=>"notes", :action=>"index"}
          POST /notes          {:controller=>"notes", :action=>"create"}
 new_note GET  /notes/new      {:controller=>"notes", :action=>"new"}
edit_note GET  /notes/:id/edit {:controller=>"notes", :action=>"edit"}
     note GET  /notes/:id      {:controller=>"notes", :action=>"show"}
          PUT  /notes/:id      {:controller=>"notes", :action=>"update"}
          DELETE /notes/:id    {:controller=>"notes", :action=>"destroy"}
               /:controller/:action/:id
```

The routes indicate which HTTP request can be issued from the Flex application to the Rails application. For example, to retrieve all of the notes, you can just call /notes.

Now that we have a Rails server, let's go back to our Flex unit tests.

Run the TestNotesResource against a Running Rails Server

Does the `NotesResource` class work? Before proceeding and coding the create, update, and delete functionality, we should ensure that the list functionality works by calling the /notes URL. We also need some data in the database; for now, we can load the fixtures generated with the scaffolding generation. Later in this chapter, you will see how to use the server running in test mode with the test database, enabling us to have separate test and development environments.

To load the fixture in the development database, issue the following command:

```
$ rake db:fixtures:load
```

Now you can start the server:

```
$ ./script/server
```

And now you can run the test: Yay! It passes (see Figure 4.3).

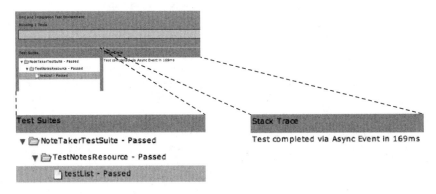

Figure 4.3   The test passes.

This time the call came back successfully from the server and the TestResponder
result callback is invoked, in this case, the asserTestList method.

```
var responder:IResponder = asyncResponder(
    new TestResponder( assertTestList, handleFault ),
                    1000, null, handleTimeOut );
```

The assertTestList method then verifies the data returned by the send() call:

```
assertEquals(2, result.result.note.length());
assertEquals("MyString", result.result.note[0].title);
```

Because we are using the default fixtures, result.result is an XML file with the
following structure:

```
<notes type="array">
  <note>
    <body>MyText</body>
    <created-at type="datetime">2007-11-09T08:40:56-07:00</created-at>
    <id type="integer">1</id>
    <title>MyString</title>
    <updated-at type="datetime">2007-11-09T08:40:56-07:00</updated-at>
  </note>
  <note>
    <body>MyText</body>
    <created-at type="datetime">2007-11-09T08:40:56-07:00</created-at>
    <id type="integer">2</id>
    <title>MyString</title>
    <updated-at type="datetime">2007-11-09T08:40:56-07:00</updated-at>
  </note>
</notes>
```

The first assertion verifies that result has two notes. The second assertion verifies that the title of the first note is "MyString."

Overview of Assertion Methods

Now is a good time to review all the different assertion methods the TestCase provides:

```
function assertEquals( expected:Object, actual:Object ):void
function assertStrictlyEquals( expected:Object, actual:Object ):void
function assertTrue( condition:Boolean ):void
function assertFalse( condition:Boolean ):void
function assertNull( object:Object ):void
function assertNotNull( object:Object  ):void
```

All these functions have a default failure message that can be overridden by adding an additional first parameter. For example, you can write assertTrue(true) and assertTrue("Expected truth", true).

An assertion method is used to express an expected outcome of your test method, and it fails if the assertion is not fulfilled. A series of failure methods lets you force the test to fail if the failure condition is met. More often than not, you will use the assertion methods. The failure methods are provided as a convenience and can be useful in specific situations.

```
function failNotEquals( message:String, expected:Object, actual:Object ):void
function failNotStrictlyEquals( message:String, expected:Object, actual:Object
):void
function failNotTrue( message:String, condition:Boolean ):void
function failTrue( message:String, condition:Boolean ):void
function failNull( message:String, object:Object ):void
function failNotNull( message:String, object:Object ):void
function fail( failMessage:String = "" ):void
```

The failure methods always require a message describing the failure.

Testing a Cairngorm-based Application

We made good progress so far, but we're not done. Now that we have a Rails application and some Flex unit tests, it's time to create a real user interface, which will enable us to add, update, and delete notes. We will follow the steps outlined in the Cairngorm Implementation section of Chapter 8, Flex MVC Frameworks, to create our user interface, and we will show how to test each of the different layers of the application. Let's assume you have read the Flex MVC Frameworks chapter and that you understand the ins and outs of Cairngorm. If you don't, read it first, then come back. Fluint is pretty cool for testing Cairngorm-based applications.

You will again create this new functionality in small increments.

1. Use the ServiceLocator and Delegate to support CRUD actions.

2. Test the delegate's CRUD actions.

3. Implement the Cairngorm commands.

4. Test the Cairngorm commands.

5. Implement ListView.

6. Test ListView.

7. Implement EditView.

8. Test EditView.

The NoteTaker User Interface

The NoteTaker application starts by showing a list of notes or an empty list if no notes exist. A new note can be added by clicking the Add button, which displays the edit note screen. If the list has some notes displayed, clicking on the note selects the note and displays it in the edit note screen.

Figure 4.4 shows an example of ListView.

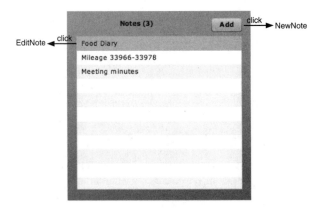

Figure 4.4   ListView.

Figure 4.5 shows an example of EditView.

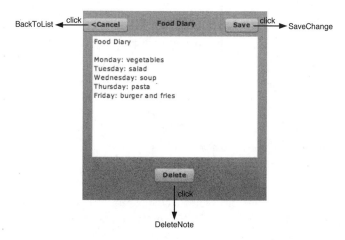

Figure 4.5   EditView.

The Cairngorm events used in ListView are the following:

- RetrieveNotesEvent—Performs a server call on application startup to retrieve the list of notes.
- NewNoteEvent—Creates a new note (in memory), selects it, and displays the edit note screen.
- EditNoteEvent—Selects the "clicked" note, and displays the edit note screen.

We added the RetrieveNotesEvent, which will be issued when the application starts. The Model attributes include the following:

- notes—The list of notes.

The edit screen lets you edit the content of the note by typing text in the text area. By pressing the Cancel button, you abandon the changes and return to the note list. By pressing the Save button, the changes are sent to the server and the notes list is displayed.

The save the command will verify if it is a new note or an update to an existing note, then invoke the appropriate HTTP service accordingly. The title of the note is set to the first line of the entered note. A note can also be deleted.

The Cairngorm events used in EditView are the following:

- SaveChangeEvent—Sends the current note to the server. Returns to the list upon saving the note.
- BackToListEvent—Cancels the change and return to the list.
- DeleteNoteEvent—Deletes the note and returns to the list.

The Model attributes include the following:

- selectedNote—The note that is edited.

We need one additional attribute in the model to indicate which view is displayed. We will name it currentView, which could be either LIST_VIEW or EDIT_VIEW.

Before we jump into testing our NoteTaker application, let's review what and how we can test. Cairngorm presents a nice MVC architecture, which allows us to test different parts of the application independently. Among the development community there are different opinions about the granularity of your tests and whether or not to even perform server calls from your Flex test. One approach would be simply to test that the delegates perform the proper remote calls and assert that the server returns the expected data. Then we could simply test the Cairngorm events and command without doing a server round trip and test the user interface by changing the model. We could use a mock delegate to test the events/commands and the UI. Another approach would be to run the Flex tests in the presence of a Rails server running in test mode and taking advantage of the Rails fixtures. The approach you choose for your project will depend on your testing preferences. For this chapter, we are using the latter approach, and we will not use a mock delegate but will instead invoke a running server.

Using the ServiceLocator and Delegate to Support CRUD Actions

Until this point in this chapter, we used NotesResource to perform the HTTP requests. In Cairngorm, we use ServiceLocator to declare all the HTTPService components that are used. So we created the Services.mxml class, which extends the cairngorm:ServiceLocator class, and we add the five HTTPServices to the Services class to support the RESTful controller. We also change the URLs to not use data binding to determine the ID because the delegate will set the URL as appropriate. The code is show in Listing 4.5.

Listing 4.5   flexonrails/examples/notetaker/business/Services.mxml

```
<?xml version="1.0" encoding="utf-8"?>
<cairngorm:ServiceLocator
  xmlns:mx="http://www.adobe.com/2006/mxml"
  xmlns:cairngorm="http://www.adobe.com/2006/cairngorm">
```

Listing 4.5   **Continued**

```
<mx:HTTPService id="notes"
  url="http://localhost:3000/notes.xml" resultFormat="e4x" />

<mx:HTTPService id="noteCreate"
  url="http://localhost:3000/notes.xml"
  method="POST"
  resultFormat="e4x"
  contentType="application/xml" />

<mx:HTTPService id="noteShow"
  url="http://localhost:3000/notes/id.xml"
  method="GET"
  resultFormat="e4x" />

<mx:HTTPService id="noteDelete"
  url="http://localhost:3000/notes/id.xml"
  method="POST"
  resultFormat="e4x">
  <mx:request xmlns="">
    <_method>delete</_method>
  </mx:request>
</mx:HTTPService>

<mx:HTTPService id="noteUpdate"
  url="http://localhost:3000/notes/id.xml?_method=put"
  method="POST"
  resultFormat="e4x"
  contentType="application/xml" />

</cairngorm:ServiceLocator>
```

We can now use these new services from the `NoteDelegate` class to implement the `list`, `create`, `show`, `update`, and `destroy` methods. In RESTful terms, the D in CRUD stands for delete, which is a reserved word in ActionScript. Therefore, we will name the delegate method `destroy` in our delegate. The code is shown in Listing 4.6.

Listing 4.6   **flexonrails/examples/notetaker/business/NoteDelegate.as**

```
package flexonrails.examples.notetaker.business
{
  import com.adobe.cairngorm.business.ServiceLocator;
  import mx.rpc.AsyncToken;
  import mx.rpc.IResponder;

  public class NoteDelegate
  {
    private var responder : IResponder;
```

Listing 4.6 *Continued*

```
  private var notesService: Object;
  private var noteCreateService: Object;
  private var noteShowService: Object;
  private var noteDeleteService: Object;
  private var noteUpdateService: Object;

  public function NoteDelegate(responder : IResponder)
  {
    this.notesService      = getService( "notes" );
    this.noteCreateService = getService( "noteCreate" );
    this.noteShowService   = getService( "noteShow" );
    this.noteDeleteService = getService( "noteDelete" );
    this.noteUpdateService = getService( "noteUpdate" );
    this.responder = responder;
  }

  private function getService(name:String):Object {
    return ServiceLocator.getInstance().getHTTPService(name);
  }

  public function list():void {
    var call:AsyncToken = this.notesService.send();
    call.addResponder(this.responder);
  }
  public function create(note:XML):void {
    var call:AsyncToken = this.noteCreateService.send(note);
    call.addResponder(this.responder);
  }
  public function show(id:Number):void {
    this.noteShowService.url = "http://localhost:3000/notes/"+id+".xml";
    var call:AsyncToken = this.noteShowService.send();
    call.addResponder(this.responder);
  }
  public function update(note:XML):void {
    this.noteUpdateService.url =
"http://localhost:3000/notes/"+note.id.toString()+".xml?_method=put"
    var call:AsyncToken = this.noteUpdateService.send(note);
    call.addResponder(this.responder);
  }
  public function destroy(id:Number):void {
    this.noteDeleteService.url = "http://localhost:3000/notes/"+id+".xml"
    var call:AsyncToken = this.noteDeleteService.send();
    call.addResponder(this.responder);
  }

  }
}
```

Testing the Delegate's CRUD Actions

Testing the delegate is similar to testing the notes resource (covered earlier in this chapter). Let's start by testing the `list` method of the delegate. This method is also asynchronous, and therefore, we are using the same approach as when using the `asyncResponder` method provided by the test case class. Again, this is required for the test framework to identify when the test is complete, which in this case is when the delegate invokes the `assertTestList` method. We use the same assertion method to test for success or fault by verifying the instance of the result to be `ResultEvent` or `FaultEvent`. We will not test the `read` functionality as the `list` functionality returns all the details of a note, and therefore, our Flex application doesn't need to retrieve these details again. Another application may need to return only a subset of the attributes for the `list` functionality and thus would require the `read` functionality when showing the details of a specific record.

testList

The code for testing the `list` method is shown in Listing 4.7.

Listing 4.7   **tests/TestNoteDelegate.as [v1]**

```
package tests
{
    import net.digitalprimates.fluint.tests.TestCase;
    import net.digitalprimates.fluint.async.TestResponder;
    import flexonrails.examples.notetaker.business.NoteDelegate;
    import mx.rpc.IResponder;
    import mx.rpc.events.ResultEvent;
    import flash.events.Event;

    public class TestNoteDelegate extends TestCase
    {
        private var delegate:NoteDelegate;

        public function testList():void {
            var responder:IResponder = asyncResponder( new TestResponder(
assertTestList, assertTestList ) , 1000 );
            var delegate : NoteDelegate = new NoteDelegate( responder );
            delegate.list();
        }
        public function assertTestList(result:Event, token:Object = null):void {
            assertTrue(result is ResultEvent);
            assertEquals(2, (result as ResultEvent).result.note.length());
            assertEquals("MyString", (result as
ResultEvent).result.note[0].title);
        }


    }
}
```

If you want to proceed incrementally and run the `testList` method before testing the `update` and `delete` actions, you need to modify the test runner and register this new test case.

Test Runner

The test runner was running a test case directly until now. As you write more tests, you will create new test cases to group related tests. We will add the `TestNoteDelegate` test case to the `TestNotesResource` test case and group them in the `NoteTakerTestSuite` shown in Listing 4.8.

Listing 4.8   **tests/NoteTakerTestSuite**

```
package tests
{
    import net.digitalprimates.fluint.tests.TestSuite;
    public class NoteTakerTestSuite extends TestSuite
    {
        public function NoteTakerTestSuite()
        {
            addTestCase(new TestNotesResource());
            addTestCase(new TestNoteDelegate());
        }
    }
}
```

Now the test runner needs to run this test suite instead of running the test case.

```
testRunner.startTests( new NoteTakerTestSuite() );
```

When testing a Cairngorm application, initialize the service and controller. Achieve this just by including them in the test runner:

```
<control:NotetakerController id="controller" />
<business:Services id="services" />
```

The whole TestRunner now looks as shown in Listing 4.9.

Listing 4.9   **TestRunner.mxml [v2]**

```
<?xml version="1.0" encoding="utf-8"?>
<mx:Application xmlns:mx="http://www.adobe.com/2006/mxml"

xmlns:fluint="http://www.digitalprimates.net/2008/fluint"

xmlns:control="flexonrails.examples.notetaker.control.*"

xmlns:business="flexonrails.examples.notetaker.business.*"

                layout="absolute"
                creationComplete="startTestProcess(event)"
                width="100%" height="100%">
```

Listing 4.9   **Continued**

```
<mx:Script>
    <![CDATA[
        import tests.NoteTakerTestSuite;

        protected function startTestProcess( event:Event ):void {
            testRunner.startTests( new NoteTakerTestSuite() );
        }
    ]]>
</mx:Script>
<fluint:TestResultDisplay width="100%" height="100%"/>
<fluint:TestRunner id="testRunner"/>

<!- Controls required to test the Cairngorm Application ->
<control:NotetakerController id="controller" />
<business:Services id="services" />

</mx:Application>
```

Now you are ready to run the tests, so let's first clear the database and start the Rails server:

```
$ rake db:fixtures:load
$ ./script/server
```

Then run the TestRunner application.

testCreate

When issuing a create request, the server returns the created note in case of success. Otherwise, the server returns the error that occurred. In the test shown in Listing 4.10, we create a simple note and test that the title we defined is actually returned by the server. We use the asyncResponder method provided by the test case, which signals that the test is only complete once the specified responder is invoked.

Listing 4.10   **TestNoteDelegate.as**

```
public function testCreate():void{
    var responder:IResponder = asyncResponder( new TestResponder(
assertTestCreate, assertTestCreate ) , 1000 );
    var delegate : NoteDelegate = new NoteDelegate( responder );
    delegate.create(<note>
                    <title>My First Note</title>
                    <body>Is this a hello world? Not even funny.</body>
                </note>);
}
public function assertTestCreate(result:ResultEvent, token:Object = null):void {
    assertEquals("My First Note", result.result.title);
}
```

testUpdate

Before writing our update test, we need to apply a small change to the fixtures. Rails 2.0 uses Foxy Fixtures, where the ID of each record defined in the fixtures is not required. Therefore, we will need a way to find out the ID of the note we want to test. In Rails, you can refer to `notes(:one).id` to retrieve the ID of the fixtures. For now, we will avoid this issue and change the fixtures to specify the ID of each record. Change the fixtures files, as shown in Listing 4.11. Specify the `id` for each entry in the fixture file.

Listing 4.11   **test/fixtures/notes.yml**

```
one:
  id: 1
  title: MyString
  body: MyText
two:
  id: 2
  title: MyString
  body: MyText
```

In the Using Fixtures section of this chapter, we will show you how to reset fixtures between each test method to write more meaningful tests.

Now we can use these IDs in our Flex tests. But first, let's reload the database:

```
$ rake db:fixtures:load
```

Now let's dive into the `testUpdate` method. As you know, when issuing an update request, the server just returns the OK status in the case of success. Of course, we should trust our server; if it tells us it's OK, then it's OK. Well, for this test, we want to make sure that the change is applied to the note, so we are retrieving the updated note and checking that the change really occurred.

Here we see that Fluint enables you to write test methods even if your test involves multiple asynchronous calls. And the test is complete when all the methods registered with `asyncHandler` are invoked. We can now write our test as shown in Listing 4.12.

Listing 4.12   **TestNoteDelegate.as**

```
public function testUpdate():void {
    var note:XML =
        <note>
          <id>1</id>
          <body>Testing Updates</body>
        </note>;
    var passThroughData:Object = {noteId:Number(note.id)}
    var responder:IResponder = asyncResponder(
        new TestResponder( assertTestUpdateSuccess,
                           assertTestUpdateSuccess ),
        1000, passThroughData );
    var delegate:NoteDelegate = new NoteDelegate( responder );
```

Listing 4.12   **Continued**

```
    delegate.update(note)
}

public function assertTestUpdateSuccess(result:Object,
                                        token:Object = null):void {
    assertTrue(result is ResultEvent);
    var responder:IResponder = asyncResponder(
        new TestResponder( assertTestUpdateData,
                           assertTestUpdateData ),
        1000 );
    var delegate:NoteDelegate = new NoteDelegate( responder );
    delegate.show(token.noteId);
}

public function assertTestUpdateData(result:Object,
                                     token:Object = null):void {
    assertTrue(result is ResultEvent);
    assertEquals("Testing Updates", result.result.body);
}
```

So when `testUpdate` is called, the test method indicates, via the usage of the `asyncResponder` method, that the test is not complete until the `assertTestUpdateSuccess` result method is invoked. We use the same method as the fault and result handler, but in addition, we ensure that the event is a `ResultEvent` and not a `FaultEvent`. In the `assertTestUpdateSuccess` method, we call again the `asyncResponder` method, which lets the test case know that a subsequent asynchronous call is required before the test method is really completed. This is a simple way to test asynchronous remote calls. Another point of interest is the use of the `passThroughData` parameter of the `aysncResponder`, which we use here to pass the note ID to the result handler and thus avoid having to duplicate this ID in two methods.

testDelete

Now that you have the knack for writing these tests, the delete test will be straightforward. Similar to the update test, you set the responder and invoke the delegate's `destroy` method; see Listing 4.13.

Listing 4.13   **TestNoteDelegate.as**

```
    public function testDelete():void {
        var responder:IResponder = asyncResponder( new TestResponder(
assertTestDelete, assertTestDelete ) , 1000 );
        var delegate : NoteDelegate = new NoteDelegate( responder );
        delegate.destroy(1);
}
```

Listing 4.13 *Continued*

```
public function assertTestDelete(result:Object, token:Object = null):void {
    assertTrue(result is ResultEvent);
}
```

Implementing the Cairngorm Commands

As you know, each user gesture is represented by a Cairngorm event, which in turn is
mapped to a Cairngorm command. The command is where all the controlling code
resides. Table 4.1 shows the commands that do not require a server round trip. Table 4.2
shows the main commands that will interact with the server. In the example code below,
we only show the important part of each execute method for each command.

Table 4.1   **Commands That Do Not Require a Server Round Trip**

Command	Example Code
EditNoteCommand	NotetakerModelLocator.getInstance().selectedNote = event.data;
	NotetakerModelLocator.getInstance().currentView = NotetakerModelLocator.EDIT_VIEW;
NewNoteCommand	NotetakerModelLocator.getInstance().selectedNote = <note><body></body></note>;
	NotetakerModelLocator.getInstance().currentView = NotetakerModelLocator.EDIT_VIEW;

Here we see that EditNoteCommand sets the selectedNote on the model and
shows the edit view. NewNoteCommand creates an empty note kept in memory and also
shows the edit view.

Table 4.2   **Commands That Do Require a Server Round Trip**

Command	Example Code
RetrieveNotesCommand	**execute:** var delegate : NoteDelegate = new NoteDelegate(this); delegate.list() **result:** NotetakerModelLocator.getInstance().notes = data.result;

SaveChangeCommand	**execute:**
	var delegate : NoteDelegate = new NoteDelegate(this)
	var note:XML = new XML(event.data.note);
	note.body = event.data.body;

```
                              note.title = note.body.split("\r")[0];
                              if (note.id.toString() == "") {
                                  delegate.create(note)
                              } else {
                                  delegate.update(note)
                              }
                              result:
                                      executeNextCommand();
                              NotetakerModelLocator.getInstance().currentView =
                              NotetakerModelLocator.LIST_VIEW;
DeleteNoteCommand             execute:
                                  var delegate : NoteDelegate = new
                              NoteDelegate( this );

                              delegate.deleteNote(DeleteNoteEvent(event).data);
                              result:
                                  executeNextCommand();
                              NotetakerModelLocator.getInstance().currentView =
                              NotetakerModelLocator.LIST_VIEW;
```

The `retrieve`, `save`, and `delete` commands pass the request along to the delegate. The `save` command handles the scenario for the `create` and the `update` commands because the note has an ID.

Let's test two of the events and commands of our awesome NoteTaker application. We will write two separate test methods to verify that the `RetrieveNotesEvent` and `SaveChangeEvent` events are operating as expected. The tests will trigger the event, listen to a model change, and assert the impact of the associated command on the model. We are also taking the opportunity to introduce a new concept of Fluint: Sequences. A sequence enables a test method to wait until multiple asynchronous events occur before triggering an assertion handler. For the test method, this capability will enable us to issue the update request, get the response, and issue the show request before asserting the result. The sequence can also issue events, so we can use a sequence to define a suite of actions that need to be executed. In the next section on testing the UI, we will use the sequence even further to emulate user input. Actually, for testing Cairngorm events and commands, we could even test chains of sequence and commands. But, let's start simple.

To host the new events- and commands-related tests, we will create a new test case class named `TestNoteCommands`, which also needs to be registered in the `NoteTakerTestSuite` class.

Testing RetrieveNotesCommand

Table 4.3 shows an extract of the `RetrieveNotesCommand` class. When the command executes, it invokes the `list` method of the delegate. Upon receiving the result, it sets the `notes` attribute on the model locator.

Table 4.3   **Overview of the RetrieveNotesCommand**

Command	Example Code
RetrieveNotesCommand	execute:
	var delegate : NoteDelegate = new NoteDelegate(this);
	delegate.list()
	result:
	NotetakerModelLocator.getInstance().notes = data.result;

The `testRetrieveNotesCommand` method will ensure that this command works as expected. To this end, as part of the `testRetrieveNotesCommand` method, we will create a `Sequence` that will wait for a change of the notes attribute of the model. We are defining the assertion method that is to be triggered once the sequence is complete, and then we will run the sequence. Finally, we trigger via the `CairngormEventDispatcher` the `RetrieveNotesEvent`. Triggering that event will execute the associated `RetrieveNotesCommand` command, which will retrieve all the notes from the server and assign these notes to the `notes` attribute of the model. The sequence will detect this change and trigger the assertion method. There we can assert that the notes are effectively assigned on the model and prove that the server returned some notes. Take a look at the test and assertion methods shown in Listing 4.14.

Listing 4.14   **tests/TestNoteCommands.as**

```
public function testRetrieveNotesCommand():void {
    var sequence:SequenceRunner = new SequenceRunner(this);

    sequence.addStep(new SequenceBindingWaiter(model, "notes", 1000));
    sequence.addAssertHandler(assertRetrieveNotesCommand, null);
    sequence.run();
    new RetrieveNotesEvent().dispatch();
}
protected function assertRetrieveNotesCommand(event:Event,
passThroughData:Object):void {
    assertNotNull("Expect model.notes not to be null", model.notes);
    assertTrue("Expect more than 0 notes", model.notes.note.length() > 0);
}
```

Testing SaveChangeCommand

`SaveChangeCommand` verifies whether a note has an ID attribute, and if it does, uses the delegate to update the note. Otherwise, it asks to create a new note. The code extract in Table 4.4 provides an overview of the code we will now test.

Table 4.4   **Overview of the SaveChangeCommand**

Command	Example Code
SaveChangeCommand	execute:
	var delegate : NoteDelegate = new NoteDelegate(this)
	var note:XML = new XML(event.data.note);
	note.body = event.data.body;
	note.title = note.body.split("\r")[0];
	if (note.id.toString() == "") {
	delegate.create(note)
	} else {
	delegate.update(note)
	}
	result:
	executeNextCommand();
	NotetakerModelLocator.getInstance().currentView = NotetakerModelLocator.LIST_VIEW;

To verify that adding a new note works, we are taking an approach similar to that for the retrieve test. We will create a new note and trigger the save change event. This action will send the new note to the server, and upon success, trigger the next event, which is the retrieve notes command. After retrieving the notes, it updates the model. The sequence is again waiting for this change and triggers the assert method, where we are testing that the view is changed back to the list view and that the last note is effectively the new note we created. This time, the command also changes the selectedNote property on the model, so we need to specify all the properties that are changed in the proper sequence to avoid the test failing. Et Voila! Listing 4.15 provides the test.

Listing 4.15   **tests/TestNoteCommands.as**

```
public function testSaveChangeCommandNewNote():void {
  var sequence:SequenceRunner = new SequenceRunner(this);
  sequence.addStep(new SequenceBindingWaiter(model, "selectedNote", 1000));
  sequence.addStep(new SequenceBindingWaiter(model, "notes", 1000));
  sequence.addAssertHandler(assertSaveChangeCommandNewNote, null);
  sequence.run();
  model.selectedNote = <note><body></body></note>;
  new SaveChangeEvent("New Note\rwith lots of info",
                      model.selectedNote).dispatch();
}
protected function assertSaveChangeCommandNewNote(event:Event,
passThroughData:Object):void {
```

Listing 4.15   *Continued*

```
assertNotNull("Expect model.notes not to be null", model.notes);
assertTrue("Expect more than 0 notes", model.notes.note.length() > 0);
assertEquals("Expected LIST_VIEW", NotetakerModelLocator.LIST_VIEW,
             model.currentView);
assertEquals("New Note",
    model.notes.note[model.notes.note.length()-1].title.toString());
}
```

Implementing the ListView Class

OK, let's go ahead and wire up the UI. ListView will mainly contain a mx:List.
When clicking the List, EditNoteEvent is dispatched. We are also adding the Add
button, which will trigger NewNoteEvent (see Listing 4.16).

Listing 4.16   **flexonrails/examples/notetaker/view/ListView.mxml**

```
<?xml version="1.0" encoding="utf-8"?>
<mx:Canvas xmlns:mx="http://www.adobe.com/2006/mxml">
<mx:Script>
  <![CDATA[
    import flexonrails.examples.notetaker.model.NotetakerModelLocator;
    import flexonrails.examples.notetaker.event.NewNoteEvent;
    import flexonrails.examples.notetaker.event.EditNoteEvent;

    [Bindable]
    private var model:NotetakerModelLocator =
                         NotetakerModelLocator.getInstance();
  ]]>
</mx:Script>
  <mx:Label id="header"
    text="Notes ({model.notes.note.length()})"
    horizontalCenter="0" />
  <mx:Button id="addBtn" right="4" y="12" label="Add"
         click="new NewNoteEvent().dispatch();"/>
  <mx:List id="list" labelField="title"
         dataProvider="{model.notes.note}"
         click="new EditNoteEvent(list.selectedItem).dispatch();"
         left="4" right="4" bottom="0"  top="39" />
</mx:Canvas>
```

In the Testing Events and Commands section of this chapter, we introduced the
Sequence class, which enables you not only to wait for events but also to dispatch events
in a sequence. We will use this feature to emulate user gestures, thus enabling us to
really test the UI and perform an end-to-end test of the impact of such a user gesture.

Let's go ahead and write some tests to ensure that the Add button effectively shows the edit screen with a new note selected, then another test to emulate the user clicking on a note and checking that the edit screen is displayed with the selected note.

A first question is this: How are we going to bring up the UI and let the test click on a grid or push a button? We will use the setUp and tearDown methods of the test case, which are invoked between each test method, to create a new ListView and a new model. So let's add these two attributes to our test case:

```
private var model:NotetakerModelLocator;
private var listView:ListView;
```

Then let's just create a new ListView instance and add it as child to the test case. In the tearDown method, we will just remove it to ensure that each test method doesn't influence another.

```
override protected function setUp():void {
  model = NotetakerModelLocator.getInstance(true);
  listView = new ListView();
  listView.addEventListener(FlexEvent.CREATION_COMPLETE,
          asyncHandler( pendUntilComplete, 1000 ), false, 0, true );
  addChild(listView);
}
override protected function tearDown():void {
  model = null;
  removeChild(listView);
  listView = null;
}
```

Now let's create the testAddNewNote method:

```
var sequence:SequenceRunner = new SequenceRunner(this);
sequence.addStep(
    new SequenceEventDispatcher(
                listView.addBtn,
                new MouseEvent( 'click', true, false ) ) );
sequence.addStep(new SequenceBindingWaiter(model, "selectedNote",1000));
sequence.addStep(new SequenceBindingWaiter(model, "currentView",1000));
sequence.addAssertHandler(assertAddNewNote, null);
sequence.run();
```

In this test, we emulate the user clicking on addBtn. Clicking on addBtn will dispatch NewNoteEvent, which in turn will trigger NewNoteCommand, which resets selectedNote and currentView. To emulate this via code, we are using SequenceRunner, which defines a sequence that dispatches the mouse client event, and then listens for the selectedNote change using SequenceBindingWaiter. It then listens to the currentView change and finally invokes the assertion handler.

In the assertion method, we just verify that the edit view is selected:

```
assertEquals("Expected EDIT_VIEW", NotetakerModelLocator.EDIT_VIEW,
model.currentView);
```

This a little more complex; let's create the `testClickNoteListShowsEditNote` test method and select the second row of the list by setting the `selectedIndex` to one and having the list dispatch the click event as highlighted in the following code:

```
var sequence:SequenceRunner = new SequenceRunner(this);
sequence.addStep(new SequenceBindingWaiter(model, "notes", 1000));
sequence.addStep(new SequenceSetter(listView.list,{selectedIndex: 1}));
sequence.addStep(
  new SequenceEventDispatcher(
      listView.list,
      new MouseEvent( 'click', true, false)));
sequence.addStep(new SequenceWaiter(listView.list, MouseEvent.CLICK, 100));
sequence.addAssertHandler(assertClickNoteListShowsEditNote, null);
sequence.run();
new RetrieveNotesEvent().dispatch();
```

And again, let's assert that the edit view is selected with the selected note.

```
assertEquals("Expected EDIT_VIEW", NotetakerModelLocator.EDIT_VIEW,
model.currentView);
assertEquals("MyString", model.selectedNote.title);
```

In the above code, we are just testing the list view and not the edit view. We could now write a similar test case to ensure that the edit view works as expected. We could test that the selected note is displayed correctly when adding a new note and also when editing an existing note. We could also test that the delete functionality is operational. Ready? Well, this is not a real question. You are ready. Just go ahead and code it.

`TestNoteListView` now is shown in Listing 4.17.

Listing 4.17   **tests/TestNoteListView.as**

```
package tests
{
  import flash.events.Event;
  import flash.events.MouseEvent;
  import mx.events.FlexEvent;
  import flexonrails.examples.notetaker.event.RetrieveNotesEvent;
  import flexonrails.examples.notetaker.model.NotetakerModelLocator;
  import flexonrails.examples.notetaker.view.ListView;
  import tests.utils.TestHelper;
  import net.digitalprimates.fluint.sequence.SequenceEventDispatcher;
  import net.digitalprimates.fluint.sequence.SequenceRunner;
  import net.digitalprimates.fluint.sequence.SequenceSetter;
  import net.digitalprimates.fluint.sequence.SequenceWaiter;
```

```
import net.digitalprimates.fluint.sequence.SequenceBindingWaiter;
import net.digitalprimates.fluint.tests.TestCase;


public class TestNoteListView extends TestCase
{
  private var model:NotetakerModelLocator;
  private var listView:ListView;

  override protected function setUp():void {
    TestHelper.resetFixtures(this, ['notes']);
    model = NotetakerModelLocator.getInstance(true);
    listView = new ListView();
    listView.addEventListener(FlexEvent.CREATION_COMPLETE,
             asyncHandler( pendUntilComplete, 1000 ), false, 0, true );
    addChild(listView);
  }
  override protected function tearDown():void {
    model = null;
    removeChild(listView);
    listView = null;
  }

  public function testAddNewNote():void {
    var sequence:SequenceRunner = new SequenceRunner(this);
    sequence.addStep(
        new SequenceEventDispatcher(
            listView.addBtn, new MouseEvent( 'click', true, false ) ) );
    sequence.addStep(
        new SequenceBindingWaiter(model, "selectedNote",1000));
    sequence.addStep(
        new SequenceBindingWaiter(model, "currentView",1000));
    sequence.addAssertHandler(assertAddNewNote, null);
    sequence.run();
  }
  protected function assertAddNewNote(event:Event,
                                    passThroughData:Object):void {
    assertEquals("Expected EDIT_VIEW",
             NotetakerModelLocator.EDIT_VIEW, model.currentView);
  }

  public function testClickNoteListShowsEditNote():void {
    var sequence:SequenceRunner = new SequenceRunner(this);
    sequence.addStep(new SequenceBindingWaiter(model, "notes", 1000));
    sequence.addStep(new SequenceSetter(
                        listView.list,{selectedIndex: 1}));
```

Listing 4.17   **Continued**

```
      sequence.addStep(new SequenceEventDispatcher(
                 listView.list, new MouseEvent( 'click', true, false)));
      sequence.addStep(new SequenceWaiter(
                 listView.list, MouseEvent.CLICK, 100));
      sequence.addAssertHandler(assertClickNoteListShowsEditNote, null);
    . sequence.run();
      new RetrieveNotesEvent().dispatch();
    }
   protected function assertClickNoteListShowsEditNote(event:Event,
                                    passThroughData:Object):void {
     assertEquals("Expected EDIT_VIEW",
              NotetakerModelLocator.EDIT_VIEW, model.currentView);
     assertEquals("MyString", model.selectedNote.title);
    }
  }
}
```

Implementing the EditView Class

The `EditView` class is mostly composed of a `TextArea` component displaying the body of the note and save, delete, and cancel buttons. As expected, the save and delete buttons trigger respectively `SaveChangeEvent` and `DeleteNoteEvent` (see Listing 4.18).

Listing 4.18   **flexonrails/examples/notetaker/view/EditView.mxml**

```
<?xml version="1.0" encoding="utf-8"?>
<mx:Canvas xmlns:mx="http://www.adobe.com/2006/mxml">
<mx:Script>
  <![CDATA[
  import flexonrails.examples.notetaker.model.NotetakerModelLocator;
  import flexonrails.examples.notetaker.event.BackToListEvent;
  import flexonrails.examples.notetaker.event.SaveChangeEvent;
  import flexonrails.examples.notetaker.event.DeleteNoteEvent;

  [Bindable]
  private var model:NotetakerModelLocator =
                        NotetakerModelLocator.getInstance();

  private function save():void {
    new SaveChangeEvent(noteBodyField.text, model.selectedNote).dispatch();
  }
  ]]>
</mx:Script>
  <mx:Label id="header" text="{model.selectedNote.title}"
          horizontalCenter="0" />
  <mx:Button left="4" y="12" label="<Cancel"
```

Listing 4.18   **Continued**

```
              click="new BackToListEvent().dispatch();"/>
   <mx:Button right="4" y="12" label="Save"
              click="save()" />
   <mx:Canvas width="100%" height="100%" >
        <mx:TextArea id="noteBodyField"
             left="4" right="4" bottom="0" top="39"
             text="{model.selectedNote.body}"/>
        <mx:ControlBar bottom="0">
          <mx:Button label="Delete"
            enabled="{model.selectedNote.id.toString() != ''}"
            click="new DeleteNoteEvent(model.selectedNote.id).dispatch()"/>
        </mx:ControlBar>
   </mx:Canvas>
</mx:Canvas>
```

Testing EditView

Armed with your newly acquired knowledge, we leave it up to you now to implement a series of tests to make sure the edit view operates as expected. You could, for instance, add a `testDeleteButtonDisabledForAddNote` method that verifies when adding a new note that the delete button is effectively disabled and also add the `testDeleteButtonEnabledForEditNote` method to ensure that the same button is enabled when editing the note. You can also add a `testSaveNoteShowNoteList` method to verify that saving the note triggers the `SaveChangeCommand` command and returns the user to the list view.

Using Fixtures

If you work with Rails, you are certainly familiar with the concept of fixtures. Fixtures are used by the test framework to reset the state of the database to the known state in place before each test method is run. This way, a test method can concentrate on one action and only assert the impact of that action without being impacted by, or having to rely on, data created or modified by another test. For example, if a test needs to verify that a retrieve works and that only two items exist, you can add two items to the fixtures and just test that the retrieve effectively returned the expected two items. Now, if another test creates a new item and performs a retrieve, three items would exist for that test. But, if the first test is run again, the database is reset, the fixtures loaded, and the test would work again (returning only two items) without being impacted by the create items in other tests. We now have repeatable tests.

To be able to reset the fixtures from Flex, we will provide and describe some infrastructure code that needs to be deployed as part of your Rails application, and we extend the TestHelper with a `resetFixtures` method, which can be used in the setup of your test cases.

Rails: FixturesController

To reset our fixtures from our Flex unit tests, we need to create a Rails fixture controller enabling the Flex application to make an HTTP request to reload the fixtures. Be sure this controller is only operational in test mode and never in production mode. We will add some code to ensure that is the case.

In Rails, to reset the fixtures, you can use the `Fixtures` class as follows:

```
def reset
  table_names = params[:fixtures][:fixture]
  Fixtures.reset_cache
  Fixtures.create_fixtures("#{RAILS_ROOT}/test/fixtures/", table_names, {})
  render :xml => "<status>ok</status>"
end
```

Rails internally uses the `Fixtures` class to manage the fixture for the rails tests, so we can create the `FixturesController` shown in Listing 4.19 to expose that functionality to Flex.

Listing 4.19   **dpuint_rails/app/controllers/fixtures_controller.rb**

```
if RAILS_ENV == "test"
  require 'active_record/fixtures'

  class FixturesController < ApplicationController

    def reset
      table_names = params[:fixtures][:fixture]
      Fixtures.reset_cache
      Fixtures.create_fixtures("#{RAILS_ROOT}/test/fixtures/", table_names, {})
      render :xml => "<status>ok</status>"
    end

    def crossdomain
      render :text => <<-EOXML
<?xml version="1.0"?>
<!DOCTYPE cross-domain-policy SYSTEM "http://www.macromedia.com/xml/dtds/cross-
domain-policy.dtd">
<cross-domain-policy>
  <allow-access-from domain="*" />
</cross-domain-policy>
      EOXML
    end

    RESULTS_FILE = File.join(RAILS_ROOT, '..', 'flex', 'bin-debug',
'test_results.txt')
    def test_results
      File.open(RESULTS_FILE, 'w') { |f| f.write params['testsuites'].to_xml(:root
=> 'testsuites') }
```

Listing 4.19   *Continued*

```
      head :ok
    end
  end

end #if test
```

In addition, we need to set up the routes, so let's add the following lines to the config/routes.rb file:

```
if RAILS_ENV == "test"
  map.resources :fixtures, :collection => {:reset => :get}
  map.crossdomain '/crossdomain.xml', :controller => 'fixtures', :action =>
'crossdomain'
end
```

Flex: TestHelper

From Flex, we can now reset the fixtures from the setUp method of the test case using the following code:

```
override protected function setUp():void {
  fixtures = new HTTPService();
  fixtures.url = "http://localhost:3000/fixtures/reset";
  fixtures.contentType="application/xml";
  fixtures.addEventListener(ResultEvent.RESULT,
        asyncHandler( pendUntilComplete, 1000 ));
  fixtures.send(<fixtures><fixture>notes</fixture></fixtures>);
}
```

But, this code is too verbose, and we can wrap it in a test helper class to provide a simple way to reset fixtures from our various test cases (see Listing 4.20).

Listing 4.20   **TestHelper.as**

```
package tests.utils
{
  import flash.events.Event;
  import mx.rpc.events.ResultEvent;
  import mx.rpc.http.HTTPService;
  import net.digitalprimates.fluint.tests.TestCase;

  public class TestHelper
  {
    static private var fixtures:HTTPService;
    static public function resetFixtures(testCase:TestCase,
                                  names:Array):void {
```

Listing 4.20   ***Continued***

```
        fixtures = new HTTPService();
        fixtures.url = "http://localhost:3000/fixtures/reset";
        fixtures.contentType="application/xml";
        fixtures.addEventListener(ResultEvent.RESULT,
            testCase.asyncHandler( pendUntilComplete, 1000 ),false, 0, true);
        var data:XML = <fixtures/>
        for each (var fixture:String in names) {
          data.fixture += <fixture>{fixture}</fixture>;
        }
        fixtures.send(data);
      }
    static public function pendUntilComplete( event:Event,
                                        passThroughData:Object ):void {
      }
    }
}
```

Now we can simply write our `setUp` method as follows:

```
override protected function setUp():void {
    TestHelper.resetFixtures(this, ['notes']);
}
```

Also note that we only define `FixturesController` when the application is in test mode. From now on, we will use the server in test mode when running our Flex unit tests. This approach also ensures that no one will, by mistake, call this test when running the server in production mode. Furthermore, it enables you to use the test and development environment in parallel, providing you with countless benefits.

To start the server in test mode, you need to add the environment flag as follows:

```
$ ./script/server -e test
```

Now we can run all our tests (see Figure 4.6). Nice!

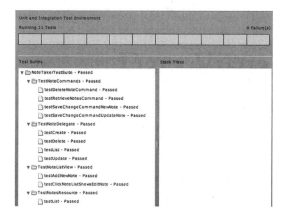

Figure 4.6   All our tests pass.

Summary

If you are not currently writing tests for your Flex and Rails application, I encourage you to do so now. With the techniques described in this chapter, you will quickly get up and running. The quality of your code will improve, you will have fewer bugs, and you will be able to implement changes and be confident that the application still runs as expected. Just do it.

5

Passing Data with AMF

This chapter shows you how to pass data to and from Flex and Rails using a slightly different method than XML: Adobe's binary AMF protocol with the RubyAMF Rails plug-in.

What Is AMF?

AMF stands for Action Message Format. This standard format is for encoding data to use in ActionScript. Macromedia created AMF as a way to make connecting a Flash interface with a "back-end" service a lot easier. As long as the service understands how to encode and decode AMF messages, applications written in ActionScript can communicate with the service as if it were a part of the running program, at least as far as the type of the objects is concerned.

This concept enables very powerful Remote Procedure Call (RPC) or Remote Method Invocation (RMI) style service interaction. Both concepts describe a way of facilitating communication from code running in one system to code running in another, separate system. The idea is that the details of communication are hidden to some degree inside the language such that a programmer can call methods or send messages from the current program to another program running on a remote system as if the remote system were a part of the current program.

As an example, the product in which AMF was introduced is Flash Remoting, which was initially developed by Macromedia for the Java platform. A developer could write a Flash application that made a remote call to a server running a Java application that had Flash Remoting installed. The Flash application could execute a method on a "remote object," passing an ActionScript object to that method. When it came out the other side to Java, it would already be translated to a Java object. Likewise, when the Java method returned a Java object, that object was encoded to AMF and sent back through Flash Remoting to be decoded by the Flash Player into an ActionScript object. As far as the Flash developer was concerned, that remote object could be treated like any other ActionScript object.

Benefits of AMF

Flex can send messages to other services, such as SOAP Web Services, XML-RPC services, RESTful services, and any other type of service with the lower-level IO classes Flash exposes. The applications could even be written such that programmers need only think about these services as local objects.

The benefit to using a service that understands how to encode and decode AMF is that the programmer is then able to take advantage of the Flash Player's native AMF encoding and decoding to have all return messages turned into ActionScript objects automatically.

Another benefit is speed. AMF is a binary format, as opposed to XML, which is text. XML is designed to be human-readable, so while it's a very useful way to describe, and even transfer, data between disparate systems, it could be considered unnecessarily verbose for communication purposes if both sides, the client and the server, could support a more concise format.

You'll find some execution and bandwidth benchmarks for various methods of transferring data to Flash at www.jamesward.org/census/. A single test run with 5,000 rows of gzip compressed data transferred to a Flex application first using XML and then using AMF showed that the AMF message size was 29K while the XML message size was 47K. The Flash player parsed the XML in 121 milliseconds using the excellent XML parsing built into ActionScript with E4X. However, parsing the AMF message took just 4 milliseconds.

Parsing and data transfer aside, a developer has some choices to make about the form of the data the application needs to work with. With E4X objects, the application can work directly with XML quickly and easily, editing properties, adding and deleting from collections of child objects, and so on. In this case, the data in the application is basically straight XML from the service.

The AMF alternative is that data from the service is turned into an ActionScript object. In this case, the developer has more flexibility in making an object act the way the application needs it to act. Remember, the definition of an object is data and methods that act on that data. An XML representation of the data is only the data.

In the case of an application displaying read-only data or providing simple CRUD functionality on data, E4X objects would work fine. If there were more complex data needs, like calculations, validations, derived data, and so on, it may make more sense to have the application deal with objects that contain those methods instead of keeping the functionality separate from the data. In that case, the Flash Player would happily decode AMF into ActionScript objects containing whatever data you chose to model with whatever methods the application needed to invoke to operate on that data.

One last small advantage to using objects instead of XML is that having a set of classes that define the objects being transferred from the server to the Flash Player client shows explicitly what data the client expects to receive. Dealing with XML would require the extra step of reading documentation or looking at server code more often to be reminded of the properties available on the data.

Now that we've seen a bit of what AMF is and how it can help development, let's look at RubyAMF.

RubyAMF

RubyAMF was written by Aaron Smith around 2006 to 2007. He wrote it to be used with any Ruby application, but it has many enhancements for Rails applications. Aryk Grosz, of Mixbook.com, helped make a lot of speed improvements in late 2007.

Installation

RubyAMF is available from Google Code at http://rubyamf.googlecode.com and is installed as a Rails plug-in. You install a plug-in directly from the web using the `script/plugin` command. The RubyAMF installation command looks like this (from the root of your project):

```
script/install http://rubyamf.googlecode.com/svn/tags/current/rubyamf
```

When the plug-in finishes installing, a new file called rubyamf_config.rb is created in the conf directory called, where RubyAMF can be configured to match your needs.

In your controller, you now can return any Ruby object (like `ActiveRecords`) using the following:

```
render :amf => object
```

and if you're using a RESTful controller, you can respond to incoming AMF requests too:

```
respond_to do |format|
  format.amf { ... }
end
```

RubyAMF Configuration

RubyAMF can be configured in conf/rubyamf_config.rb. The documentation in the comments is fairly comprehensive, but this section presents a list of all the `ClassMappings` options to show you the different ways you can configure RubyAMF. None of these options is required; at least, you don't have to change the settings since all have a default. Some of the `ClassMapping` RubyAMF configuration options appear in Table 5.1.

Table 5.1   Some of the ClassMapping RubyAMF Configuration Options

Option	Default
ClassMappings.ignore_fields	[created_at, created_on, updated_at, updated_on]
ClassMappings.translate_case	false
ClassMappings.assume_types	false
ClassMappings.use_ruby_date_time	false
ClassMappings.use_array_collection	false
ClassMappings.check_for_associations	true

The `ignore_fields` option lets you configure an array of properties which, coming from Flex, will be ignored by RubyAMF when translating to Ruby objects.

This may seem odd, but there's a common use case: the `created_on/at` and `updated_on/at` properties of `ActiveRecords` are automatically populated with the date and time the object was created and last updated, respectively. Those data may be important to show on the UI, but we want Rails to control what values appear there. By ignoring them, we can make sure that no values coming in to be saved are used and instead let Rails choose what goes in those properties.

The `translate_case` option is a simple one, but it is helpful for maintaining coding standards. ActionScript developers tend to name properties and methods using "camel case," where the spaces between the words that make up that element are indicated by a change from lowercase to uppercase, for example, `aPropertyName` or `firstAndLastName`. For properties and method names, Ruby developers conventionally use "snake case," which simply replaces spaces with underscores, as in: `a_property_name`. Using the `ClassMappings.translate_case` option, RubyAMF lets you decide to keep those conventions in place on both sides. It will also automatically translate an incoming ActionScript object's properties from camel case to snake case and outgoing Ruby object's properties from snake case to camel case.

The `assume_types` option lets objects coming in from Flex automatically be translated into corresponding Ruby objects, and vice versa, without the need for explicitly mapping ActionScript classes to Ruby classes.

This follows the "Convention over Configuration" and "DRY" principles of Rails development. The name of the incoming class is configured in the ActionScript with the `RemoteClass` metadata:

```
[RemoteClass(alias="MyClass")]
class MyClass {
  ...
}
```

That alias doesn't have to match the qualified name of the ActionScript class. All it needs to be is a unique string to identify the class as belonging to RubyAMF. If `ClassMappings.assume_types` is set to true and you follow the convention of naming

the `RemoteClass` alias to the name of the corresponding `ActiveRecord` class, then
RubyAMF will automatically translate the incoming class to the right `ActiveRecord`.
We'll hear more about this option in the section on workflow.

Incoming dates from ActionScript are turned into Ruby Time objects by default. If
`ClassMappings.use_ruby_date_time` is true, they're turned into `DateTime` objects
instead.

Outgoing array objects are turned into ActionScript array objects by default. If
`ClassMappings.use_array_collection` is true, they're turned into ActionScript
`ArrayCollection` classes instead.

If `ClassMappings.check_for_associations` is true, RubyAMF will automatically
load any associated members of outgoing objects like `has_many`, `belongs_to`, and
so on, one level deep.

The `ParameterMappings` settings concern incoming parameters instead of incoming
objects. Two such settings are presented in Table 5.2.

Table 5.2   **ParameterMappings Settings**

Option	Default
`ParameterMappings.always_add_to_params`	`true`
`ParameterMappings.scaffolding`	`false`

Rails controllers always provide a hash called `params` that contains incoming data.
RubyAMF sends data in a hash called `rubyamf_params` but also adds all data to `params`
if `ParameterMappings.always_add_to_params` is `true`, which it is by default. This
setting is useful if you want to depend on `rubyamf_params` and keep large object
graphs out of the Rails logs.

`ParameterMappings.scaffolding` helps you work with Rails scaffold-generated
controllers a bit more easily. When `ParameterMappings.scaffolding` is true, the first
incoming object is named the snake-cased name of the class so that code in the controller like this works:

```
@person = params[:person]
```

One last convenience is that if RubyAMF finds an object with no type mapping
(such as an anonymous object), it will turn that object into the `params` hash. We'll look
at that mechanism in the examples.

If `ParameterMappings.scaffolding` is `false`, any entering objects appear in both
the `rubyamf_params` and `params` hashes starting at key `0` and counting up. To specify
names to the incoming params, see `ParameterMappings.register`.

RubyAMF allows automatic class translation if `ClassMappings.assume_types` is
true. Why would you want to be more explicit about class mappings?

First, if you have some properties that aren't a one-to-one correlation, you could use
mappings to let RubyAMF know how to translate them.

Second, you may want to have certain properties ignored at a class level instead of a
global level, as with `ClassMappings.ignore_fields`.

Third, there may be a case where you want to call a method on a Rails model and put the results in a property of an ActionScript object.

Last, but not least, RubyAMF gains a speed advantage if you map every property and association you expect it to translate.

A basic class mapping looks like this:

```
ClassMappings.register(:actionscript => '<incoming class alias>', :ruby => '<ruby
class name>')
```

If the Ruby class is an `ActiveRecord`, then that's specified like this:

```
ClassMappings.register(
    :actionscript => '<incoming class alias>',
    :ruby => '<ruby class name>',
    :type => 'active_record'
)
```

You can also be more explicit about the properties you want translated by using the `:attributes`, `:ignore_fields`, and `:associations` keys, as in this example:

```
ClassMappings.register(
    :actionscript => 'com.myapp.Person',
    :ruby => 'Person',
    :type => 'active_record',
    :attributes => ['first_name', 'last_name'],
    :ignore_fields => ['address_line_3'],
    :associations => ['orders', 'coupons'],
    :methods => ['friends_full_names']
)
```

If you want even more fine-grained control over which attributes get deserialized, you can set up mapping scopes. These allow you to name a few sets of attributes that you want deserialized in different circumstances. Consider this mapping:

```
ClassMappings.register(
    :actionscript => 'com.myapp.BlogPost',
    :ruby => 'BlogPost',
    :type => 'active_record',
    :attributes => { :list_view => ['title', 'tag_list', ], :full_view =>
['body', 'title', 'tag_list', 'updated_on' ] }
)
ClassMappings.default_mapping_scope = :full_view
```

In this case, the `:attributes` key points to a hash instead of to an array. Each key is a different mapping scope. That means the developer can choose which attributes to send back by choosing the mapping scope. This isn't an everyday need, but it's a great performance enhancement to help with sending large object graphs back to Flex. If you don't need the attributes, there's no need for RubyAMF to encode them, right?

To choose a non-default mapping scope, add it to the render statement like this:

```
render :amf => blogs, :class_mapping_scope => :list_view
```

Table 5.3 presents a couple of final RubyAMF configuration settings.

Table 5.3   **Final RubyAMF Configuration Settings**

Option	Default
ClassMappings.force_active_record_ids	true
ParameterMappings.register	NA

If you define the attribute list you want RubyAMF to translate with `ClassMappings.register`, and you set `force_active_record_ids` to true, you can omit the `id` property from the registrations, and RubyAMF will still make sure the `id` property is encoded and decoded.

`ParameterMappings.register` enables you to name any incoming parameters. This capability is helpful if you're either sending primitives or sending multiple objects at once.

To name a parameter, you choose which controller, optionally, which action to name the parameters for, and then which position in the incoming parameter array to name. If you don't specify an action, the names work for all actions on that controller. Here's an example:

```
ParameterMappings.register(
    :controller => :OrdersController,
    :action => :verify_card,
    :params => { :card_number => "[0]", :name_on_card => "[1]" })
```

Now, when calling to the `OrdersController#verify_card` action, the params hash will contain two keys:

```
card_number = params[:card_number]
name_on_card = params[:name_on_card]
```

Parameters can be deeply mapped, too:

```
ParameterMappings.register(
    :controller => :OrdersController,
    :action => :verify_card,
    :params => { :card_number => "[0][number]", :name_on_card =>
 "[0][name]" })
```

The mapping shown here would find the same `params` keys as above, but get them both from one incoming object.

RubyAMF Generators

RubyAMF provides a few tools, in the form of generators, to help you get going. Generators are run with a command like `script/generate <something>`, for instance, `script/generate scaffold Person`, which creates a model, migration, tests, fixtures, controller, and views. Table 5.4 presents two generators and example commands.

Table 5.4   **Two Generators with Sample Commands**

Generator	Command
ClassMapping Generator	script/generate rubyamf_class_mappings
RubyAMF Standard Scaffold	script/generate rubyamf_scaffold

This generator doesn't actually modify anything or create any files, but it does facilitate mapping your `ActiveRecords` without a lot of typing. It goes over all the `ActiveRecords` in your app/models directory and prints out the full mapping for those classes to the console. You can then copy and paste any parts you need into the configuration in conf/rubyamf_config.rb.

With Rails 2.0, the standard scaffold generates a controller that provides a RESTful service. A lot can be read about the finer points of a RESTful service around the web. RubyAMF provides a `respond_to` type to fit in nicely with a RESTful service and respond to any AMF client requests.

If your Rails application will only act as a back-end to a Flex client, you probably want your controllers to look cleaner and more fine-tuned than a RESTful controller. You also probably don't need to generate any of the HTML views or standard view tests either.

Generating a RubyAMF standard scaffold gives you:

- A Model
- A Migration
- A Unit Test and Fixtures
- A Controller with these actions:
  - `find_all` returns all objects of class `type`
  - `find_by_id`, given an ID, returns corresponding object or nil (null)
  - `save` creates or updates object or throws `FaultObject`
  - `destroy`, given an ID, destroys object and returns `true`

This controller matches a simpler set of needs than the Rails standard scaffold controller and is set up to expect RubyAMF objects.

Workflow with RubyAMF

Seeing all the tools and options RubyAMF provides may seem a little overwhelming all in one place. It's a very flexible plug-in, but there's no need to use every configuration option. In this section, we cover a few common use cases with steps and configuration options.

Before we look at those use cases, let's look at the workflow around `ClassMappings`. Unless you have a well-defined data model, you're probably going to be making a lot of changes. RubyAMF's `ClassMappings` provides good documentation of what the application means to send between the client and server and also gives a serialization speed increase over using `ClassMappings.assume_types`. We don't necessarily need those things during development, though.

That's what `ClassMappings.assume_types` is for. Just like Rails, it enables you to define the class name in an ActionScript `RemoteClass` alias, where it needs to be defined anyway, and then not have to repeat yourself. Make as many changes as necessary, and then once you're ready to push to production, add `ClassMappings` and change `ClassMappings.assume_types` to false.

The four use cases include development, data model complete/production ready, using RESTful controllers, and using the RubyAMF standard controller.

Development
The development use case goes as follows:

1. Install RubyAMF out of the box.
2. Change `ClassMappings.assume_types` to `true`.
3. Develop the data model.

Data Model Complete/Production Ready
The data model complete/production ready use case also follows three steps:

1. Use `script/generate rubyamf_class_mappings` to rough out the `ClassMappings`.
2. Set up `ClassMappings` in conf/rubyamf_config.rb.
3. Set `ClassMappings.assume_types` to `false`.

Using RESTful Controllers
To implement RESTful controllers, you follow these steps:

1. Change `ParameterMappings.scaffolding` to `true`.
2. Add `respond_to format.amf` blocks to the scaffold-generated controller.
3. You may need to add a `save` method for RubyAMF, since the `create` and `update` actions don't work well with incoming RubyAMF `params`. We'll see more about this in the examples.

Using the RubyAMF Standard Controller
Using the RubyAMF standard controller is very simple:

1. No configuration changes are necessary.
2. Write the controller as necessary, or generate a RubyAMF standard scaffold.

Using Flex with RubyAMF

We've seen a lot of the Ruby side of working with RubyAMF, but not much of the Flex side. If you've ever worked with any other brand of remoting, like AMFPHP or remoting through LiveCycle Data Services, you'll notice no difference. Even if you're unfamiliar with Flex, there's not much more you need to know to connect it with RubyAMF.

The first thing to take note of is the `RemoteClass` metadata, which we've already seen above.

When the Flash player sends AMF-encoded data, it wants to know the type of the object it's encoding. It could just take the qualified name of the object it's working with, but it honors a metadata annotation called `RemoteClass`, which lets the programmer decide what name to put on the object.

This convention is helpful when integrating systems, for instance, when integrating a Flex application with a J2EE application where it makes sense for some reason to have a different package structure and name for transferred objects. The `RemoteClass` alias can take the name of the Java object without the need to rename the ActionScript object.

A pattern commonly used when integrating remote systems is the Transfer Object, or Data Transfer Object, or as it's called in the Flex programming community, the Value Object (VO). A VO is an object used to transfer chunks of data from one system to another, which is easier than transferring individual pieces of data a piece at a time. For instance, instead of transferring `firstName` and then `lastName`, you transfer the whole Person object. As long as the translation from system to system is automatic or sufficiently hidden, communicating with the remote system seems like sending objects to a local method.

Using VOs to describe the persistent data part of your application is a good idea anyway. This part of the logical structure of your application is called the model, and in most Flex and Rails applications, the model part of your Flex application will mirror your `ActiveRecord` models. To make this relationship clear, a good practice is to make the `RemoteClass` alias the same as the `ActiveRecord` model name. The only place this practice breaks down is if there's a name conflict. That is the situation where there's some reason to name two objects the same name but keep them in a different directory structure. That doesn't happen often, so you should be safe. If it does happen, there's always RubyAMF `ClassMappings`. As we've said, it doesn't matter what you name your ActionScript class. The `RemoteClass` alias is what the AMF-encoded object will be named. Regardless, it's probably a good practice to name each model class the same name as the corresponding `ActiveRecord` class. As a side note, if a class has no alias, it comes across as an Object.

So given an `ActiveRecord` that looks like this:

```
class Person < ActiveRecord::Base
end
```

The ActionScript VO would look like this:

```
package com.example {
  [RemoteClass(alias="Person")]
  public class Person {
    ...
  }
}
```

The next thing to understand to integrate RubyAMF and Flex is the RemoteObject class. RemoteObject is how Flex makes remote method calls. Here's the RemoteObject tag that would match a Rails controller. Table 5.5 discusses each property and runs down the RemoteObject properties.

```
<mx:RemoteObject
    id="personService"
    destination="rubyamf"
    endpoint="http://localhost:3000/rubyamf_gateway"
    source="PersonController"
    showBusyCursor="true" />
```

Table 5.5   **RemoteObject Properties**

Property	Description
id	Refers to the RemoteObject in other tags
destination	destination usually refers to a location in the configuration file used to configure the Flex services. With RubyAMF the value rubyamf is all you need.
endpoint	The endpoint is the URL of the service. In most of these examples, you'll see an explicit localhost:3000 which probably won't work in a production environment.
source	The source is the name of the class to instantiate and call on the remote side. In the case of RubyAMF, we use the name of the controller here.
showBusyCursor	This property tells Flex whether or not to show a busy cursor while there's an outstanding call to this RemoteObject.

A Simple RubyAMF Example

Let's take a look at an example application that uses RubyAMF: a contact manager (see Figure 5.1).

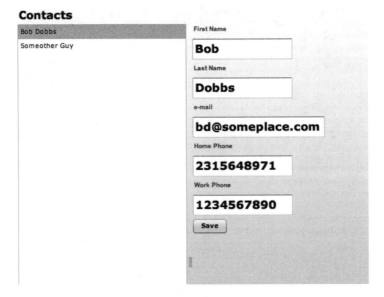

Figure 5.1   Example application.

This is a simple application with only one model, contact. We used the RubyAMF scaffold generator with these arguments to create the migration, model, and controller:

```
script/generate rubyamf_scaffold contact first_name:string last_name:string
email:string office_phone:integer home_phone:integer
```

That gives us a migration that looks like what is shown in Listing 5.1.

Listing 5.1   **db/migrate/001_create_contacts.rb**

```
class CreateContacts < ActiveRecord::Migration
  def self.up
    create_table :contacts do |t|
      t.string :first_name
      t.string :last_name
      t.string :email
      t.integer :office_phone
      t.integer :home_phone

      t.timestamps
    end
  end

  def self.down
    drop_table :contacts
  end
end
```

It also gives us a controller that works well for a RubyAMF-style service (see Listing 5.2).

Listing 5.2   **app/controllers/contacts_controller.rb**

```ruby
class ContactsController < ApplicationController

  # return all Contacts
  def find_all
    respond_to do |format|
      format.amf {render :amf => Contact.find(:all) }
    end
  end

  # return a single Contact by id
  # expects id in params[0]
  def find_by_id
    respond_to do |format|
      format.amf { render :amf => Contact.find(params[0]) }
    end
  end

  # saves new or updates existing Contact
  # expect params[0] to be incoming Contact
  def save
    respond_to do |format|
      format.amf do
        @contact = params[0]

        if @contact.save
          render :amf => @contact
        else
          render :amf => FaultObject.new(@contact.errors.full_messages.join('\n'))
        end
      end
    end
  end

  # destroy a Contact
  # expects id in params[0]
  def destroy
    respond_to do |format|
      format.amf do
        @contact = Contact.find(params[0])
        @contact.destroy
```

Listing 5.2   *Continued*

```
        render :amf => true
      end
    end
  end
end
```

Table 5.6 presents the RubyAMF actions. There are fewer actions than with the standard Rails RESTful controller, but these are all a RubyAMF service needs for basic CRUD operations.

Table 5.6   **RubyAMF Actions**

Action	Description
find_all	Returns all contacts
find_by_id	Given an `id` as the first argument, returns the matching contact
save	Creates or updates a contact
destroy	Given an `id` as the first argument, deletes the matching contact

Also, some configuration changes to the RubyAMF configuration will make things work smoothly. Those changes from the default are listed in Table 5.7.

Table 5.7   **Changes to RubyAMF Configuration**

Configuration	New Setting
translate_case	true
assume_types	true
use_array_collection	true

Now let's look at the Flex side. Just to get an easy look at the code to make the connection, we have two somewhat monolithic files, but we'll be looking at ways to better organize Flex applications in later chapters.

First, the list of all the contacts, ContactList.mxml, has calls to load all contacts and to delete the selected contact in the list. The service is accessed through a `RemoteObject` like that shown in Listing 5.3.

Listing 5.3   **src/flexonrails/examples/view/ContactList.mxml: #91–100**

```
<mx:RemoteObject
    id="contactListService"
    destination="rubyamf"
    source="ContactsController"
    endpoint="http://localhost:3000/rubyamf_gateway"
    fault="serviceFault(event)"
```

Listing 5.3   *Continued*

```
      showBusyCursor="true">
      <mx:method name="find_all" result="contactsLoaded(event)" />
      <mx:method name="destroy" result="contactDestroyed(event)" />
</mx:RemoteObject>
```

Adding the method tags to the RemoteObject is not necessary to make the calls to the service, but it does enable us to call a method when the service responds, the contactsLoaded event for the find_all service call, and to call the contactDestroyed method when the destroy method returns.

So then, in the init method, which is called when the application starts, we have what is shown in Listing 5.4.

Listing 5.4   **src/flexonrails/examples/view/ContactList.mxml: #32–34**

```
private function init():void {
   contactListService.find_all();
}
```

A call to the contactListService will call through to the Rails service, and when it returns, the contactsLoaded method will be called (see Listing 5.5).

Listing 5.5   **src/flexonrails/examples/view/ContactList.mxml: #37–40**

```
private function contactsLoaded(data:Object):void {
   var re:ResultEvent = data as ResultEvent;
   contactList = re.result as ArrayCollection;
}
```

And all that's needed is to take the result and make it the array collection that the list of contacts uses as a data provider. A big reason is the RemoteClass metadata in the Contact ActionScript class, which makes sure that the Flash Player knows that any AMF messages coming in with the name of Contact in the class are automatically converted to objects of the type shown in Listing 5.6.

Listing 5.6   **src/flexonrails/examples/vo/Contact.as**

```
package flexonrails.examples.vo {

   [RemoteClass(alias="Contact")]
   [Bindable]
   public class Contact {

      public var id:int;
      public var firstName:String;
      public var lastName:String;
```

Listing 5.6   *Continued*

```
        public var email:String;
        public var homePhone:String;
        public var officePhone:String;
        public var createdAt:Date;
        public var updateAt:Date;

        [Transient]
        public var newContact:Boolean = true;
    }
}
```

Notice the [Transient] metadata tag too, which tells the Flash player not to try to encode or decode this property to or from AMF.

One other interesting feature to note is the FaultObject from the Rails side. Let's look again at the save action on our generated controller (see Listing 5.7).

Listing 5.7   **app/controllers/contacts_controller.rb: #20–32**

```
def save
  respond_to do |format|
    format.amf do
      @contact = params[0]
      if @contact.save
        render :amf => @contact
      else
        render :amf => FaultObject.new(@contact.errors.full_messages.join('\n'))
      end
    end
  end
end
```

If the save doesn't return true on the incoming Contact, there will be validation errors you may want to display on the client. The generated controller's behavior is to group these as strings separated by newline characters and put them in the message of a FaultObject. Whenever a FaultObject is rendered from RubyAMF, the Flash player knows there was an error in execution on the service and it calls the corresponding fault method of the service that was called instead of a result method, which in the case of our RemoteObject points to serviceFault (see Listing 5.8).

Listing 5.8   **src/flexonrails/examples/view/ContactList.mxml: #52–55**

```
private function serviceFault(data:Object):void {
    var fe:FaultEvent = data as FaultEvent;
    Alert.show("An error occurred: " + fe.fault.faultString);
}
```

In our example application, we just put that right into an Alert message.

This is a good example of a simple, standard RubyAMF service with a front end accessing it. Now let's look a little bit at the ins and outs of working RubyAMF into a RESTful service.

A RESTful RubyAMF Integration

Rails gives developers the power to respond to different types of requests when building a service, and RubyAMF fits into that plan. Listing 5.9 shows a typical RESTful service, generated by the Rails generator but changed to work with AMF requests.

Listing 5.9   **src/flexonrails/examples/view/ContactList.mxml: #32–34**

```
class ContactsController < ApplicationController
  # GET /contacts
  # GET /contacts.xml
  def index
    @contacts = Contact.find(:all)
    respond_to do |format|
      format.html # index.html.erb
      format.xml  { render :xml => @contacts }
      format.amf  { render :amf => @contacts }
    end
  end


  # GET /contacts/1
  # GET /contacts/1.xml
  def show
    @contact = Contact.find(params[:id])
    respond_to do |format|
      format.html # show.html.erb
      format.xml  { render :xml => @contact }
      format.amf  { render :amf => @contact }
    end
  end


  # GET /contacts/new
  # GET /contacts/new.xml
  def new
    @contact = Contact.new
    respond_to do |format|
      format.html # new.html.erb
      format.xml  { render :xml => @contact }
      format.amf  { render :amf => @contact }
    end
  end
end
```

Listing 5.9 *Continued*

```
# GET /contacts/1/edit
def edit
  @contact = Contact.find(params[:id])
end


# POST /contacts
# POST /contacts.xml
def create
  @contact = Contact.new(params[:contact])
  respond_to do |format|
    if @contact.save
      flash[:notice] = 'Contact was successfully created.'
      format.html { redirect_to(@contact) }
      format.xml  { render :xml => @contact, :status => :created, :location =>
@contact }
    else
      format.html { render :action => "new" }
      format.xml  { render :xml => @contact.errors, :status =>
:unprocessable_entity }
    end
  end
end


# PUT /contacts/1
# PUT /contacts/1.xml
def update
  @contact = Contact.find(params[:id])
  respond_to do |format|
    if @contact.update_attributes(params[:contact])
      flash[:notice] = 'Contact was successfully updated.'
      format.html { redirect_to(@contact) }
      format.xml  { head :ok }
    else
      format.html { render :action => "edit" }
      format.xml  { render :xml => @contact.errors, :status =>
:unprocessable_entity }
    end
  end
end


# DELETE /contacts/1
# DELETE /contacts/1.xml
def destroy
  @contact = Contact.find(params[:id])
  @contact.destroy
  respond_to do |format|
    format.html { redirect_to(contacts_url) }
```

Listing 5.9   **_Continued_**

```
      format.xml   { head :ok }
      format.amf   { render :amf => true }
   end
 end


 # For RubyAMF
 def save
   @contact = params[:contact]
   respond_to do |format|
     if @contact.save
       format.amf   { render :amf => @contact }
     else
       format.amf   { render :amf => FaultObject.new(@contact.errors.full_
messages.join("\n")) }
     end
   end
 end
end
```

Actions like `index` and `show` work fine with little modification, just an extra block for the AMF format. The `create` and `update` actions don't quite work out of the box because they expect an incoming hash in the `params` hash that would be converted to an `ActiveRecord`, but RubyAMF already has an `ActiveRecord`. You have a few ways to react to this situation. You can try to refactor those actions to work a little differently in case of an AMF input, or as we did, you can break out a separate `save` action more along the lines of a RubyAMF generated controller. Of course, the only changes to Flex in this case would be to rename the methods called on the `RemoteObject`.

Table 5.8 presents the RubyAMF configuration settings that go along with this controller.

Table 5.8   **RubyAMF Configuration Settings for the Controller**

Configuration	New Setting
`translate_case`	true
`assume_types`	true
`use_array_collection`	true
`ParameterMappings.scaffolding`	true

Summary

There you have RubyAMF. It's a very flexible plug-in that lets you either fit in to an existing Rails application or tailor your Rails project to support Flex. It provides a speed increase over parsing XML and a development time savings because of the simplicity of integration with Flex.

6

Debugging

One way to introduce the concept of debugging is to begin with a definition:

> Debugging is a methodical process of finding and reducing the number of bugs, or defects, in a computer program or a piece of electronic hardware thus making it behave as expected.
>
> (http://en.wikipedia.org/wiki/Debugging)

The definition assumes that the code you write has bugs, which isn't the case, is it? Next chapter!

For the rest of us still here, figuring out what's happening inside your running code is the best way to understand how to get it back to working the way it's expected to work.

A lot has been written on the fine art of tracking down bugs. It takes intuition, a good knowledge of the particular code you're working on, and enough experience with general types of problems to recognize patterns. For instance, go to Google and look up the "off-by-one error," the "fencepost error"—a special case of the "off-by-one,"—"race condition," or "infinite loop," and you'll find loads of common patterns to the problems that face programmers. You've probably run into these, and more besides, plenty of times already in your programming career.

Understanding your code and common programming bug patterns is important to troubleshooting bugs, but as we've said, sometimes you must get into the running program and figure out what bad data or faulty logic caused your application to fail.

Client/server applications present special problems when they get buggy because so many pieces could be misbehaving. Is the problem because of bad data in the database? Is there bad logic on the server side? Is the server side doing its job, but the front end somehow is causing problems? Maybe the problem is that what you're sending from one tier to the next isn't getting there in the form you expect, or worse, there's no communication at all between the front end and back-end of the application.

Let's look at how to debug the front end, back-end, and communication between both sides of a Flex and Rails application.

Table 6.1 lists the tools we'll be covering

Table 6.1   **Tools by Context and Technology**

Context	Flex	Rails
Logging	Actionscript logging framework	Rails logger
IDE debugger	Flex builder debugger	Aptana debugger
Command line debugger	Fdb	Ruby-debug
Network communication		Charles

Logging

The easiest way to get an idea of the less-visible steps your application takes is to write to a log. Logging is simply writing a message to a file so you can report that a method ran, a database query took a certain amount of time to run, or what the value of a variable is at a certain point.

Rails uses a class from the Ruby Standard Library called Logger, and plenty of logging happens right out of the box, which we'll explore in a bit.

Flex's situation is different, since it has a big limitation. Flex browser applications run in Flash Player, which doesn't have access to the file system due to security concerns. We can view some logging a few different ways, though, using either Flex Builder or fdb.

Rails Logging

Logging is configured and running by default in Rails. In your Rails application directory, you'll notice a directory that looks something like that shown in Figure 6.1.

```
log
|-- development.log
|-- production.log
|-- server.log
|-- test.log
```

Figure 6.1   Log directory in your rails application directory.

Logger, like other logging packages you may be familiar with (e.g., log4j), uses a concept of levels or severities. Certain log messages may have a higher severity than others, which allows you to filter out certain levels. The levels are, in order of lowest to highest severity:

1. debug
2. info
3. warn
4. error
5. fatal

Rails filters debug-level messages from the production environment, but no filters are available in any of the other environments. Change filter access in any of the environment-specific configuration files by setting `config.log_level` to one of the strings (or a related symbol) above.

To see the logger in action, just start up a Rails application and navigate around it while watching the console output. All the information in the console is put there by the logger, and log file is written to the console.

Of course, you have access to the logger too; otherwise it wouldn't be that useful. Each controller has an instance variable called `logger` and a method for each level, such as debug, info, warn, and so on.

Let's make a simple Rails application, and try out the logger. First, create a Rails application:

```
$ rails widgets
create
create app/controllers
...
```

Then set up the databases, configure the `database.yml` file, and run the migrations. Next, create a simple widget scaffold with a name attribute:

```
$ ruby script/generate scaffold widget name:string
exists  app/models/
exists  app/controllers/
...
```

Open up the widgets controller, and insert a logging statement (see Listing 6.1):

Listing 6.1   **app/controllers/widgets_controller.rb, lines 4–11**

```
def index
  logger.info '>>> searching for all widgets' # insert this logging statement
  @widgets = Widget.find(:all)
  respond_to do |format|
    format.html # index.html.erb
    format.xml  { render :xml => @widgets }
  end
end
```

Then run the server, navigate to http://localhost:3000/widgets, and look at the console output:

```
Parameters: {"action"=>"index", "controller"=>"widgets"}
SQL (0.000000)  SET SQL_AUTO_IS_NULL=0
>>> searching for all widgets
Widget Load (0.031000)  SELECT * FROM 'widgets'
Rendering template within layouts/widgets
Rendering widgets/index
```

```
Widget Columns (0.015000)  SHOW FIELDS FROM 'widgets'
Completed in 0.09400 (10 reqs/sec) | Rendering: 0.03200 (34%) | DB: 0.04600 (48%
) | 200 OK [http://localhost/widgets]
```

Notice your logging output right there.

> **Tip**
>
> If you see a lot of strange characters in your console output in Windows, it's because the Windows console doesn't understand how to display ANSI colors. `ActiveRecord` puts some color into SQL logging statements to make them more readable, but this option actually makes them less readable on Windows.
>
> To fix this, you could try one of these things:
>
> - Get a Mac :)
> - Install Linux :)
> - Or, more reasonably, put this line in your config/environments/development.rb:
>
>   ```
>   ActiveRecord::Base.colorize_logging = false
>   ```

`ActiveRecords` have loggers, too. Let's use a life-cycle callback method in the widget model to write a log message every time a widget is created. Add the code in Listing 6.2 to your widget model.

Listing 6.2   **app/models/widget.rb**

```
class Widget < ActiveRecord::Base
  after_create do |widget|
    logger.debug ">>> Widget named #{widget.name} created"
  end
end
```

The `after_create` block will be called after any widget is first inserted into the database. Try it out by going to http://localhost:3000/widgets/new and creating a new widget. Look at the new console output to see your logging message.

Rails lets you customize what information is stored in the log, so you can track any special notes you want to keep about the path through your running application. Setting the debug log level (which will not be logged in production by default) to be fairly verbose and setting the higher-severity log levels to report exceptional situations makes it a little easier to run through the logs and decide what's happening around unexpected problems.

Flex and Logging

As mentioned above, Flex doesn't have access to logging in the same way that Rails does. Some third-party applications help with this issue and provide a more standard logging approach, with severity levels and filtering. Most of these solutions have platform or browser requirements, so if you'd like to investigate further, this part is left as an exercise to the reader. Here are some of the applications:

- ThunderBolt—http://flash-thunderbolt.googlecode.com/
  Logging through JavaScript to Firebug, a Firefox JavaScript debugger.

- SOS—http://sos.powerflasher.com/english.html
  Logging over a local socket. Windows only.

A simple logging command is still available in ActionScript: the trace statement. This statement enables messages to be written to the console inside Flex Builder or to the console debugger, fdb.

The console debugger is not as straightforward to set up and run as Flex Builder is, so if you're not using Flex Builder, you can see what a trace statement looks like and then skip ahead to see how to run fdb to view the trace output.

Here's an example of a very simple Flex application with a trace statement:

```
<?xml version="1.0" encoding="utf-8"?>
<mx:Application
    xmlns:mx="http://www.adobe.com/2006/mxml"
    layout="absolute"
    applicationComplete="init()">

    <mx:Script>
    <![CDATA[

        public function init():void {
            trace("application started")
        }

    ]]>
    </mx:Script>
</mx:Application>
```

To view trace statements, you need to run the application in debug mode. To do that in Flex Builder, click the debug icon's down arrow and select Debug As, Flex Application. Flex Builder will open your browser and run the application in debug mode. Any trace statements that are run will be output to the Flex Builder console.

Logging has its role in the debugging process by telling you the "story" of how your application is run. That story is helpful for telling you where in the execution of the application issues may be hidden. Often though, a debugger is key to actually tracking down problem areas in your code.

Debuggers

A debugger is a tool that enables a programmer to examine the environment of a running program. Debuggers enable program execution to be paused at certain intervals, called breakpoints, which the programmer can set before or during a debugging session. Debuggers also enable stepping—incremental, line-by-line execution through the program, pausing after each line is executed.

Scope

Let's define some terminology here. First of all, you should already understand the concept of scope in an object-oriented language. Basically, a variable can be defined at one of many levels or areas in a program and is only available when that level or area is reached during execution. For instance, if I define a Class "Foo" and say that it has an instance variable `instance_var`, I can only access that variable if I have an instance of that class available.

More to the point, if I have a method named `do_something` on class Foo, and inside that method a variable `local_var` is defined, when program execution is inside `do_something` it has access to the variable `local_var` and the variable `instance_var`. If execution moves to another method in the same object, that new method only has access to the variable `instance_var`, because variable `local_var` has gone out of scope. Variable `local_var` is of a type called **method local**, which means it only has meaning inside of that method, and referencing outside that method will cause an error in most languages. If execution then passes on to a different object, it no longer has access to variable `instance_var` either, at least not in the same way (depending on access rules of the language and the definition of the object).

Keep in mind, then, that the goal of stepping through a program with a debugger is to inspect the values of the variables in a given scope.

Call Stack and Stack Frames

Another concept is that of a **call stack**. If a program has a method M that calls to another method N, which calls to method O, each of those methods does something and then returns execution to the method that called it: M -> N -> O -> N -> M. Each method has its own context of local variables, objects it has permission to access, and, of course, all the method instructions. This chain of methods is called the **stack**, because down deep in the inner workings, it's implemented as a stack of instructions, with each **frame** in the stack having its own context and the frame to call back to when execution completes.

When stepping through the execution of a program with a debugger, it's possible to "step into" another frame, step through execution there, look back at the context of a previous frame, continue stepping through execution of the current frame, return execution to the previous frame, and so on. It's important to keep track of what frame you're in, especially if you have a program with any recursion in it.

Table 6.2 provides a quick list of debugging terms.

Table 6.2   **Debugging Terminology**

Term	Explanation
Scope	The context; the set of variables and objects available to the currently executing code.
Call stack (or just "stack")	The chain of the execution of the program from calling method to called method.
Frame	A certain point in the call stack.

Debugging Flex

Flex's debugging framework is built from a few different parts. First, to have an ActionScript program connect to the debugger, the SWF needs to be running in the Flash Player Content Debugger, the long name for the debugger version of Flash Player. If you've installed Flex Builder, this version is running in your browser already, but if you're not using Flex Builder, you may download the debugger player from here: www.adobe.com/support/flashplayer/downloads.html.

Then there is the debugger itself. If you have Flex Builder, the debugger is built in and you operate the debugger almost exactly the same way you operate the debugger in the Eclipse JDT; it should be familiar to anyone who's ever debugged a Java application. If you don't have Flex Builder, you can still use `fdb`, the console debugger that comes with the Flex SDK.

We're going to postpone discussing `fdb` for a little while and talk about `ruby-debug` and `fdb` together, since console debuggers can be daunting. First, let's debug a simple problem inside a small Flex application.

Open the sample code for this project in Flex Builder, and consider the simple Flex application in Listing 6.3.

Listing 6.3   **src/flex_debugging.mxml**

```
<mx:Application xmlns:mx="http://www.adobe.com/2006/mxml" layout="absolute"
initialize="init()">
    <mx:Script>
    <![CDATA[
        import mx.controls.Alert;

        private var greeting:String;

        private function init():void {
            var greeter:Greeter = new Greeter();
            greeting = greeter.sayHello();
            Alert.show(greeting);
        }

    ]]>
    </mx:Script>
</mx:Application>
```

Upon initialization, the `init` function is called. It creates a `greeter` object, which is a class that looks like what is shown in Listing 6.4.

Listing 6.4   **src/Greeter.as**

```
public class Greeter {
    public function sayHello(target:String="World"):String {
        return "Hello" + target;
    }
}
```

`Greeter` has a method, `sayHello`, that makes the obligatory "Hello World" greeting. This application is very simple one, but it has a few features to help us work through the debugger.

First, to make things a little easier to explain, open up the Flex Debugging Perspective as shown in Figure 6.2.

Figure 6.2   Open the Flex Debugging perspective.

In this perspective, a few more panels are available and the configuration of the panels is slightly different. The editors are still in the middle, but you'll find in the top right three tabs, Variables, Breakpoints, and Expressions, and in the top left, the Debug tab.

Debug

This tab shows whether the debugger is connected to a debugging session. If execution is paused, it also shows the current call stack. Clicking an item in the call stack list opens the source code to the line of code associated with that frame (if source code is available).

This is also where you control the debugger, with the controls described in Table 6.3.

Table 6.3   **Debugger Controls**

Name	Icon	Description
Resume		Resume tells the debugger to continue execution of the application. If the player reaches another breakpoint, the debugger will stop at that breakpoint.
Suspend		Suspend keeps the debugger connected but doesn't stop at any breakpoints during execution.
Terminate		Stops the debugger.
Disconnect		Disconnects the debugger (effectively the same as Terminate).
Step Over		Steps to the next line and stops.
Step Into		Steps into any method called from the current line and stops on the first line of that method. If multiple methods are called from the current line, it steps into the methods in order.
Step Return		Returns from current method to its calling method at the line it was called.

Variables

Figure 6.3 shows the Variables tab. If a frame is selected in the Debug tab, all the variables associated with the immediate scope of that frame are listed. The variables are listed in a tree with objects as the branches. If you want to change the value of a variable, click into the cell in the value column to change it.

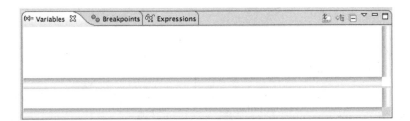

Figure 6.3   The Variables tab.

Breakpoints

This tab lists any breakpoints you have set. Double-clicking opens an editor at the line where the breakpoint occurs.

Expressions

It's possible to "watch" variables, to keep a list of interesting variables in this panel. If you right-click a variable in the Variables panel and select Create Watch Expression, a **watch**

expression is created. It shows the value of a variable with that name whenever it exists. This method is useful for showing specific variables when the Variables panel is full of them. To try out the debugger, go to the mxml application in Flex Builder and make sure you have line numbers turned on. Look to the left of your code, and if you don't see a number for each line of code in the file, right-click the gutter to the left of your code and select Show Line Numbers. Make sure the **init** function begins on line 10 and ends on line 13.

Now we're going to set a **breakpoint** to tell the debugger to pause execution once it gets to a certain line in the code. Right-click the 11 in the line number gutter, and select Toggle Breakpoint. You should see a blue dot appear to the left of the line number, as shown in Figure 6.4.

```
10        private function init():void {
11            var greeter:Greeter = new Greeter();
12            greeting = greeter.sayHello();
13            Alert.show(greeting);
14        }
15
```

Figure 6.4   A blue dot appears to the left of the line number.

You should also see a new breakpoint in the Breakpoints tab in the top right pane of Flex Builder in the Debugging Perspective, as shown in Figure 6.5.

Figure 6.5   The new breakpoint under the Breakpoints tab.

Now, to debug the application, go to the toolbar, click the arrow next to the bug icon, and select Debug As, Flex Application (see Figure 6.6).

Figure 6.6   Select Debug As, Flex Application.

Flex Builder will open the application in your browser just as if it were going to run it, but the Flash Content Debugger will connect to the debugger in Flex Builder. The Flex application will run until the first breakpoint and then pause the execution, which means the application becomes unusable. In fact, you won't be able to use your browser at all while the Flash Player is paused during debugging.

Back in Flex Builder, a list of stack frames now appears in the Debug tab (see Figure 6.7).

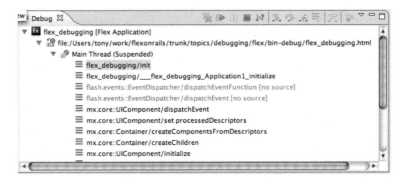

Figure 6.7   The list of stack frames.

There also is a list of variables in the Variables tab (see Figure 6.8).

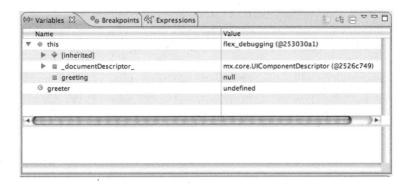

Figure 6.8   The list of variables.

The variables are under a tree item with a label of "this," which corresponds to the current object. To make it easier to get some context, the inherited properties are grouped together in the (inherited) item. The instance variable greeting is in the variables list, with a value of null.

If you click-step past line 12 where the greeting is set, you'll notice that the value of greeting changes in the Variables panel (see Figure 6.9).

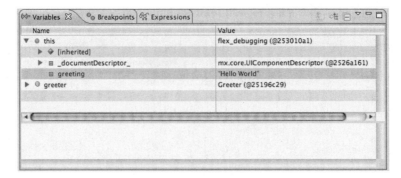

Figure 6.9   The value of greeting changes.

If you click the Resume button, program control resumes, and since there are no more breakpoints, the init method finishes and the Alert shows in the browser.

Let's try that one more time and study a different feature. Close the browser window, which terminates the debugger, and then start the debugger again by clicking the debugger icon. Once you've debugged the current application, you can rerun the last application by clicking the button once.

Once again, the debugger stops at line 11. Instead of clicking Resume, this time, step over line 11 and click Step Into on line 12. Now Flex Builder opens up the Greeter class to the line where the sayHello method begins. If you step once into that method, you'll notice the method local variable target from the arguments starts out with a value of World because it has a default. From here, you can either step once or click Step Return. Since the sayHello method has only one line, the next thing that happens here is the execution returns to the init method in the application.

If you debug the application one more time and wait for it to stop on line 11, we can try out one more thing. Once the application stops, open the Greeter class and set a breakpoint on line 6 in the sayHello method. Now click Resume. The debugger should go to the sayHello method. This step shows how Resume works when multiple breakpoints exist and also shows that you can set a breakpoint anytime you'd like, even when the debugger is running.

Those are the basics of a debugger. Flex Builder debugging is the same as most Eclipse-based IDEs, which will help you debug Flex and Java but also works the same for Aptana, the Eclipse-based Rails IDE we'll talk about next.

Debugging Rails

If you're using the Aptana Rad Rails IDE for Rails, you also have the capability to debug Rails applications.

If you haven't already, make sure that you have the ruby-debug-id gem installed by typing `gem install ruby-debug-ide` at a console.

Once you've opened Aptana and imported the Rails project from this chapter's sample code, go to the Servers tab at the bottom of the IDE, right-click, and select Add.

Add a configuration for a mongrel server, and then right-click that server and select Debug. Once you start the server in debug mode, it connects back to the debugger in Aptana and we can start debugging Rails code.

Now that you have Aptana configured to debug and you're running the server in debug mode, everything else is much the same as debugging in Flex Builder. To test debugging, open `widgets_controller.rb` and put a breakpoint in the index action. Then go to http://localhost:3000/widgets, and you'll see a debugging session start in Aptana and stop at your breakpoint. Step once, and you'll see a variable `@widgets` appear near the bottom of the tree in the Variables pane.

Now it's a lot easier to see what's happening in the actual code in Flex and Rails. This is true not only of your own code but of the framework code as well. If you step through your code enough times, you'll end up in Flex or Rails framework code, which is a great way to learn about the inner workings of both. Not only that, but you can debug both sides of the application, the Flex and the Rails side, at the same time. This feature lets you get to the bottom of problems very quickly.

IDEs aren't everyone's bag though, and some people prefer to work in a lighter-weight text editor, like the Rails-standard TextMate. It's a tradeoff in functionality for system resources or familiarity, or perhaps it's just a preference. In any case, you have choices to help figure out why your code is working (or not working) the way it is.

Command Line Debuggers

In this section, we cover command line debuggers for Flex and Rails. The command line debugger for Flex, as you know by now, is `fdb`. The command line debugger for Rails is `ruby-debug`.

Debugging Flex with fdb

The Flex SDK comes with a console debugger called `fdb`. To use the debugger, the SWF you want to debug needs to be compiled with the debug option `-debug=true` using mxmlc. Flex Builder compiles the SWF with debugging on by default, but mxmlc does not. When `debug=true`, the debugger is provided extra information in the SWF about the ActionScript files, source code, and variables.

To test `fdb`, compile the source for this chapter with the debug option on, and then open a console in the directory of the SWF. If you used Flex Builder to compile the SWF already and are just curious about `fdb`, simply open a console to the bin-debug directory in the sample directory for this chapter.

To illustrate how to use `fdb`, we'll go through a few sessions and point out a few things along the way. First, run the debugger by typing this command:

```
$ fdb flex_debugging.swf
```

You should see something like the following output:

```
Adobe fdb (Flash Player Debugger) [build 189825]
Copyright (c) 2004-2006 Adobe, Inc. All rights reserved.
Attempting to launch and connect to Player using URL
flex_debugging.swf
Player connected; session starting.
Set breakpoints and then type 'continue' to resume the session.
[SWF] Users:tony:work:for:trunk:topics:debugging:flex:bin-debug:
flex_debugging.swf - 604,378 bytes after decompression
(fdb)
```

The (fdb) is the debugger prompt, so the next set of commands to type will be prefixed by that prompt.

When a debugging session starts, it immediately pauses execution before any code is run, so you can set breakpoints in framework classes. Let's take a look around the debugger before continuing.

Type help at the debugger prompt:

```
(fdb) help
New to fdb? Do 'tutorial' for basic info.
List of fdb commands:
bt (bt)          Print backtrace of all stack frames
break (b)        Set breakpoint at specified line or function
cf (cf)          Display the name and number of the current file
...
```

You'll see something similar to the text above. If you're ever lost or need help with a specific command, type help or help <command name> and fdb will print some help text. If you'd like, you can type tutorial and get commonly used commands in a sample session. Otherwise, type continue so fdb will continue to load our application:

```
(fdb) continue
Additional ActionScript code has been loaded from a SWF or a frame.
To see all currently loaded files, type -info files'.
Set additional breakpoints as desired, and then type 'continue'.
(fdb)
```

Now that our application is loaded, we can see what files are available as source to help us debug them.

```
(fdb) info files
---
AddRemoveEffectTargetFilter.as#197
Alert.as#143
AlertForm.as#191
Application.as#78
ApplicationBackground.as#159
ApplicationGlobals.as#100
ApplicationLayout.as#139
```

```
...
mx_internal.as#10
---
Greeter.as#144
flex_debugging.mxml#79
(fdb)
```

That's a lot of files. Each file that makes up the Flex source is listed here, which means that we can set breakpoints in any of those files. Notice that, at the bottom of the list, the two source files in our application are listed below the ---. If you type info sources instead of info files, you'll see only the source files for the current application:

```
(fdb) info sources
Greeter.as#144
flex_debugging.mxml#79
(fdb)
```

After each file listed by either command is a number. For most commands that take a file name, the number can be substituted for the name of the file. Next, let's set a breakpoint.

```
(fdb) break flex_debugging.mxml:init
Breakpoint 1 at 0x45782: file flex_debugging.mxml, line 10
(fdb)
```

Breakpoints can be set on a file at a certain line or at a function, as we've done above. Breakpoints are also numbered. As you can see, the first one we set gets the number 1.

```
(fdb) continue
Breakpoint 1, init() at flex_debugging.mxml:10
 10             private function init():void {
(fdb)
```

Now, typing continue again runs the application, either to its end or until the next breakpoint is reached. In this case, we have reached the breakpoint we just set. fdb prints the current line after reaching a breakpoint and identifies that that line is the 10th in this file. To see a little more context, we can type list:

```
(fdb) list
 5      <![CDATA[
 6              import mx.controls.Alert;
 7
 8              private var greeting:String;
 9
=10             private function init():void {
 11                     var greeter:Greeter = new Greeter();
 12                     greeting = greeter.sayHello();
 13                     Alert.show(greeting);
 14             }
(fdb)
```

Notice that fdb puts the = next to the current line. Now that we've hit a breakpoint, we can start stepping through the code.

```
(fdb) next
 11                      var greeter:Greeter = new Greeter();
(fdb)
```

fdb shows us the current line each time. If we want, we can also inspect variables by using print:

```
(fdb) print greeter
$1 = undefined
(fdb)
```

Oops. The line that sets greeter hasn't be executed yet; it was only just reached by fdb. Let's step one more time and then see what greeter looks like:

```
(fdb) next
 12                      greeting = greeter.sayHello();
(fdb) print greeter
$2 = [Object 807280473, class='Greeter']
(fdb)
```

fdb tells us that we have an object of type Greeter. Now we can continue stepping through or just allow the application to continue:

```
(fdb) continue
```

Notice that fdb doesn't take any more input at this point, since the application is running and has not paused at a breakpoint. Now close the browser, and let's try another session that shows us a few more fdb tricks.

```
[UnloadSWF] Users:tony:work:for:trunk:topics:debugging:flex:bin-
debug:flex_debugging.swf
Player session terminated
(fdb)
```

Notice that fdb keeps running after the session is over, which is nice for multiple debugging sessions, since information like breakpoints is kept from session to session. Now let's start another session by running the SWF that we specified on the command line before and then running a few commands like we did last time:

```
(fdb) run flex_debugging.swf
Attempting to launch and connect to Player using URL
flex_debugging.swf
Player connected; session starting.
[SWF] Users:tony:work:for:trunk:topics:debugging:flex:bin-
debug:flex_debugging.swf - 604,378 bytes after decompression
Set breakpoints and then type 'continue' to resume the session.
(fdb) continue
Additional ActionScript code has been loaded from a SWF or a frame.
```

```
To see all currently loaded files, type 'info files'.
Set additional breakpoints as desired, and then type 'continue'.
(fdb) info sources
Greeter.as#144
flex_debugging.mxml#79
(fdb)
```

Now we're in the same place we were when we set a breakpoint on the application last time, but that breakpoint should still be there. Here on out, I'll use the short names of commands (listed next to the command in the help menu) to save typing. Instead of info breakpoints, I can type i b for short, for instance:

```
(fdb) i b
Num Type           Disp Enb Address    What
1   breakpoint     keep y   0x00045782 in init() at flex_debugging.mxml:10
(fdb)
```

And, I have a list of all the breakpoints currently set. The breakpoint on line 10 at the init method in the application is listed here. Now we'll set a breakpoint on the Greeter.as file at the sayHello method. I use shorthand not only for commands but also for files. As long as the file name is not ambiguous, you could type as little of the file-name as you'd like, and fdb will try to match what you typed to a filename.

```
(fdb) b Greet:sayHello
Breakpoint 2 at 0x56ada: file Greeter.as, line 5
(fdb)
```

Now I should have a breakpoint at the sayHello method in Greeter. Let's continue:

```
(fdb) c
Breakpoint 1, init() at flex_debugging.mxml:10
 10            private function init():void {
(fdb) l
 5       <![CDATA[
 6             import mx.controls.Alert;
 7
 8             private var greeting:String;
 9
=10           private function init():void {
 11               var greeter:Greeter = new Greeter();
 12               greeting = greeter.sayHello();
 13               Alert.show(greeting);
 14            }
(fdb)
```

After listing the context of the current line when the breakpoint at init is reached (with the shorthand l), I'd like to tell fdb to automatically print the contents of a variable whenever it hits breakpoints. I know that later on in the Greeter class I'll have a variable called target, so I'll tell fdb to print target whenever I hit a breakpoint:

```
(fdb) display target
(fdb)
```

This is just like a **watched expression** in Flex Builder's debugger. Now, if we continue, the variable target will be printed:

```
(fdb) continue
Breakpoint 2, Greeter.as:5
5               public function sayHello(target:String="World"):String
{
1: target = Variable target unknown
(fdb)
```

Continue one more time to actually step into the method:

```
(fdb) continue
Breakpoint 2, Greeter.as:5
 5               public function sayHello(target:String="World"):String
{
1: target = "World"
(fdb)
```

You'll see that target has a value now. You'll also notice that we've changed files from flex_debugging.mxml to Greeter.as. If we type `where`, `fdb` will show us the current stack trace:

```
(fdb)where
#0   this = [Object 801196905,
class='Greeter'].Greeter/sayHello(target="World") at Greeter.as:5
#1   this = [Object 735064225,
class='flex_debugging'].flex_debugging/init() at flex_debugging.mxml:12
#2   this = [Object 735064225,
class='flex_debugging'].flex_debugging/___flex_debugging_Application1_
initialize(event=[Object 790020785, class='mx.events::FlexEvent'])
at flex_debugging.mxml:2
(fdb)
```

Now we'll step to the next line and see target printed one more time:

```
(fdb) step
 6                      return "Hello " + target;
1: target = "World"
(fdb)
```

Now, let's say we wanted to change the value of the target variable to see what will happen:

```
(fdb) set target="Console"
(fdb) p target
$1 = "Console"
(fdb)
```

Now target is `Console` instead of `World`. Let's continue:

```
(fdb) c
```

We'll see that reflected in the Alert box that's shown.

Console debuggers may not be as user friendly as an IDE debugger at first glance, but once you get used to the commands, they may be faster since you can easily limit the view to information you care about, as long as you don't mind interacting with a command line. These commands certainly cause less system overhead, which may or may not be a concern to you.

Debugging Rails with ruby-debug

Now let's have a look at `ruby-debug`, which is similar to `fdb`, with a few syntactic differences. We'll be dealing with the Rails sample code for this chapter. By the way, if you haven't already installed `ruby-debug`, you can do so quickly with `gem install ruby-debug` as previously mentioned.

Rails 2 added support for `ruby-debug` by default. The only thing you need to do to kick off a debugging session is to start the server in debug mode by specifying the debug command line option with `script/server`:

```
$ ruby script/server —debug
```

There's no phase to set breakpoints once the server starts, though, so we need to jump into debugger mode by calling `debugger` in our code. For example, if we wanted to debug the widget_controller's index action, our code would look like that shown in Listing 6.5.

Listing 6.5   **rails/app/controllers/widget_controller.rb lines 4–13**

```
def index
  debugger # we call out to debugger to start a debugging session
  widgets = Widget.find(:all)
  respond_to do |format|
    format.html # index.html.erb
    format.xml  { render :xml => widgets }
  end
end
```

Then, once the debugger is started, we can set breakpoints easily in any file we'd like. This is a little messy, since we have to modify a file to add the debugger line to set the first breakpoint. Just make sure you remember to remove these statements from the code before you check files into source control: although these debugger statements don't cause any problems, only warnings in Rails 2 and greater, earlier versions will throw an error.

Let's look at a quick session with `ruby-debug` by calling the widget's index action at http://localhost:3000/widgets:

```
Processing WidgetsController#index (for 127.0.0.1 at 2008-01-01 20:02:04) [GET]
  Parameters: {"action"=>"index", "controller"=>"widgets"}
/Users/tony/work/for/trunk/topics/debugging/rails/app/controllers/
widgets_controller.rb:6 widgets = Widget.find(:all)
(rdb:5)
```

First, you'll notice that since the server is in debug mode, the debugging happens right alongside the log output. Once the code reaches the spot where we placed the `debugger` statement, we're kicked into debug mode and `rdb` (as I'll call ruby-debug here) tells us what line we're on and in which file, and then gives us an `rdb` prompt.

First, let's try the `list` command, which should be familiar to us from the previous `fdb` section:

```
(rdb:5) list
[1, 10] in /Users/tony/work/for/trunk/topics/debugging/rails/app/controllers/
widgets_controller.rb
    1  class WidgetsController < ApplicationController
    2    # GET /widgets
    3    # GET /widgets.xml
    4    def index
    5      debugger
=>  6      widgets = Widget.find(:all)
    7
    8      respond_to do |format|
    9        format.html # index.html.erb
   10        format.xml  { render :xml => widgets }
(rdb:5)
(rdb:5) l
...
```

It looks like it works the same, with some small formatting differences. The shorthand command `l` also works. Most commands are similar, in fact, and just as in `fdb`, if you ever wonder about a command, you can always use `help`:

```
(rdb:5) help
ruby-debug help v0.9.3
Type 'help <command-name>' for help on a specific command
Available commands:
backtrace break catch cont delete display down eval exit finish frame
help irb list method next p pp quit reload restart save script set
step thread tmate trace undisplay up var where
(rdb:5)
```

Let's try another similar command, `where`:

```
 (rdb:5) where
-> #0 .../for/trunk/topics/debugging/rails/app/controllers/widgets_controller.
rb:6 in 'index'
    #1 /opt/local/lib/ruby/gems/1.8/gems/actionpack-
2.0.2/lib/action_controller/base.rb:1158 in 'send'
    #2 /opt/local/lib/ruby/gems/1.8/gems/actionpack-
2.0.2/lib/action_controller/base.rb:1158 in 'perform_action_without_filters'
```

`where` tells us where we are in the call stack. `rdb` also has some nice methods to navigate around the call stack.

```
(rdb:5) frame 1
#1 /opt/local/lib/ruby/gems/1.8/gems/actionpack-
2.0.2/lib/action_controller/base.rb:1158 in 'send'
(rdb:5)
```

By using the `frame` command and the frame number listed in the output from where, we can jump to any frame in the stack. Keep in mind that frame 0 is always the current frame. Now, in frame 1, we can do a `list`:

```
(rdb:9) l
[1153, 1162] in /opt/local/lib/ruby/gems/1.8/gems/actionpack-2.0.2/lib/
action_controller/base.rb
   1153          render
   1154        end
   1155
   1156        def perform_action
   1157          if self.class.action_methods.include?(action_name)
=> 1158            send(action_name)
   1159            default_render unless performed?
   1160          elsif respond_to? :method_missing
   1161            method_missing action_name
   1162            default_render unless performed?
(rdb:9)
```

We're looking at code from ActionController::Base . . . Rails source code! That's a great way to understand how Rails works, by watching the code that ends up calling your own code. There are a few more simple frame navigation commands, too:

```
(rdb:5) up
#2 /opt/local/lib/ruby/gems/1.8/gems/actionpack-2.0.2/lib/
action_controller/base.rb:1158 in 'perform_action_without_filters'
(rdb:5) down
#1 /opt/local/lib/ruby/gems/1.8/gems/actionpack-2.0.2/lib/
action_controller/base.rb:1158 in 'send'
(rdb:5) down
#0 /Users/tony/work/for/trunk/topics/debugging/rails/app/controllers/
widgets_controller.rb:6 in 'index'
(rdb:5)
```

Here, using `up` and `down`, we've moved up to frame 2, back down to frame 1, and then down again to 0, the current frame.

Back to our code, we also have familiar commands to list variables, such as `print`:

```
(rdb:5) p params
{"action"=>"index", "controller"=>"widgets"}
(rdb:5) pp params
{"action"=>"index", "controller"=>"widgets"}
(rdb:5) help pp
ruby-debug help v0.9.3
pp expression   evaluate expression and pretty-print its value
(rdb:5)
```

There's also its sibling pp, which stands for "pretty print." Not only can we print the variables in the current scope, but also we can evaluate any Ruby expression:

```
(rdb:5) 5+5
10
(rdb:5)
```

This may remind you of an irb session. In fact, at any point, we can drop in and out of an irb session with the current environment loaded, just as if we'd called it from script/console:

```
(rdb:5) irb
irb(#<WidgetsController:0x34ed40c>):001:0>
irb(#<WidgetsController:0x34ed40c>):001:0> exit
(rdb:5)
```

And then, when we're done with the current context, we can continue:

```
(rdb:5) c
  SQL (0.000658)    SET NAMES 'utf8'
  SQL (0.001116)    SET SQL_AUTO_IS_NULL=0
  Widget Load (0.001405)    SELECT * FROM 'widgets'
Rendering template within layouts/widgets
Rendering widgets/index
  Widget Columns (0.081906)    SHOW FIELDS FROM 'widgets'
Completed in 290.20263 (0 reqs/sec) | Rendering: 0.03571 (0%) | DB: 0.08508 (0%) |
200 OK [http://localhost/widgets]
```

In this case, continuing enables the index action to complete.

Now let's try another quick example, but this time we'll ask for the results of all the widgets in XML instead by calling http://localhost:3000/widgets.xml.

```
/Users/tony/work/for/trunk/topics/debugging/rails/app/controllers/
widgets_controller.rb:6 widgets = Widget.find(:all)
(rdb:13)
```

Now we're back in rdb. We can do a list again to get an idea where we are:

```
(rdb:13) l
[1, 10] in /Users/tony/work/for/trunk/topics/debugging/rails/app/controllers/
widgets_controller.rb
    1  class WidgetsController < ApplicationController
    2    # GET /widgets
    3    # GET /widgets.xml
    4    def index
    5      debugger
=> 6      widgets = Widget.find(:all)
    7
    8      respond_to do |format|
    9        format.html # index.html.erb
   10        format.xml  { render :xml => widgets }
(rdb:13)
```

However, it gets a little irritating to have to do a list every move you make, every step you take (that's a debugging joke right there). ruby-debug has a feature called autolist for this:

```
(rdb:13) set autolist
autolist is on.
(rdb:13)
(rdb:13) n
```

```
Processing WidgetsController#index (for 127.0.0.1 at 2008-01-01 20:32:20) [GET]
  Parameters: {"format"=>"xml", "action"=>"index", "controller"=>"widgets"}
/Users/tony/work/for/trunk/topics/debugging/rails/app/controllers/
widgets_controller.rb:8 respond_to do |format|
[3, 12] in /Users/tony/work/for/trunk/topics/debugging/rails/app/controllers/
widgets_controller.rb
    3    # GET /widgets.xml
    4    def index
    5      debugger
    6      widgets = Widget.find(:all)
    7
=>  8      respond_to do |format|
    9        format.html # index.html.erb
   10        format.xml  { render :xml => widgets }
   11      end
   12    end
(rdb:13)
```

Now, whenever we step around the code, we get a listing automatically. Another time saver is autoeval:

```
(rdb:14) set autoeval
autoeval is on.
(rdb:14) params
{"format"=>"xml", "action"=>"index", "controller"=>"widgets"}
(rdb:14)
```

If autoeval is on, all you need to do to print it is type the name of a variable instead of typing p each time. On the command line, every character counts!

That's a simple overview of ruby-debug. It's easy to get it up and running, and it's very helpful for figuring out what's going on in your Rails code or, if you'd like to poke around, in the Rails source itself.

Debugging Communication

One last tool for your debugging toolbox is Charles. Charles is a web proxy debugger, which means it puts itself between all web communication on your computer and then logs all traffic by address. This means you can look at any requests to, say, localhost:3000,

and see what's actually going over the wire and coming back. What's even better is that
Charles knows how to decode AMF, so that makes it very nice for debugging Flex
applications that use `RemoteObject`.

Charles is shareware, so you can try it and see if you like it. You can download it from
http://charlesproxy.com

Once you install Charles according to the instructions on the web site, open it. Then
run a Rails server task, perhaps one from the debugging sample code, and make a
request from a browser. Charles sees that a request has been made to localhost:3000, and
an item for that location shows up in the tree on the left to contain all the requests and
responses Charles sees both to and from that address. Make a few requests, and see what
kind of data Charles shows about each.

Figure 6.10 shows a sample response from Rails using the same code from the
RubyAMF example code from Chapter 5, Hierarchical Data with RubyAMF.

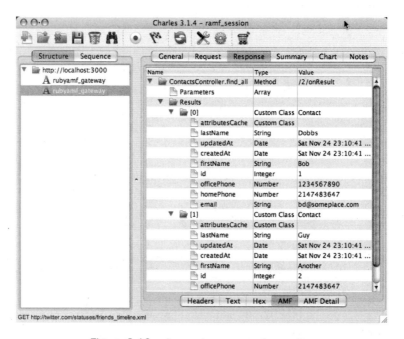

Figure 6.10   A sample response from rails.

Charles knows about AMF and how to decode AMF objects that show up in requests
and responses to and from Rails using RubyAMF. You can see how useful Charles
might be, since no matter what, you know what's actually being sent and received
between Flex and Rails.

Summary

Debugging is a part of building any significantly complex application. Testing helps make sure that your application works the same across changes, but debugging with the tools we've seen here helps you understand and fix more complex problems. Of course, next you should prove that the problems are fixed by writing a test.

7

Data Visualization

Flex Builder Professional provides a new data visualization framework enabling you to manage and display complex data structures by supplying three main types of visual components: the advanced data grid, the OLAP data grid, and the charting components. The three components let you create some impressive data analysis applications. The advanced data grid provides progressive features, such as multicolumn sorting, data grouping, and summaries. The OLAP data grid enables display of multidimensional data, which is a common use in executive dashboards. Like a spreadsheet, it organizes data into rows and columns to show aggregated data in a very condensed way. Finally, the data visualization framework includes the Flex charting classes, which can be used to display a large variety of charts, including bar charts, pie charts, plot charts, bubble charts, line charts, area charts, HLOC charts, candlestick charts, and stack charts.

In this chapter, we will build a Stock Portfolio application to show that Ruby on Rails is a perfect companion for this data visualization framework.

But first, a note of caution. The data visualization framework comes only with Flex Builder Professional, which costs $699 at the time of this writing. A trial version of the IDE is available for 60 days, but a watermark displays across the application saying it's a trial version. Students may get it for free.

Figure 7.1 shows the application we will build using these new data visualization components in conjunction with Rails.

This application enables you to buy and sell stock, as well as track which stock you hold. Of course, this is just a demo application, so we will just ignore many aspects of stocks that a real-world application would need to address, such as stock splits. Let's look at the user interface. On the top right of the application, you see the OLAPDataGrid, which displays an overview of all the managed accounts. If you wonder what OLAP is, I will explain the concepts in the next section of this chapter and, of course, show how to use the Flex OLAP framework. In this OLAP grid, we see that Tony didn't invest in the Financial sector, and we also see the total estimated value of each account and the total estimated value of all the accounts. Additionally, this OLAP data grid can be pivoted, which consists of swapping the rows with the columns to provide a different perspective of the same data. On the top right corner of the application, we display the

Figure 7.1   The stock portfolio application.

positions for a specific account. Use the combo box to select an account, then the positions for that account are displayed in the Advanced Data and are grouped by stock sector. When selecting a given position in the grid, the application displays the historical price data and trading volume in the chart area in the bottom half of the application. We also annotate the historical price chart with the buy and sell movements, providing a good overview of whether we bought or sold the stock at the right time.

This application is a good example of how well Rails and Flex can work together. We will walk through the source code in three steps. First, we will explore how to use the OLAPDataGrid and show how Rails generates the required XML data to summarize the accounts. Then we will look at the Advanced DataGrid, which can group data and display hierarchical data, as well as provide advanced features such as multicolumn sorting, data grouping, and summaries. Finally, we will see how Rails can provide data series that can be connected directly to the Flex charting components.

The Rails data model to keep the account information is quite simple. An account has many positions in a given stock. Each position has many movements created when the stock is bought or sold. The financial data is retrieved from the Yahoo Finance web site using the very easy-to-use yahoofinance gem. Connect to the Internet if you want to code along while we go through the chapter. We will explore how each of the Flex components is connected to the XML returned by our Rails application. When going through the examples, you may want to reference the model diagram shown in Figure 7.2. Again, an account has many positions, and a position has many movements. A position can return an array of historical price data. Account, Position, and Movement are all ActiveRecords, and when accessing the history, the yahoofinance gem is used to retrieve the data from the Yahoo Finance web site. We don't store the historical data.

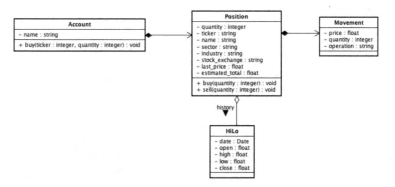

Figure 7.2   Model of the stock portfolio application.

Online Analytical Processing (OLAP)

Before diving into the Flex OLAP framework, let's look at the definition of the term OLAP from Wikipedia:

> Online Analytical Processing, or OLAP (IPA: /ˈoʊlæp/), is an approach to quickly provide answers to analytical queries that are multidimensional in nature. OLAP is part of the broader category business intelligence, which also encompasses relational reporting and data mining. The typical applications of OLAP are in business reporting for sales, marketing, management reporting, business process management (BPM), budgeting and forecasting, financial reporting and similar areas. The term OLAP was created as a slight modification of the traditional database term OLTP (Online Transaction Processing).
>
> Databases configured for OLAP employ a multidimensional data model, allowing for complex analytical and ad-hoc queries with a rapid execution time. They borrow aspects of navigational databases and hierarchical databases that are speedier than their relational kin. http://en.wikipedia.org/wiki/OLAP, 3/3/2008

Flex Builder 3.0 Professional introduces the mx.olap framework that provides a set of classes to visualize and drill down into multidimensional data. We will learn in this chapter how to use the principal classes provided by this new Flex framework, namely, the OLAPCube, which is a dynamic array that can hold multidimensional data; the OLAPQuery classes, which we will use to extract data from the OLAPCube; and, of course, the OLAPDataGrid, which is used to display the queried data. The nature of OLAP is to provide users a means for looking at aggregated information and extracting meaning from what would otherwise be an overwhelming amount of data.

Before we continue, let's define some concepts of what multidimensional data is and what challenges and benefits it represents. A multidimensional database is organized in dimensions and measures. A dimension is a categorization of your data.

A measure is often also called a fact. For an online sales application, you may want to categorize sales by the year and month when the sale occurred, as well as by the product category and the region and state. So, you would have a time dimension, which composes a hierarchy with year and month; a location dimension, which composes a hierarchy with region and state; and a product category dimension. For each sale, you may want to track some facts, like total amount, number of items sold, and cost of items. Organizing your data lets you identify trends that would not be visible simply by looking at the thousands of records of sales. Now you can see sales activity for a given state in a given month, and you can identify which state has the highest sales. One obvious benefit to categorizing lower-level data is that you gain a higher-level view of the data.

In multidimensional data, the amount of data under consideration can quickly become large. Let's assume we want to analyze sales data over the last 5 years for each month, each state, 33 products, and two measures (items and amount). That corresponds to 198,000 values (5 $\star$ 12 $\star$ 50 $\star$ 33 $\star$ 2 = 198,000), which in turn could correspond to millions of sales records. That's still too much data to analyze, so instead of looking by month, we can look by quarter, thus dividing the number of cells by three, or 66,000 values. Then we can summarize the states by region, assuming three regions, thus reducting the total to 3960 values (= 5 $\star$ 4 $\star$ 3 $\star$ 33 $\star$ 2). This total still seems like a lot of data, but OLAP provides a means to visualize this data in a data grid with a hierarchy of headers and rows, enabling you to effectively display this amount of data. In our situation, you could have 99 rows (3 regions with 33 products each), and 20 columns (5 years with 4 quarters each), and you could consider one measure at time. I agree this is still a large set of data, but now you can start comparing all the states over a 5-year period in one glimpse.

Do we really need multidimensional data? Doesn't a relational database contain all the data we need? We could simply query the data as needed, whenever we need a summary report, for example. When speaking about OLAP and multidimensional databases, we must understand that they are used to keep information over many years. Often we are trying to compare data that aggregates in large amounts. Not only is it time-consuming to query these large amounts of data, but also, such queries would certainly impact the performance of your application. This is where data warehouses, which enable us to store data multidimensionally, come into play. They are used to reorganize data to enable more efficient querying without impacting the existing systems. One approach to a data warehouse is to have an extraction phase where data is gathered from your main application and stored into a data warehouse. A data warehouse can use a custom storage system, which is not relational, or like the Rails ActiveWarehouse framework, your relational database can be used in a manner that is more efficient for the type of queries that OLAP requires. In such a case, the tables are organized in a "star schema," where the facts are stored in a facts table pointing to all the dimensions in a dimensions table, forming a "star" if you were to set it out on a diagram. Using a separate database for your data warehouse enables you to perform many queries while not impacting the performance of the main application. Also, OLAP is mostly concerned with analyzing data over time, like comparing month-over-month or year-over-year sales figures, and therefore, it's acceptable, for the most part, to not have the latest daily information. Like everything, the point in time when the data is extracted is mostly a tradeoff between reducing the performance impact on the running application and having the greatest number of data points you can get. Therefore, extraction is mostly performed when the application usage is the lowest.

Was that explanation too abstract for you? Still scratching your head? Let's look at some code that will shine light on the above information and will give you some useful techniques you can use right away on your projects.

The Flex mx.olap Framework

To present the Flex mx.olap framework, let's create an example unrelated to our Stock Portfolio application so we can walk through some of the concepts. For this example, we will analyze what products Tony and Daniel bought over the last couple of years. We will create a cube with three dimensions: `Products`, `Owner`, and `Year`, and measure the number of products and the amount each product cost.

To use the framework, you will need to get familiar with the `OLAPCube`, the `OLAPQuery`, and the `OLAPDataGrid`. These components are usually used in the following way

1. Create an `OLAPCube` defining all the dimensions. This can be done easily using MXML.

2. Set the `dataProvider` on the cube to load data in the cube.

3. Create an `OLAPQuery`, defining which dimension to display in which row and column and how to aggregate the data.

4. Have the cube execute the query. This is asynchronous.

5. Set the result of the query to the `OLAPDataGrid` data provider.

Let's dive in to our example. We will load the cube from the following array of data:

```
var array:Array =
    [ {name:'Tony', product:'MediaPlayer', type:'iPod', year:2007, value:299},
      {name:'Tony', product:'Computer', type:'MacBook Pro', year:2007, value:2990},
      {name:'Tony', product:'Computer', type:'iMac', year:2008, value:1499},
      {name:'Daniel', product:'Computer', type:'MacBook Pro', year:2007, value:2990},
      {name:'Daniel', product:'MediaPlayer', type:'iPod', year:2007, value:299},
      {name:'Daniel', product:'MediaPlayer', type:'iPod Nano', year:2008, value:149}
    ]
```

To define the cube, we need to specify dimensions and measures, so in the following example, we declare the cube using MXML and define three dimensions: `Owner`, `Product`, and `Year`. We specify two additional measures: number and value of product. If you think in spreadsheet terms, the dimension will be used to organize the data in rows and columns, and the measures will be used to calculate the cells. When defining the dimension, specify the `dataField` that identifies a given record of the array as being part of that dimension. So the dimensions are mapped to the name, product, and year attributes of the objects in the above array.

```
<mx:OLAPCube id="cube">
   <!-- Dimension 1 Owner-->
   <mx:OLAPDimension name="Owner" >
      <mx:OLAPAttribute dataField="name" name="Name"/>
   </mx:OLAPDimension>
   <!-- Dimension 2 Product-->
   <mx:OLAPDimension name="Product" >
      <mx:OLAPAttribute dataField="product" name="Product"/>
   </mx:OLAPDimension>
   <!-- Dimension 3 Year-->
   <mx:OLAPDimension name="Year" >
      <mx:OLAPAttribute dataField="year" name="Year"/>
         <mx:OLAPHierarchy name="YearHierarchy" hasAll="true" >
            <mx:OLAPLevel attributeName="Year" />
         </mx:OLAPHierarchy>
   </mx:OLAPDimension>
   <!-- Measures -->
  <mx:OLAPMeasure name="NUMBER_OF_PRODUCTS" dataField="value" aggregator="COUNT"
/>
  <mx:OLAPMeasure name="VALUE_OF_PRODUCTS" dataField="value" aggregator="SUM" />
</mx:OLAPCube>
```

Once defined, the cube can be loaded with the array. Processing for the cube is asynchronous, thus enabling the UI to provide progress feedback if needed. Here we just set an event listener to trigger the `runQueryYearByProduct` method once the cube data is loaded and processed.

```
cube.dataProvider = new ArrayCollection(array);
cube.addEventListener(CubeEvent.CUBE_COMPLETE, runQueryYearByProduct);
cube.refresh();
```

Once the query is loaded, we can perform various queries. We will look at different ways to analyze the data contained in the cube. In essence, a query enables you to specify which dimension to include for the columns and rows axes of the grid and which measure to use for the cells.

Add the `Year` dimension to the column axis:

```
// runQueryYearByProduct
var query:OLAPQuery = new OLAPQuery();
var yearSet:IOLAPSet = new OLAPSet();
yearSet.addElements(
     cube.findDimension("Year").findAttribute("Year").children);
var colAxis:IOLAPQueryAxis = query.getAxis(OLAPQuery.COLUMN_AXIS);
colAxis.addSet(yearSet);
```

Then add the `Product` dimension to the row axis:

```
var productSet:IOLAPSet = new OLAPSet();
productSet.addElements(
     cube.findDimension("Product").findAttribute("Product").children);
query.getAxis(OLAPQuery.ROW_AXIS).addSet(productSet);
```

The cube can now execute the query we specified. This process is again asynchronous, and we specify the `displayResult` method as `responder`:

```
var token:AsyncToken = cube.execute(query);
token.addResponder(
   new AsyncResponder(displayResult, olapFaultHandler));
```

The `displayResult` method receives an `OLAPResult`, which can be set as the data provider of the grid as follows:

```
olapGrid.dataProvider = result as IOLAPResult;
```

The grid then displays `Year` dimension values in the column axis and `Product` dimension values on the row axis. Because we didn't specify a measure, the first measure declared in the cube is used by the query, and the grid uses the count measure of the products for the cells. Figure 7.3 shows the resulting data grid.

Product	Year	
	2007	2008
MediaPlayer	2	1
Computer	2	1

Figure 7.3   The data grid from running a query on the data by year and product.

So far, this still looks like a standard grid. The main difference between a standard grid and an OLAP data grid is that the rows and columns can have several levels. So let's create a query that results in the data grid shown in Figure 7.4. We want to add the `Owner` name to the rows, and we now use the count of the products as a measure.

Product	Name	Year	
		2007	2008
MediaPlayer	Tony	1	NaN
	Daniel	1	1
Computer	Tony	1	1
	Daniel	1	NaN

Figure 7.4 Data grid including product owner.

We start creating the query in the same way as the previous one and associate the `Year` dimension with the column axis.

```
var query:OLAPQuery = new OLAPQuery();
var yearSet:IOLAPSet = new OLAPSet();
yearSet.addElements(
          cube.findDimension("Year").findAttribute("Year").children);
query.getAxis(OLAPQuery.COLUMN_AXIS).addSet(yearSet);
```

To add two dimensions to the row axis, we use the `crossJoin` method of OLAP, which in turn will create the Cartesian product of the two dimensions. In our case, that is all combinations of products and owners.

```
var productSet:IOLAPSet = new OLAPSet();
var ownerSet:IOLAPSet = new OLAPSet();
ownerSet.addElements(cube.findDimension("Owner")
           .findAttribute("Name").children);
productSet.addElements(cube.findDimension("Product")
           .findAttribute("Product").children);

query.getAxis(OLAPQuery.ROW_AXIS)
    .addSet(productSet.crossJoin(ownerSet));
```

In this case, we add the product set, joined to the owner set, to the row axis. This results in the first two columns of the grid being `Product` and `Owner`, organized in a hierarchical way where owners are grouped by product.

Now let's create another grid where we move the `Owner` dimension to the column axis, which results in the grid shown in Figure 7.5.

The one difference is that, this time, we joined the year set with the owner set. We also see that Daniel didn't buy a computer in 2008.

Let's have a look at a couple more features of the framework, namely selecting a different measure and adding totals for the dimensions. Until now, we used the default

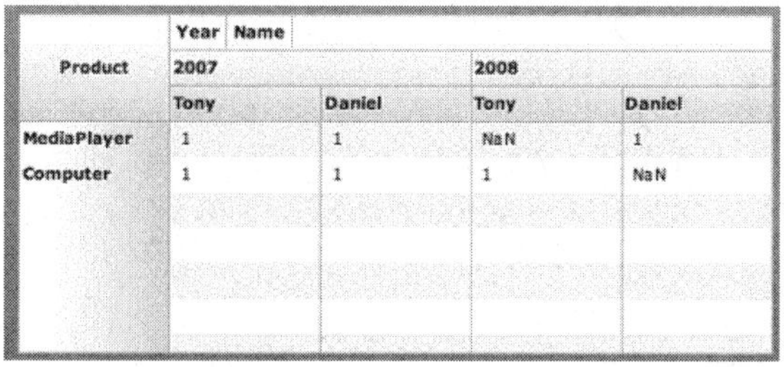

	Year	Name			
Product	**2007**			**2008**	
	Tony		**Daniel**	**Tony**	**Daniel**
MediaPlayer	1		1	NaN	1
Computer	1		1	1	NaN

Figure 7.5 The `Owner` dimension is now on the column axis.

measure, which is the first declared measure, NUMBER_OF_PRODUCTS, in our case. Now
let's use the VALUE_OF_PRODUCTS measure by using the slicer axis as follows:

```
var slicerQueryAxis:IOLAPQueryAxis = query.getAxis(OLAPQuery.SLICER_AXIS);
var valueSet:OLAPSet= new OLAPSet();
valueSet.addElement(
    cube.findDimension("Measures").findMember("VALUE_OF_PRODUCTS"));
slicerQueryAxis.addSet(valueSet);
```

To display the total of a dimension, we need to use the **members** of the attribute
instead of the **children**. Doing so results in displaying the total of a dimension at the top
of the column, and by default, the cell uses the label "(All)."

```
yearSet.addElements(cube.findDimension("Year").findAttribute("Year").members);

productSet.addElements(cube.findDimension("Product").findAttribute("Product").
members);
```

Using these sets would result in the grid shown in Figure 7.6.

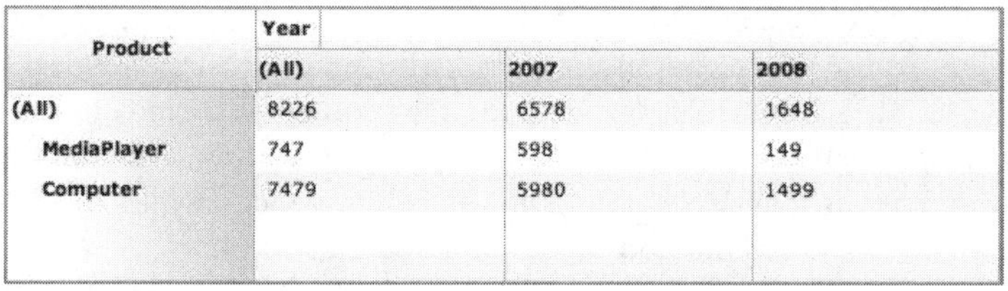

Product	Year		
	(All)	**2007**	**2008**
(All)	8226	6578	1648
MediaPlayer	747	598	149
Computer	7479	5980	1499

Figure 7.6   Value of the product is displayed instead of the number of
products.

If you want the total for the year to appear as the last column, pass `true` to the
hierarchize method of the set object, which indicates that the children should precede
the parents.

```
yearSet.hierarchize(true)
```

If we had done the same for the product dimension, the product total would appear as the last row in a row titled "(All)."

To review, we can have one or many dimensions as column axes, one or many dimensions as row axes, and we can select one measure as the cell content. The queries enable you to extract summary data at different levels and display the result in a very concise manner. It's now time to create an OLAPCube and the OLAPDataGrid for our Stock Portfolio application.

Using the OLAPCube for the Stock Portfolio Application

The Flex code shown in this section can be found in 07_Data_Visualization/flex/src/views/PortfolioSummary.mxml

On the top left part of the Stock Portfolio application, we display an OLAPDataGrid providing a summary of the estimation of all the accounts by sector (see Figure 7.7).

All Accounts Overview by Sectors

Sector	Account		
	daniel	tony	(All)
Consumer Goods	53.96	13240	13293.96
Financial	2455	NaN	2455
Technology	51923.8	8121.99	60045.79
(All)	54432.76	21361.98999999	75794.75

Figure 7.7   A summary of the estimation of all the accounts by sector.

The Flex application receives that data in XML format by using the HTTPService component querying our Rails application. The RESTful configuration and the use of HTTPService is explained in detail in Chapter 3, Flex with RESTful Services. For now, let's just see what XML is returned and how the Flex component can consume it.

To query for all positions with account information, Flex invokes the following URL http://localhost:3000/accounts/positions_with_accounts, which invokes the positions_with_accounts method of AccountsController.

```
class AccountsController < ApplicationController
  def positions_with_accounts
    @positions = Position.find(:all, :include => :account)
    render :xml => @positions.to_xml(:dasherize => false)
  end
end
```

This controller returns all positions for all accounts in XML format. The `:dasherize` setting is set to `false` to ensure that XML formats the element names with an underscore and not a dash, and returns, for example, `<last_price />` instead of `<last-price />`. The former is easier to reference from Flex. `Position.find (:all, :include => :account)` specifies that the account table be included. This is an optimization to retrieve all the account information in one query together with the positions. This enables the `to_xml` method of the Position active record to include the account name without having to query again the account table for each position. We had to override the `to_xml` method in the position active record to add the `last_price` and `estimated_total` calculated values. The `to_xml` method takes a `:methods` attribute, which invokes the specified methods and adds the result to the returned XML with an element named after the method.

```
class Position < ActiveRecord::Base
  belongs_to :account
  def to_xml(options = {})
    super(options.merge({:methods => [:last_price, :estimated_total,
:account_name]}))
  end
end
```

The XML returned looks like this:

```
<positions type="array">
  <position>
    <account_id type="integer">1</account_id>
    <created_at type="datetime">2008-06-13T13:56:40Z</created_at>
    <id type="integer">1</id>
    <industry>Internet Information Providers</industry>
    <name>GOOGLE</name>
    <quantity type="integer">80</quantity>
    <sector>Technology</sector>
    <stock_exchange>NasdaqNM</stock_exchange>
    <ticker>GOOG</ticker>
    <updated_at type="datetime">2008-06-16T13:38:41Z</updated_at>
    <last_price type="float">569.46</last_price>
    <estimated_total type="float">45556.8</estimated_total>
    <account_name>daniel</account_name>
  </position>
  <position>
    <account_id type="integer">1</account_id>
    <created_at type="datetime">2008-06-13T13:56:55Z</created_at>
    <id type="integer">2</id>
    <industry>Diversified Computer Systems</industry>
    <name>SUN MICROSYSTEMS </name>
    <quantity type="integer">100</quantity>
    <sector>Technology</sector>
```

```
    <stock_exchange>NasdaqNM</stock_exchange>
    <ticker>JAVA</ticker>
    <updated_at type="datetime">2008-06-13T13:56:55Z</updated_at>
    <last_price type="float">11.62</last_price>
    <estimated_total type="float">1162.0</estimated_total>
    <account_name>daniel</account_name>
  </position>
  ...
</positions>
```

I left out a couple of records for briefness. Now we can assign this XML to the cube.
However, the cube expects an `mx.collections.ICollectionView`, so let's look at the
following code:

```
var positions:XML = <positions>...</positions>
cube.dataProvider = new XMLListCollection(positions.position)
```

Let's assume the `positions` variable contains the returned XML. Again, we don't
show all the XML here; we replaced the `<position>` elements with an ellipsis. We can
now extract all `<position>` tags from the XML using the `.position` e4X instruction
and wrap the resulting `XMLList` into an `XMLListCollection`. This method takes more
steps than just passing an array of objects to the cube, but it works really well with
XML. Then we can refresh the cube and run the query.

The cube defines the `Account` and `SectorIndustry` dimensions, which will be
mapped to the `account_name`, `sector`, and `industry` data fields of the XML returned
by the server.

```
<mx:OLAPCube id="cube">
  <mx:OLAPDimension name="Account" >
    <mx:OLAPAttribute dataField="account_name" name="Account"/>
    <mx:OLAPHierarchy name="AccountHierarchy">
        <mx:OLAPLevel attributeName="Account" />
    </mx:OLAPHierarchy>
  </mx:OLAPDimension>

  <mx:OLAPDimension name="SectorIndustry" >
      <mx:OLAPAttribute dataField="sector" name="Sector"/>
      <mx:OLAPAttribute dataField="industry" name="Industry"/>
      <mx:OLAPHierarchy name="SectorIndustryHierarchy">
      <mx:OLAPLevel  attributeName="Sector" />
      <mx:OLAPLevel  attributeName="Industry" />
    </mx:OLAPHierarchy>
   </mx:OLAPDimension>

  <mx:OLAPMeasure name="Estimated" dataField="estimated_total" aggregator="SUM" />
</mx:OLAPCube>
```

We wrapped the query creation logic in the getQuery method, which also takes the pivot and showIndustry boolean arguments. Pivoting is not provided by the Flex framework, but we can achieve this result by adding the pivot argument to our query method, which simply enables swapping the column and row axis, thus providing the pivot effect. The showIndustry argument defines whether the axis shows the sector and should further show the breakdown by industry.

```
private function getQuery(pivot:Boolean=false,
                          showIndustry:Boolean=false):IOLAPQuery {
  var query:OLAPQuery = new OLAPQuery;
  var firstAxis:IOLAPQueryAxis =
      query.getAxis(pivot ? OLAPQuery.ROW_AXIS : OLAPQuery.COLUMN_AXIS);
  var sectorSet:IOLAPSet = new OLAPSet();
  sectorSet.addElements(
    cube.findDimension("SectorIndustry").findAttribute("Sector").members);
  if (showIndustry) {
    var industrySet:IOLAPSet = new OLAPSet();
    industrySet.addElements(
      cube.findDimension("SectorIndustry")
          .findAttribute("Industry").members);
    firstAxis.addSet(
        sectorSet.hierarchize(true)
          .crossJoin(industrySet).hierarchize(true));
  } else {
    firstAxis.addSet(sectorSet.hierarchize(true));
  }
  var secondAxis:IOLAPQueryAxis =
      query.getAxis(pivot ? OLAPQuery.COLUMN_AXIS : OLAPQuery.ROW_AXIS);
  var accountSet:IOLAPSet = new OLAPSet();
  accountSet.addElements(
      cube.findDimension("Account").findAttribute("Account").members);
  secondAxis.addSet(accountSet.hierarchize(true));
  return query;
}
```

When selecting pivot and showIndustry for the query, we get the data grid shown in Figure 7.8. The row axis has the additional Industry column.

I encourage you to play with the Flex OLAP framework, as it is straightforward to use and can provide a useful addition to your application. I didn't show in this section several aspects, such as a cell styling and formatting, that enable further customization of the grid.

Now on to the next Flex Data Visualization component, the Advanced DataGrid.

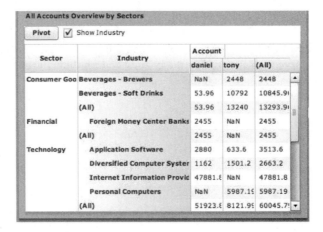

Figure 7.8   Choosing pivot and `showIndustry` yields the Industry column.

Advanced DataGrid

If you have used Flex, chances are you used the DataGrid component, which enables you to display data in a tabular format. The Flex Advanced DataGrid can be used in the same way and provides additional functionality, such as multicolumn sorting, data grouping, advanced cell selection, advanced styling for rows and columns, and much more. We will now explore some of these possibilities.

The Flex code shown in this section can be found in Chapter 7/stockportfolio/flex/src/views/PositionList.mxml

So let's see how we can define the data grid shown in Figure 7.9.

Let's start with the Estimation and Industry columns, which, as you can see, have subcolumns. They are simply a visual group of the header and not a grouping of the data. We achieved this by using the `groupedColumns` property of the advanced data

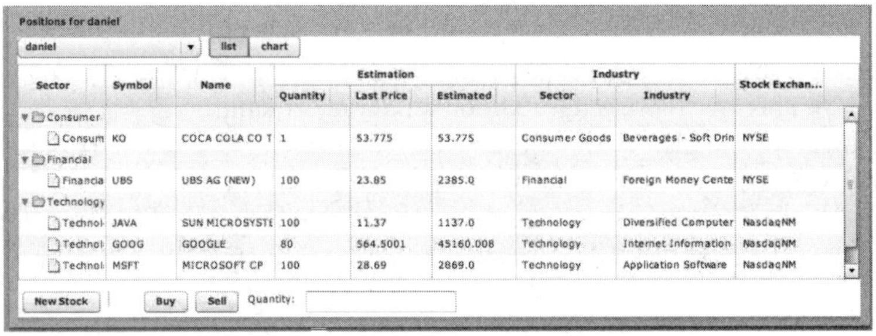

Figure 7.9   Example data grid.

grid instead of the columns attribute and wrapping the columns in a column group, as follows:

```
<mx:groupedColumns>
    <mx:AdvancedDataGridColumnGroup headerText="Estimation">
        <mx:AdvancedDataGridColumn headerText="Quantity" dataField="quantity"/>
        <mx:AdvancedDataGridColumn headerText="Last Price"
dataField="last_price"/>
        <mx:AdvancedDataGridColumn headerText="Estimated"
dataField="estimated_total"/>
    </mx:AdvancedDataGridColumnGroup>
</mx:groupedColumns>
```

The grid groups the positions by sector, which results in a tree-like structure in the first column where a sector can be opened and collapsed. For our grid, we are grouping a flat list of positions, but the advanced data grid can also display hierarchical data. To group the position list, we wrap it in GroupingCollection, which defines the field to use for the group. This Flex class converts the flat position list into a hierarchy. Because we are using XML where the position node contains subnodes for each attribute, we need to trick the GroupingCollection class into not treating them as subnodes but rather as attributes. We do this by specifying the childrenField as a value that does not map to an element of the position node (we used "subnodes" in this case), and therefore, the GroupingCollection class will not try to dive deeper in the hierarchy. This is the only subtle aspect of using XML with the advanced data grid. The grouping collection definition follows:

```
<mx:GroupingCollection id ="groupingCollection" childrenField="subnodes">
  <mx:grouping>
    <mx:Grouping>
      <mx:GroupingField name="sector" />
    </mx:Grouping>
  </mx:grouping>
</mx:GroupingCollection>
```

The rest of the advanced data grid definition consists of declaring the data grid column. The whole declaration of the grid goes as follows:

```
<mx:AdvancedDataGrid id="positionGrid" width="100%" height="100%" >
  <mx:dataProvider>
    <mx:GroupingCollection id ="groupingCollection"  childrenField="subnodes">
        <mx:grouping>
            <mx:Grouping>
                <mx:GroupingField name="sector" />
            </mx:Grouping>
        </mx:grouping>
```

```
          </mx:GroupingCollection>
        </mx:dataProvider>
    <mx:groupedColumns>
      <mx:AdvancedDataGridColumn headerText="Sector" dataField="sector"/>
      <mx:AdvancedDataGridColumn headerText="Symbol" dataField="ticker"/>
      <mx:AdvancedDataGridColumn headerText="Name" dataField="name"/>
      <mx:AdvancedDataGridColumnGroup headerText="Esitmation">
        <mx:AdvancedDataGridColumn headerText="Quantity" dataField="quantity"/>
        <mx:AdvancedDataGridColumn headerText="Last Price" dataField="last_price"/>
        <mx:AdvancedDataGridColumn headerText="Estimated"
dataField="estimated_total"/>
      </mx:AdvancedDataGridColumnGroup>
      <mx:AdvancedDataGridColumnGroup headerText="Industry">
        <mx:AdvancedDataGridColumn headerText="Sector" dataField="sector"/>
        <mx:AdvancedDataGridColumn headerText="Industry" dataField="industry"/>
      </mx:AdvancedDataGridColumnGroup>
      <mx:AdvancedDataGridColumn headerText="Stock Exchange"
dataField="stock_exchange"/>
    </mx:groupedColumns>
</mx:AdvancedDataGrid>
```

Now that we have a grid, let's load some data into it. For this grid, we request the positions for the selected account. If the selected account has an ID of 1, then the URL is the following: http://localhost:3000/accounts/1/positions. This invokes the index method of the positions controller, which returns the list of positions in XML format.

```
class PositionsController < ApplicationController
  before_filter :get_account
  def index
    @positions = @account.positions.find(:all, :include => :account)
    render :xml => @positions.to_xml(:dasherize=>false)
  end
end
```

The main difference compared to the accounts controller is that the positions are scoped to the current account. The returned XML is in the same format as that used for the OLAP grid shown in the previous section of this chapter.

We don't set the data provider directly on the data grid in this case, since the grid is connected to the grouping collection. So we just change the source of the grouping collection with the XMLList returned by the `positions.position` statement and refresh the grouping collection, which in turns updates the data grid display.

```
groupingCollection.source = positions.position;
groupingCollection.refresh();
```

The advanced data grid provides many more features, such as multicolumn cell renderers, styling and formatting, and displaying of hierarchical data. Chances are, if your application demands it, the advanced data grid may provide it.

Charting

Using charts in your application not only adds a nice touch but also provides a different view of the data that is displayed. Charts help the user quickly identify facts that would otherwise be buried somewhere deep in a long list of data. The Flex charting framework that comes with Flex Builder Professional supports a wide variety of 2D charts, such as bar charts, pie charts, plot charts, bubble charts, line charts, area charts, HLOC charts, candlestick charts, and stack charts, each type providing a different view of your data or supporting different types of data. These charts can be interactively animated and visually decorated. We will explore here only a subset of that functionality, but the discussion will show how easily these charts can render XML returned by our Rails application.

PieChart

In the upper right corner of the application, we can select to display the positions of the selected account as the chart shown in Figure 7.10 rather than as a grid. This chart provides a nice visual clue about the composition of the account. Here we see that Tony has a large part of his portfolio vested in Coca-Cola (KO).

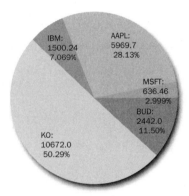

Figure 7.10   Portfolio visualized through a pie chart.

This chart uses the same data as the advanced data grid but calculates the percentage based on the `estimated_total` field of each stock. Here is the XML returned by the Rails position controller (we included only the relevant fields in the following list; the controller returns all the fields for each position as required by the grid display):

```
<positions type="array">
  <position>
    <ticker>MSFT</ticker>
```

```
      <estimated_total type="float">636.46</estimated_total>
   </position>
   <position>
     <ticker>AAPL</ticker>
     <estimated_total type="float">5969.7</estimated_total>
   </position>
   <position>
     <ticker>IBM</ticker>
     <estimated_total type="float">1500.24</estimated_total>
   </position>
   <position>
     <ticker>KO</ticker>
     <estimated_total type="float">10672.0</estimated_total>
   </position>
   <position>
     <ticker>BUD</ticker>
     <estimated_total type="float">2442.0</estimated_total>
   </position>
</positions>
```

Now we can declare the mx:PieChart to use estimate_total as the field and the ticker as nameField.

```
<mx:PieChart id="pie" width="100%" height="100%" dataProvider="{positions}">
  <mx:series>
    <mx:PieSeries
      nameField="ticker"
      displayName="Estimated Amount"
      field="estimated_total"
      labelPosition="insideWithCallout"
      labelFunction="formatLabel"
      />
  </mx:series>
</mx:PieChart>
```

We provide a label function that enables customization of the formatting of the label associated with each slice. The label function also receives the percentage, as calculated by the chart component.

```
private function formatLabel(data:Object, field:String, index:Number,
percentValue:Number):String {
  var temp:String= (" " + percentValue).substr(0,6);
  return data.ticker + ": " + '\n' + data.estimated_total + '\n' + temp + "%";
}
```

The labelPosition property of the chart lets you specify whether the label should appear inside, outside, or, as in our case, insideWithCallout, which moves the label outside of the slice if there is not enough space to display it.

HLOCChart

Now let's look at a more complex chart that will show the historical price for the selected stock, and we will add a second axis to the same chart to display the trading volume of that stock. Finally, we will annotate the chart with a buy-and-sell indicator for each of the movements of that position. The High, Low, Open, Close chart is made to display financial data that include the opening, closing, high, and low price of a stock for a given day. It just happens that the Yahoo Finance API exposes this data and that our Rails position controller simply transforms it into an XML series. Here is code used in the Rails application. To retrieve the time series, the Flex application makes an HTTP request to this URL: http://localhost:3000/accounts/1/positions/1/history.

This triggers the `history` method of the positions controller. There we find the specified position in the account and request the history from that position.

```
class PositionsController < ApplicationController
  before_filter :get_account
  def history
    @position = @account.positions.find(params[:id])
    render :xml => @position.history.to_xml
  end
end
```

In fact, all the magic happens in the position active record. We don't store the historical price but request it using the `YahooFinance` class that is provided by the yahoofinance gem. As you see, the call is fairly straightforward; we need to pass two arguments, the first being the ticker, for example, GOOG for the Google stock, and the number of historical days we want to retrieve. For simplicity, we are always retrieving 200 days. In a real application, you may want to make this variable. Note the call returns an array of pricing information with the most recent pricing in first position. The pricing information looks as follows ["2008-06-19," "555.35," "563.78," "550.81," "560.20," "5683100," "560.20"] and represents the date, open, high, low, and close prices, followed by the volume and an additional adjusted closing price. To make our life easier in the Flex application, the following `history` method turns this information into an array of hash maps with the key of the hash matching the pricing information names.

```
class Position < ActiveRecord::Base
  def history
    items = YahooFinance::get_historical_quotes_days( ticker, 200 )
    items.reverse!
    items.each_with_index do |item, index|
      hash = {}
      %w{date open high low close volume adjusted_close}.each_with_index do
|field, position|
```

```
        hash[field] = item[position]
      end
      items[index] = hash
    end
  end
end
```

The positions controller can then simply call the `to_xml` method on the array of hash returned by the history method to transform it into the following XML. The `to_xml` method is a nice addition to the `Array` and `Hash` classes provided by Rails.

```xml
<records type="array">
  <record>
    <close>681.53</close>
    <high>695.00</high>
    <date>2007-12-03</date>
    <adjusted-close>681.53</adjusted-close>
    <volume>4325100</volume>
    <low>681.14</low>
    <open>691.01</open>
  </record>
  <record>
    <close>684.16</close>
    <high>692.00</high>
    <date>2007-12-04</date>
    <adjusted-close>684.16</adjusted-close>
    <volume>4231800</volume>
    <low>677.12</low>
    <open>678.31</open>
  </record>
  ...
</records>
```

This XML is then returned to the Flex application, and assuming we assign it to the `priceHistory` variable, we can now define the following chart. First, I'll let you look at the whole chart declaration here, and then we can walk through its different parts:

```xml
<mx:HLOCChart id="hlocchart"
        showDataTips="true" dataProvider="{priceHistory.record}">
  <mx:horizontalAxis>
    <mx:CategoryAxis id="haxis" categoryField="date" title="Date"  />
  </mx:horizontalAxis>

  <mx:horizontalAxisRenderers>
    <mx:AxisRenderer axis="{haxis}" canDropLabels="true"  />
  </mx:horizontalAxisRenderers>
```

```
<mx:verticalAxisRenderers>
  <mx:AxisRenderer placement="left" axis="{v1}" />
  <mx:AxisRenderer placement="right" axis="{v2}"/>
</mx:verticalAxisRenderers>

<mx:series>
  <mx:HLOCSeries id="hlSerie"
    openField="open" highField="high"
    lowField="low" closeField="close" >
    <mx:verticalAxis>
        <mx:LinearAxis id="v1"  baseAtZero="false" title="Price" />
    </mx:verticalAxis>
  </mx:HLOCSeries>

  <mx:ColumnSeries id="dateSerie"
    xField="date" yField="volume"
    fill="{serieColor}" stroke="{null}">
    <mx:verticalAxis>
        <mx:LinearAxis id="v2"  baseAtZero="false" title="Volume" />
    </mx:verticalAxis>
  </mx:ColumnSeries>
</mx:series>


<mx:annotationElements>
  <mx:CartesianDataCanvas id="canvas" verticalAxis="{v1}"
includeInRanges="true"/>
</mx:annotationElements>
</mx:HLOCChart>
```

The first thing is to set the chart data provider to `priceHistory.record`, which is
an e4x expression returning an XMLList. The chart has no problem displaying this
XMLList. Each data element contains the price information and the volume information, so we define two series that will refer to the same data provider but will use and
display different attributes of the data. So the chart has the `series` attribute, which takes
one or more series and, in our example, we create one `HLOCSeries` for the historical
pricing and one `ColumnSeries` for the trading volume. For the first series, we need to
declare which field from each data point represents the high, low, open, and close, and
we do this by setting the respective `openField`, `highField`, `lowField`, and
`closeField` on the `HLOCSeries` object. For the `ColumnSeries`, we define the `xField`
and `yField` as the date and volume attribute of the data point. We also specify not to
use a stroke for the series and to use the color as declared hereafter to draw the volume
columns. Not using the stroke removes the border of each column, and using the following color with an alpha set to 0.7 makes for a slightly transparent column bar, thus
enabling both series to overlap while still being visible.

```
<mx:SolidColor id="serieColor" color="0xCCCCCC" alpha=".7"/>
```

We also define a linear axis for both series; we could have used a logarithmic axis, which can be used to represent data with a wider range of values, but in our case, this isn't needed. Now, to put each of the series on a different vertical axis, we can define the vertical axis renderers and specify that the axis representing the high-low series is placed on the left and that the axis for the volume data is on the right. To associate the axis with the renderer, we pass the ID of the axis to the renderer as follows:

```
<mx:verticalAxisRenderers>
  <mx:AxisRenderer placement="left" axis="{v1}" />
  <mx:AxisRenderer placement="right" axis="{v2}"/>
</mx:verticalAxisRenderers>
```

Both series share the same horizontal axis, so we need to define just one that is using the date field of each data point. We also need to specify a renderer for this axis to inform the chart to drop some of the date labels, since we couldn't display 200 dates horizontally across the chart.

```
<mx:horizontalAxisRenderers>
  <mx:AxisRenderer axis="{haxis}" canDropLabels="true" />
</mx:horizontalAxisRenderers>
```

Let's look at one last detail of this chart; if you look at the top of the chart declaration, you will see that we set the showDataTips attribute to true; this makes the chart react to the mouse and displays a data tooltip when hovering over the series showing the pricing information.

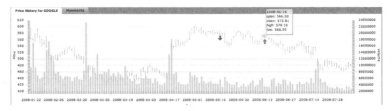

Figure 7.11   Price history and volume chart.

Summary

The advanced data visualization that comes with Flex Builder professional enables you to quickly add some advanced features to your application that are well worth the price of the components. These components offer more features than we presented in this chapter, but you can quickly get good results without having to grasp all the nitty-gritty details and possibilities offered. So just go try them.

## 8

Flex MVC Frameworks

This chapter discusses what we mean by an MVC framework, where the Flex framework leaves room for other frameworks, and two architectural frameworks for Flex: Cairngorm and PureMVC.

What Do We Mean by a Framework?

Rails is a framework. Flex is a framework. So why are we talking about frameworks again? For that matter, what do we mean when we say "framework"? Framework is kind of an overloaded term, to be sure, but in this instance, we mean: "A collection of utilities, classes, and patterns to help organize code and promote consistency."

Framework classes help you follow the rules of the framework, and the patterns, when followed, help enforce the philosophy or style of the framework. The style or philosophy of the framework reflects what the framework authors believe to be a good way to architect and build applications of a certain type and may or may not use special language features.

Code organization follows the conventions of the framework. It may seem like a small thing, but it's helpful when, from application to application, programmers can find things exactly where they expect to find them. For instance, you know that for every Rails application you come across, the `ActiveRecord` models are in the app/models directory and extend `ActiveRecord::Base`. Consistency helps keep teams of developers from stepping on each other's toes and makes it easy to understand where to find resources of a certain type.

Frameworks can be the focus of "holy wars," too, just like languages can be. Beware of taking at face value any assertion that a framework is "the best." As we mentioned, different frameworks have different styles and philosophies, and you should weigh the merits of a framework and decide if it fits your project's needs. Comparing different frameworks by their merits will give you a good idea which one matches your needs.

Roll Your Own

You could write a framework to fit your needs rather than use one written by someone else. The way Flex works—by enabling you to write ActionScript classes that you can describe in an XML-based language or by extending the Flex components—means you can easily write whatever you need to build the type of application you need. It's a good idea to know what the available prewritten frameworks offer, though, so you can avoid reinventing the wheel.

Cairngorm and PureMVC are the most commonly used frameworks, and a look at both of them will help you choose which one might fit your needs.

Cairngorm at a High Level

Let's start our attempt to understand Cairngorm by taking a high-level view of it.

Origin

When people hear the word "Cairngorm" for the first time, they generally have a quizzical look on their faces, and they need a few tries to pronounce it correctly. It may be a funny-sounding word, but it's not made up. The Cairngorms is a mountain range in Scotland, which is where most employees of the former iteration::two are from. iteration::two was one of the first rich Internet application (RIA) consultancies and was located in the United Kingdom.

The folks at iteration::two were some of the first developers to realize how powerful Flex was when it was first being developed (codenamed Royale). In fact, iteration::two wrote the first Flex book. iteration::two also developed the Cairngorm microframework to make it easier for Flex developers to fit to their application's "enterprise" patterns—patterns that applications integrating with enterprise systems often use. Most of these patterns can be found in the seminal *Design Patterns: Elements of Reusable Object-Oriented Software,* written by the "Gang of Four."[1] iteration::two was acquired by Adobe and is now the Adobe Consulting European practice. Any other information you need about Cairngorm can be found at http://labs.adobe.com/wiki/index.php/Cairngorm.

Goals and Concepts

The goal of Cairngorm is to help developers separate the concerns of the application—the model, view, and controller—to achieve a more flexible and less coupled architecture. Cairngorm defines itself as a prescriptive framework, which means it helps enforce what it believes to be good practices. Cairngorm provides a single model that multiple views can reference, and it relies heavily on Flex's powerful binding system to make it very simple to configure the various screens of an application to automatically respond to changes in the model.

---

[1] Erich, Gamma, Richard, Helm, Ralph, Johnson, and John Vlissides, *Design Patterns: Elements of Reusable Object-Oriented Software.* Boston: Addison-Wesley, 1994.

Cairngorm is event based. Each view captures a "user gesture" (e.g., a click or a drag of a form submission) and dispatches an event, which Cairngorm interprets as a command. A command is a very useful pattern in any kind of an application, especially a visual application. A command has a very specific responsibility and does nothing more than whatever is needed to fulfill the responsibility.

Commands are often associated directly with an application's specific need, such as "save document," "submit order," and "delete comment." Commands never deal with the specifics of what part of the application triggers them, and in this way, they're decoupled and reusable. Therefore, it's easier for a developer to invoke the same command in different ways, for instance, both from a menu option and a hot key.

The life cycle of a command is often in this form:

- Execution

- Service interaction (optional—through business layer)

- Modification of application state by updating the model

Service interaction is a big part of Cairngorm as well. A good practice when working with a different system exposed through a service—a back-end—is to provide a "level of indirection," which is code that acts as a layer between the rest of the application and the service. This practice provides insurance that any changes to the service only affect a small part of the application. Then it's relatively easy, or at least straightforward, to change from, say, a PHP back-end to a Rails service, or perhaps from an XML over REST service to AMF. Once the service interaction layer is changed to do what it needs to do, as long as any classes interacting with this layer—hopefully only the commands—require no change, the rest of the application will continue to function as it did before the change.

Now let's look more specifically at the cast of characters, the classes, that a Cairngorm application interacts with.

The Cairngorm Players

The players include model, view, controller, and service layer.

Model

The Cairngorm model is called the ModelLocator and is a singleton, which means only one instance per application is ever possible. (Think of the movie *The Highlander* here—"There can be only one!"—even if you don't need that image to help you remember, it's still fun.) In ActionScript, as in Java and other similar languages, the singleton instance is accessed through a static method on the model class called getInstance. Cairngorm provides an interface called IModelLocator, which doesn't expose any methods, so it's a placeholder interface and is sometimes omitted.

Other de facto parts to the model are often called Value Objects, or VOs for short. These objects describe your "problem domain," such as Users or Products. Your model will most likely have properties of these types, and they will probably be returned as the result of service calls. Cairngorm makes no demands on these parts of your application.

View

The ModelLocator is so named because any place in the application that needs to reference the model can access the singleton instance by using the model's `getInstance` method. This method is like looking the model up or locating it. The model is always marked with a `[Bindable]` metadata tag, and any view that needs to display a property of the model usually does so by binding directly to the property. In that way, Flex's binding takes care of any changes to the state of the application automatically.

Other than that convention, Cairngorm doesn't have much else to say about the view of the application. It does have some helper classes, called ViewHelpers, but they're not officially encouraged and we won't cover them here. Basically, they're a way to get access to any view in the application through an API, which isn't bad in itself, but a well-architected Cairngorm application doesn't generally use them.

Controller

The Cairngorm controller is made up of one class, a FrontController, and a lot of other pairs of classes, such as Events and Commands. The FrontController is what interprets into a command an event triggered by a user gesture. The only interaction a developer has with the FrontController is to subclass it and, inside it, to register every event used in the application to a corresponding command. Once the FrontController is configured to match an event to a command, when the view dispatches an event, the corresponding command will start life with its execute method being called.

The events in these cases are all subclasses of `CairngormEvent`, which are subclasses of `flash.events.Event`, the basic Flash event. The job of the event is to carry information about the user gesture to the command. Once the event is dispatched from the view, the command is instantiated and the instance of the event that was dispatched is passed as an argument to the command's execute method. This may seem like a lot of jumping through hoops, but again, it provides a level of indirection so that views don't have to know about the commands they trigger. It's then possible to swap out a different command that corresponds to the event, meaning the command logic could totally change, but the view wouldn't have to be changed.

Once the command is executed, it follows the lifecycle mentioned above. There are two types of commands: commands and responders. Basic commands must implement an interface that requires an execute method. Responders implement an interface, in addition, which specifies a method called `result` and a method called `fault`. These methods are callback methods, which will be called by the Flash Player's service classes when a service call returns. I'll bet you can guess which one is called when a call is completed successfully and which one is called on a service call exception.

Commands that only have an execute method typically make some change to the model in one way or another directly in the execute method. Responders generally wait for a response to a service call and then modify the model, perhaps by requesting to load a collection of data objects, the VOs we talked about earlier. When the service returns them, they place the collection on the model for a list on the view to contain, which is updated by binding.

Service Layer

The service layer, as we mentioned above, is the layer between the rest of the application and the service. In fact, the only other parts of the application that interact with the service layer are the commands. The Cairngorm classes that the commands use are called business delegates, and they are instantiated directly in the command when it wants to make a service call. A simple command may call a delegate—there's no restriction—but it needs to be a responder if you want a response when the service call is finished.

Business delegates generally have a list of methods that correspond roughly to methods on a back-end service. When a command calls a delegate method, the delegate gets a reference to a service and makes a call to the service, and then control passes to the Flash Player itself. Everything about service interaction is asynchronous—meaning when you make a call to a service, the method you called from doesn't wait for a response. That's why the responder implements a result method; the result method has a certain signature that the Flash Player expects to call back when a service call is complete. The delegate makes the call and designates the command that called it as the object to call back when the command is complete, and then the delegate is done.

One more piece to the service layer is the service locator. Extending Cairngorm's service locator as an mxml file is a way to keep in one place a configuration of all the services you expect to call—HTTP services, remote objects, web services, and so on. The delegate then requests the service definition from the service locator and makes a call on it.

That's a lot of parts and pieces to get a handle on. Let's look at a diagram that shows a typical Cairngorm interaction from the view to the service and back, and let that cement some ideas about what each piece does. Figure 8.1 presents an overview of such a Cairngorm interaction.

As a developer putting together an application that uses Cairngorm, you'll spend very little upfront time creating the directory structure and configuring the services. You'll spend some time creating business delegates, which mostly correspond directly to the service methods your back-end service exposes. But you'll spend the bulk of your time creating new events and commands, configuring the front controller to register these, and then modifying the model to contain the properties or getter/setter pairs that it needs to correctly model the application's needs.

Those are the pieces and parts that make up a Cairngorm application. Now let's look at where to put them in the project structure.

A typical project using Cairngorm has the directory structure shown in Figure 8.2 underneath the obligatory com.domain directories. Of course, the names may vary to suit taste. Let's briefly look at the contents of the directories:

- business: Contains all business delegates and the service locator configuration file, by convention named Services.mxml.

- commands: As you might expect, contains all commands.

- control: Usually contains only the front controller.

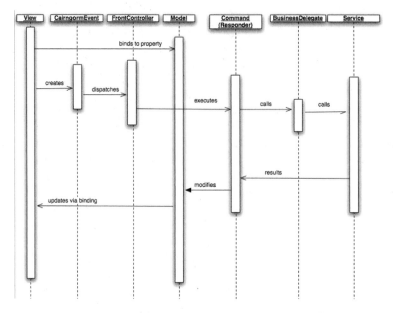

Figure 8.1   A Cairngorm interaction from view to the service and back.

Figure 8.2   Typical Cairngorm directory structure.

- events: No surprise, this directory contains all the events. Occasionally, I'll add non-Cairngorm events here, but some may find it more helpful to add these to view/events.

- model: In general, this directory contains only the model locator, but from time to time, I've also included helper files that relate only to the model.

- view: This is generally a very deep directory, and once again, Cairngorm makes no special demands on how the view is structured, so this directory can be organized in whatever way makes sense for your application.

- vo: This is where to keep objects that describe the domain model, the DTOs, or as most of the Flex community calls them, VOs.

PureMVC at a High Level

PureMVC, as you may expect from the name, is a framework that helps developers separate the concerns of their application into model, view, and controller. The chief architect, Cliff Hall, initially created the framework as an ActionScript 3 (AS3) framework—ActionScript, not Flex, mind you—but at this time of writing, projects are underway for ActionScript 2, ActionScript 3 MultiCore, C#, ColdFusion, Java, Perl, PHP, Python, and Ruby.

As you can see from the list of ports above, one of the goals is to make PureMVC language agnostic as much as possible, by not relying on special features of a language that others don't have. Specifically for Flex, the AS3 version doesn't rely on binding or any Flex framework classes.

The goals of the AS3 version, which we'll be using, are these, taken from the PureMVC website at www.puremvc.org:

- Simple but appropriate framework scope.
- Reduce confusion over application layers, class roles, responsibilities, and collaborations.
- Balance speedy implementation with scalability and maintainability.
- Provide clear and adequate documentation.
- Avoid platform dependencies.
- Hide complexity from developer.
- A well-planned framework that doesn't require continual upgrade and maintenance to keep up with new features, deprecations and refactorings.

One more thing about the framework—although the AS3 version doesn't make use of binding, you're free to use bindings inside of your views. Also, one other spec is that all PureMVC classes conform to interfaces, so you're free to replace any part of the framework you need to replace. All you need to do is write your class to the appropriate interface provided with the framework.

Let's look at the parts of a PureMVC application.

Controller

In PureMVC, access to any part of the framework in your application is through what's called a Facade. The Facade is responsible for either keeping a reference or constructing any framework objects, as needed. Your application generally has a singleton subclass of a class called Facade, which implements the interface for the Facade. Inside your subclass is where you do all the registration of notifications to commands, which tells the framework what should happen when certain notifications are received.

It's rare, though, to actually interact directly with the Facade, since most of the time, you access it through convenience methods implemented by the framework. You'll understand this better when you see some code, but for now, keep the Facade in mind.

Notifications, as you may have guessed, are messages that different parts of the framework can send and receive to tell those parts when a certain action has taken place. Notifications are the glue that loosely holds the various parts of your application together. Anything can register to receive a notification, and multiple objects can respond to the same notification.

One of the objects that the Facade accesses and tracks for you is the Controller. The Controller, much like Cairngorm's front controller, responds to notifications, which we've seen correspond to commands. That's right, here's a pattern we've seen before—probably because it's such a useful one.

PureMVC commands are stateless and are constructed by the controller as needed. We've seen that anything can register to receive a notification and choose whichever action to perform in response, but the only way a command can be executed is in response to a notification.

The PureMVC command class implements an interface that requires one method, named execute, just as in Cairngorm's command class (they both implement the same pattern). The framework offers a convenience class, called SimpleCommand, which you'll probably extend most of the time because it provides access to the facade through some helper methods, making it a convenience to extend. You're, of course, free to implement the command interface as you see fit.

Again, the command's responsibility is to execute business logic and then modify the model. Interacting with the model is done by accessing what PureMVC calls a proxy.

Model

The PureMVC model does nothing more than hold a collection of named proxies. These proxies are instances of classes that you write to work with a certain part of your data model. The model is not a singleton as it is in Cairngorm, but if you know a proxy's name, you can access it from anywhere in the application. The API you implement in your application's proxies provides access to methods for things like adding and removing objects from a collection and creating, updating, and deleting objects.

The type of objects the proxies manage are whatever object types your application needs. For instance, given a data model that had Customers, Products, and Orders, the application may have a `CustomerProxy`, an `OrderProxy`, and a `ProductProxy`. Where the `CustomerProxy` may deal with updating a certain customer's preferences, the `ProductProxy` could deal with loading information about a collection of products according to the customer's search terms. The `OrderProxy` could keep a shopping cart and the customer's order information.

View

In contrast to Cairngorm, where the glue between the view and the model is Flex's binding framework, PureMVC takes a more explicit role in the inner workings of your application's view. This role is filled by mediators. A mediator's responsibility is to listen for events on a particular instance of a view and take appropriate action, as well as to make sure that any change to the model is reflected on the view, which it does by listening to application-wide notifications usually dispatched by commands.

Since the mediator takes such an active role in listening for actions on the view, most views can be built more like a component should be. In other words, your application can be made up of view components that emit "pure" ActionScript events, not PureMVC specific events, so that your views don't need to be tied to PureMVC. Although you may not often find yourself reusing the views you make for one application in another unrelated application, this feature is still a win since your application isn't tied to a certain framework—and you may also find yourself thinking harder about how to componentize your application's views, which is a Good Thing.

Not every view needs a mediator, and it may make sense for your application to have some mediators that mediate more than one view. Mediators are named, just like proxies, so a certain mediator can be accessed by name from anywhere in the application.

Service Layer

PureMVC doesn't have as much to say about how your application accesses the service layer. These types of tasks could be done in either the commands or proxies. Another approach is to borrow some patterns from Cairngorm and use business delegates. This is what some of the PureMVC examples on the web do and what we've done in the sample application.

Figure 8.3 provides an illustration of a typical sequence in PureMVC.

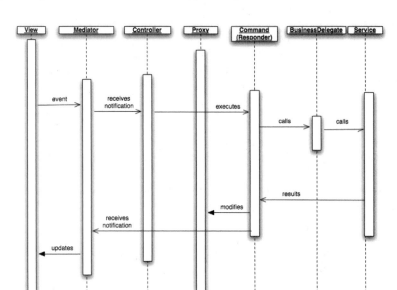

Figure 8.3   A typical sequence in PureMVC.

Figure 8.4 shows a standard PureMVC project directory structure.

Figure 8.4   Typical PureMVC project directory structure.

Let's briefly look at each of the directories:

- business: As mentioned, PureMVC doesn't have a lot to say about service interaction, but some examples take a page from Cairngorm's book and use business delegates. If this is the case, the business folder could contain those delegates.

- controller: The controller directory simply contains all the command classes.

- model: The model directory contains all the proxy classes, as you'd expect, but if your application makes use of VOs, they can go here as well, or in a subdirectory called vo.

- view: The view directory contains the components of the view and any mediators. In most small examples, the mediators go in the root of the view directory and the components that they mediate go in the components subdirectory. This could break down as the view gets bigger, so you could also choose to keep mediators in a separate mediator directory, or organize the directory more along the functional lines of your application and put the mediators wherever the view files go.

As you develop using PureMVC, you'll find yourself spending some time creating proxies and service interaction code, either in business delegates, commands, or proxies. You'll find that you spend most of the time developing view components and related mediators, wiring up events to the mediators, and creating commands to perform the business logic on the data held in the proxies.

Now that we've looked at these frameworks from a high level, let's see how they feel to work with by looking at an example application.

Stuff

GTD, Getting Things Done, is a way of thinking about productivity introduced a few years ago by David Allen (www.davidco.com/). A few software applications have been made to help keep track of things following the GTD model, such as Things (http://culturedcode.com/things/) and OmniFocus (www.omnigroup.com/applications/omnifocus/) for Mac or the cross-platform ThinkingRock (www.thinkingrock.com.au/).

Stuff is a web application that's going to blow all of those away with its simple yet effective interface and stunning good looks . . . (OK, maybe not). In any case, a GTD-style application should provide a simple but meaningful data model to look at putting both PureMVC and Cairngorm to use. The code for Stuff is in the example code. Figure 8.5 provides a look at Stuff.

Stuff has two important entities: contexts and tasks. Contexts are a concept from GTD that help you decide what tasks you should be working on right now, for instance "At work" or "Going to the store." Choosing from the list on the left shows all the tasks belonging to that context in the main area on the right. From there, the user can add or delete a task, edit a task's description, delete a task, or mark it complete.

It is a very simple data model. Let's have a look at the use cases too:

- CRUD (CReate, Update, Delete) context
- CRUD task
- Display all contexts
- Display selected context's tasks
- Complete task

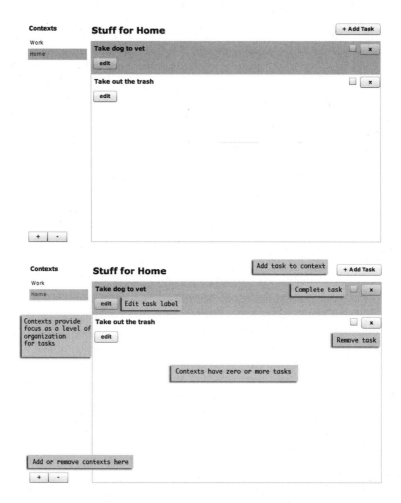

Figure 8.5   A look at the Stuff web application.

Figure 8.6 shows you how the application is organized:

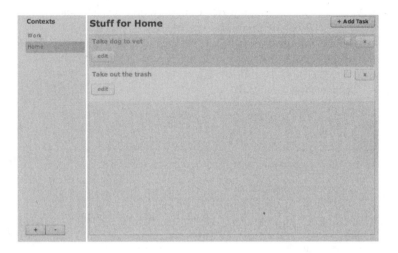

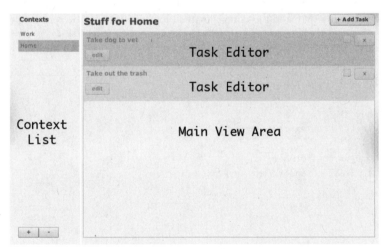

Figure 8.6   Organization of the Stuff Web application.

The context list displays contexts and lets the user add or remove contexts. The main view area displays tasks for the current context and lets the user add tasks. Each task in the task list gets its own task editor, which enables editing, deleting, and completing that task.

The Rails services are pretty simple, too. We'll be dealing with models that look like those shown in Listings 8.1 and 8.2.

Listing 8.1   **app/models/context.rb**

```ruby
class Context < ActiveRecord::Base
  has_many :tasks
end
```

Listing 8.2   **app/models/task.rb**

```ruby
class Task < ActiveRecord::Base
  belongs_to :context
end
```

We'll use RubyAMF, and the controllers will look like those shown in Listings 8.3 and 8.4.

Listing 8.3   **app/controllers/contexts_controller.rb**

```ruby
class ContextsController < ApplicationController

  def load_all
    @contexts = Context.find :all

    respond_to do |format|
      format.amf { render :amf => @contexts }
    end
  end

  def save
    respond_to do |format|
      format.amf do
        if params[:context].save
          render :amf => params[:context]
        else
          render :amf =>
FaultObject.new(params[:context].errors.join("\n"))
        end
      end
    end
  end
```

Listing 8.3   *Continued*

```ruby
  def destroy
    @context = Context.find params[:id]
    @context.destroy

    respond_to do |format|
      format.amf do
        render :amf => true
      end
    end
  end

end
```

Listing 8.4   **app/controllers/tasks_controller.rb**

```ruby
class TasksController < ApplicationController

  before_filter :find_context

  def load_all
    @tasks = @context.tasks

    respond_to do |format|
      format.amf { render :amf => @tasks }
    end
  end

  def save
    respond_to do |format|
      format.amf do
        if params[:task].save
          render :amf => params[:task]
        else
          render :amf =>
FaultObject.new(params[:task].errors.join("\n"))
        end
      end
    end
  end

  def destroy
    @task = @context.tasks.find params[:id]
    @task.destroy
```

Listing 8.4 *Continued*

```
  respond_to do |format|
    format.amf { render :amf => true }
  end
 end


 protected
  def find_context
    @context = Context.find params[:context_id]
  end
end
```

The controllers have very simple methods to load, save, or delete (destroy) contexts and tasks. Notice that the `TaskController` has a before filter that calls `find_context`, which requires a context ID in the `params` of any call. The RubyAMF config has the settings shown in Listing 8.5.

Listing 8.5 **app/config/rubyamf_config.rb**

```
  ParameterMappings.scaffolding = true
  ClassMappings.translate_case = true
  ClassMappings.register(
    :actionscript  => 'Context',
    :ruby          => 'Context',
    :type          => 'active_record',
    :attributes    => ["id", "label", "created_at", "updated_at"])

  ClassMappings.register(
    :actionscript  => 'Task',
    :ruby          => 'Task',
    :type          => 'active_record',
    :attributes    => ["id", "label", "context_id", "completed_at",
"created_at", "updated_at"])
```

These settings will tell RubyAMF to translate all properties from camel case to snake case or vice versa (with `translate_case`), allow anonymous objects passed to controllers to become the `params` object (with scaffolding), and translate the objects found in service calls with the attributes listed in the class mappings.

The ActionScript side of the data model is as shown in Listing 8.6.

Listing 8.6 **Context.as**

```
  [Bindable]
  [RemoteClass(alias="Context")]
  public class Context {
```

Listing 8.6   *Continued*

```
        public var id:int;
        public var label:String;
        public var createdAt:Date;
        public var updatedAt:Date;

        [Transient]
        public var tasksLoaded:Boolean;

        [Transient]
        public var tasks:ArrayCollection;
    }


Task.as
    [Bindable]
    [RemoteClass(alias="Task")]
    public class Task {

        public var id:int;
        public var contextId:int;
        public var label:String;
        public var completedAt:Date;
        public var createdAt:Date;
        public var updatedAt:Date;

        [Transient]
        public var newTask:Boolean;
    }
```

Note a few things here: First, we have some [Transient] annotations on tasksLoaded and tasks in Context, and on newTask in Task. These properties won't be serialized as AMF and will only be used on the client. Also note that tasks don't have properties that point to a parent context; they only have contextId properties. Since we expect to load tasks at a different time than contexts, we can't have RubyAMF try to encode the context object with the task. It won't match the context object that is already loaded by the Flash Player.

Now let's look at the specifics of the application implemented with each framework.

Cairngorm Implementation

Figure 8.7 provides an overview of all the classes that make up the Cairngorm application and a description of what they do. Remember the standard Cairngorm directory structure and the types of classes we've discussed as you look through this list.

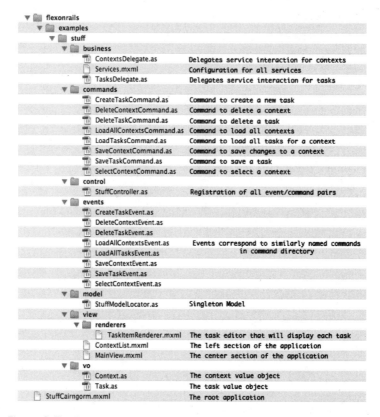

Figure 8.7   Classes that make up the Cairngorm version of the application.

Now let's look at some code. We'll start from the services and go backwards. All services that the application interacts with are defined in Services.mxml (see Listing 8.7).

Listing 8.7   **flexonrails/examples/stuff/business/Services.mxml**

```
<cairngorm:ServiceLocator ...>

    <mx:RemoteObject
        id="contextsService"
        destination="rubyamf"
        endpoint="http://localhost:3000/rubyamf_gateway/"
        source="ContextsController"
        showBusyCursor="true"
    />
    <mx:RemoteObject
        id="tasksService"
        destination="rubyamf"
```

Listing 8.7   *Continued*

```
        endpoint="http://localhost:3000/rubyamf_gateway/"
        source="TasksController"
        showBusyCursor="true"
    />
</cairngorm:ServiceLocator>
```

Notice that the base class extended here is the singleton `ServiceLocator`. Since ActionScript doesn't have true private constructors, this is made possible with mxml. The result is that this mxml class acts like a configuration file for the `ServiceLocator`, which is used throughout the application whenever a reference to a service is needed.

In the configuration, we instantiate two remote objects, which correspond to the two controllers we have on the Rails side. We could do some more work to pull out the endpoint URLs so they're not hardcoded into the file, but we can leave that as an exercise for the reader for now.

The delegates are both similar, so let's look at the task delegates to see how they work. Look at Listing 8.8.

Listing 8.8   **flexonrails/examples/stuff/business/TasksDelegate.mxml, #17–20**

```
        public function TasksDelegate(responder:IResponder) {
            this.responder = responder;
            this.service =
ServiceLocator.getInstance().getRemoteObject('tasksService');
        }
```

The constructor takes an argument of type `IResponder`. You may remember from our discussion about Cairngorm that it is implemented by some commands, the type of commands that expects an asynchronous callback from a service call. It holds a reference to that responder for later. It also creates an instance of a service, which it gets from the `ServiceLocator`. In our case, this is a reference to one of the remote objects we defined in the service configuration (see Listing 8.9).

Listing 8.9   **flexonrails/examples/stuff/business/TasksDelegate.mxml, #22–25**

```
        public function loadAll(context:Context):void {
            var call:AsyncToken = service.load_all({context_id:context.id});
            call.addResponder(responder);
        }
```

The `loadAll` method is a good example of the type of method delegates have. It takes whichever arguments make sense given the requirements of the service for that method call, and then calls the service with those arguments. Remember that since we turned on the scaffolding option for RubyAMF, we can pass an anonymous object to the service and it will become the `params` object once it reaches the controller.

The call to a `RemoteObject` returns something called an `AsyncToken`, which is an object that waits for a callback from a service and then calls the appropriate method on a responder, either the `result` method or the `fault` method depending on the success of the call. After we send off the call by calling the `load_all` method, we tell the `AsyncToken` to respond to the command that called the delegate, and then the application continues on its way—expecting a callback but not waiting for it. This is called a non-blocking call, meaning the call to the service doesn't halt the Flash Player's execution until it returns.

Before we review the next level, the controller, let's look at how to load the service definition. The service configuration is generally referenced on the root of the application, as shown in Listing 8.10.

Listing 8.10   **StuffCairngorm.mxml, #26–27**

```
<business:Services id="services" />
<control:StuffController id="controller" />
```

The services are instantiated and ready to go by the time the application needs them. Right below the services configuration is our application's front controller, which is instantiated in the same way.

As we mentioned before, the controller layer of a Cairngorm application is mostly contained in the events and commands that we create. We need to configure the FrontController, though, which listens for events being dispatched and executes the appropriate command. This configuration is simple and looks something like what is shown in Listing 8.11.

Listing 8.11   **flexonrails/examples/stuff/control/StuffController.as, #16–23**

```
addCommand(CreateTaskEvent.CreateTask_Event,
    CreateTaskCommand);
addCommand(SelectContextEvent.SelectContext_Event,
    SelectContextCommand);
addCommand(LoadAllContextsEvent.LoadAllContexts_Event,
    LoadAllContextsCommand);
addCommand(LoadAllTasksEvent.LoadAllTasks_Event,
    LoadTasksCommand);
addCommand(SaveContextEvent.SaveContext_Event,
    SaveContextCommand);
addCommand(DeleteContextEvent.DeleteContext_Event,
    DeleteContextCommand);
addCommand(SaveTaskEvent.SaveTask_Event,
    SaveTaskCommand);
addCommand(DeleteTaskEvent.DeleteTask_Event,
    DeleteTaskCommand);
```

The `addCommand` method takes a string, which should be unique, and registers that string to the command. When an event is constructed, it passes that same name to the

`CairngormEvent` constructor (the constructor of the class it extends), which sets the event's type property to that string key (see Listing 8.12).

Listing 8.12   **flexonrails/examples/stuff/events/LoadAllContextsEvent.as, #5–11**

```
public class LoadAllContextsEvent extends CairngormEvent {
    public static const LoadAllContexts_Event:String =
"<LoadAllContextsEvent>";

    public function LoadAllContextsEvent()  {
        super(LoadAllContexts_Event);
    }
}
```

When the event is dispatched and the FrontController gets the event, it can look up the command by that string and execute the correct command. Let's look at an event/command sequence from start to finish. You've seen the `LoadAllContextsEvent` registered and explained in Listing 8.12; Listing 8.13 shows one actually being dispatched:

Listing 8.13   **flexonrails/examples/stuff/StuffCairngorm.mxml, #19–21**

```
public function init():void {
    new LoadAllContextsEvent().dispatch();
}
```

This `init` method is registered as a callback to the `applicationComplete` event on the application (see the definition on line 12), so when the application is ready, it calls this method. To dispatch a Cairngorm event, all you need to do is instantiate and call `dispatch`, the way this method does. Once the event is dispatched and the event is caught by the FrontController, the `LoadAllContextsCommand` is constructed and executed as shown in Listing 8.14.

Listing 8.14   **flexonrails/examples/stuff/commands/LoadAllContextsCommand.as, #19–23**

```
public function execute(event:CairngormEvent):void {
    var evt:LoadAllContextsEvent = event as LoadAllContextsEvent;
    var delegate:ContextsDelegate = new ContextsDelegate(this);
    delegate.loadAll();
}
```

The event is passed to the `execute` method of the command, which is the way data added to an event gets to its command. Then the command constructs a delegate and calls the appropriate method on it. Once the call returns, the `AsyncToken` from the delegate will call either `result` or `fault` depending on whether the service call failed or succeeded (see Listing 8.15). Again, a failure could be called if the service is down or an error is thrown by the service, or, from RubyAMF, you can programmatically cause a fault (see Chapter 5, Passing Data with AMF).

Listing 8.15   flexonrails/examples/stuff/commands/LoadAllContextsCommand.as, #25-32

```
public function result(data:Object):void {
    var result:ResultEvent = data as ResultEvent;
    this.model.contexts = new ArrayCollection(result.result as Array);
}


public function fault(info:Object):void {
    var fault:FaultEvent = info as FaultEvent;
}
```

Our app doesn't do anything special in the case of failure, but it could have popped up an alert or something like that. On the off chance that the service call succeeds, though, this command takes all the contexts it loaded and puts them in a new `ArrayCollection` on the model. Speaking of the model, since it's so simple for this application, let's look at the whole thing in Listing 8.16.

Listing 8.16   flexonrails/examples/stuff/model/StuffModelLocator.as

```
package flexonrails.examples.stuff.model {

    [Bindable]
    public class StuffModelLocator {

        private static var instance:StuffModelLocator;

        public var contexts:ArrayCollection;
        public var selectedContext:Context;

        public function StuffModelLocator(access:PrivateAccess) {
            if (access == null) {
                throw new CairngormError(CairngormMessageCodes.SINGLETON_EXCEPTION,
                        "StuffModelLocator");
            }
        }
        public static function getInstance():StuffModelLocator {
            if (instance == null) {
                instance = new StuffModelLocator(new PrivateAccess());
            }
            return instance;
        }


    }
}
/**
 * Inner class which restricts constructor access to Private
 */
class PrivateAccess {}
```

First, notice that although ActionScript doesn't allow private constructors, which is how languages like Java generally enforce singletons, we can still get similar behavior by requiring an instance of a class, `PrivateAccess`, which is defined in the same file outside the package block and therefore not accessible anywhere else for instantiation. This isn't a requirement of Cairngorm; it just depends on how sure you need to be that no other code in your application is instantiating the model. Apart from the singleton accessor method `getInstance` and the singleton variable, the rest of the model is for storing data meant to drive the view of the application. In our case, this only ends up being lines 17 and 18, but it could be as many properties and methods as you need.

Since the class is marked bindable, all public properties will dispatch a change event when their value changes, and any views binding to the model will automatically update. The `LoadAllContextsCommand` loads all of the contexts from the service into the contexts property of the model. Now that we've seen where that is on the model, let's look at an example of a view binding to a model property (see Listing 8.17).

Listing 8.17   **flexonrails/examples/stuff/view/ContextList.mxml, #12**

```
    [Bindable] private var model:StuffModelLocator =
StuffModelLocator.getInstance();
```

First, any view that needs a reference to the model sets up a `bindable` property like what is shown in Listing 8.17. Then a data-aware control, like a list control, can bind to `model.contexts`, and it will automatically have all the contexts loaded by the `LoadAllContextsCommand`, as shown in Listing 8.18.

Listing 8.18   **flexonrails/examples/stuff/view/ContextList.mxml, #61**

```
    <mx:List id="contextList" ... dataProvider="{model.contexts}"
itemClick="contextSelected()" />
```

The `LoadAllContextsEvent` was dispatched when the application was ready, on `applicationComplete`. The `itemClick` event on the `contextList` on Listing 8.18 is dispatched when the user selects an item in the list. It's worth looking at that sequence as well for a few slight differences from what we've seen so far. When the `itemClick` event is dispatched from the list, the `contextSelected` method is called (see Listing 8.19).

Listing 8.19   **flexonrails/examples/stuff/view/ContextList.mxml, #15-19**

```
    private function contextSelected():void {
        var item:Object = contextList.selectedItem;
        var context:Context = item as Context;
        new SelectContextEvent(context).dispatch();
    }
```

This method gets the new selected item in the list, or null if one isn't selected, and casts it to a Context. It then dispatches a SelectContextEvent, which expects a context in the constructor. That call will work through the system until the SelectContextCommand is executed, as shown in Listing 8.20.

Listing 8.20   **flexonrails/examples/stuff/commands/SelectContextCommand.as, #21–29**

```
public function execute(event:CairngormEvent):void {
    var evt:SelectContextEvent = event as SelectContextEvent;
    context = evt.context;
    model.selectedContext = context;
    if (!context.tasksLoaded) {
        var delegate:TasksDelegate = new TasksDelegate(this);
        delegate.loadAll(context);
    }
}
```

The command casts the selected context off the event and then sets that context onto the model's selectedContext property. This is an example of what a command would do if it didn't have to interact with a service: manipulate the model directly in the execute method. Of course, this command goes on to load all the tasks for the new selected context, but only if the context hasn't already had its tasks loaded, as noted by the tasksLoaded property.

Have a look around the rest of the application and see how things work in response to user-initiated events. Follow each control through to the result of the command at the end of the chain. This is a classic Cairngorm application and will be what you'd expect to find with any other application using Cairngorm. When you have a good idea how this simple application works using Cairngorm, then move on and see how it would work using PureMVC.

PureMVC Implementation

On our tour through the PureMVC implementation of the same application, we're going to take the same route so you can get a good comparison of the two frameworks' styles. First, review all the files in the PureMVC implementation (see Figure 8.8).

In the Cairngorm implementation, we started with the service layer, but as we mentioned, the PureMVC version uses the same delegate pattern (and code) to access the service. So we'll jump right to the configuration of the controller.

As you'll remember, the common point of contact for all the parts of a PureMVC application is the Facade. The Facade is where commands are registered to strings, which are keys passed along with the PureMVC notifications. Mediators can register to different notification types, but commands are only instantiated as needed, so the Facade initialization is the place to configure these commands (see Listing 8.21).

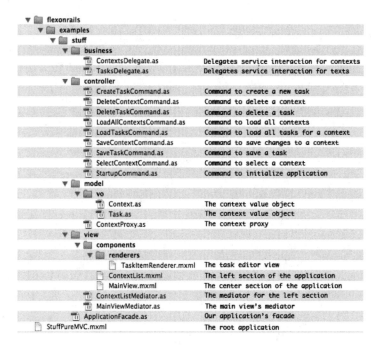

Figure 8.8   Files in the PureMVC implementation.

Listing 8.21   **flexonrails/examples/stuff/ApplicationFacade.as, #51–61**

```
override protected function initializeController():void {
    super.initializeController();
    registerCommand(STARTUP,
StartupCommand);
    registerCommand(LOAD_CONTEXTS,
LoadAllContextsCommand);
    registerCommand(DELETE_CONTEXT,
DeleteContextCommand);
    registerCommand(SAVE_CONTEXT,
SaveContextCommand);
    registerCommand(LOAD_TASKS,
LoadTasksCommand);
    registerCommand(ADD_TASK,
CreateTaskCommand);
    registerCommand(SAVE_TASK,
SaveTaskCommand);
    registerCommand(DELETE_TASK,
DeleteTaskCommand);
}
```

You can see that the commands are registered to strings that are keyed up as constants on our implementation of the facade. The rest of our implementation of the facade is just boilerplate. Let's look at what actually kicks the application off, though, and tells the facade to initialize itself. Savvy readers may have already guessed that this happens in the root application (see Listing 8.22).

Listing 8.22   **StuffPureMVC.mxml, #18–22**

```
    public var facade:ApplicationFacade =
ApplicationFacade.getInstance();

    public function init():void {
        facade.notifyObservers(new
Notification(ApplicationFacade.STARTUP, this));
    }
```

The `init` method will be called on `applicationComplete`, and it simply sends a notification with the key for the `StartupCommand` from the facade. Notice an important point: the second argument to the `Notification` constructor is some data to pass along in the body of the notification, and here we're sending a reference to the application.

On receiving the notification, the facade knows that a command has been registered, the `StartupCommand`, so that's what's executed next (see Listing 8.23).

Listing 8.23   **flexonrails/examples/stuff/controller/StartupCommand.as, #19–27**

```
    override public function execute(note:INotification):void {
        facade.registerProxy(new ContextProxy());

        var app:StuffPureMVC = note.getBody() as StuffPureMVC;
        facade.registerMediator(new
ContextListMediator(app.contextList));
        facade.registerMediator(new
MainViewMediator(app.mainView));
        sendNotification(ApplicationFacade.LOAD_CONTEXTS);
    }
```

Notice that by virtue of extending the framework's `SimpleCommand`, we have access to the `ApplicationFacade` through the `facade` variable, and also the method `sendNotification` to dispatch other notifications.

This command's responsibility is to start up the application, and to do that, it needs to register some mediators. This is why we passed the reference to the application through with the notification, so we could get a reference to the components that make up the view and pass references to the mediators as they're constructed and registered. Let's look at one of those mediators, the `ContextListMediator`, which is responsible for the context list (see Listing 8.24).

Listing 8.24   **flexonrails/examples/stuff/view/ContextListMediator.as, #190–200**

```
public function ContextListMediator(viewComponent:Object) {
    super(NAME, viewComponent);

    contextList.addEventListener(ContextList.NEW, newContext);
    contextList.addEventListener(ContextList.DELETE,
deleteSelectedContext);
    contextList.addEventListener(ContextList.SELECT, contextSelected);
    contextProxy = facade.retrieveProxy(ContextProxy.NAME) as
ContextProxy;
    contextList.contexts = contextProxy.contexts;
}
```

The constructor first has to pass up the view component and a unique name for the mediator to the superclass, `Mediator`. The unique name can be whatever you like, but a convention is to put a static constant on the class called NAME with the name of the mediator in it. The unique name enables code anywhere to get a reference to a particular mediator, and the static constant makes it easy to know what that name should be.

Next, the mediator registers for a number of events that its view component will dispatch. Again, this practice keeps business logic out of the view; view components can stick to just sending out notifications of user interaction.

The last two lines of the constructor are important to note. First, the mediator gets a reference to the `ContextProxy`, which is responsible for dealing with a collection of contexts. It does this by the process described above for getting a reference to the mediator; we use the same process to get a reference to a proxy from anywhere in the application.

After getting a reference to the proxy, the mediator "wires up" the contexts property of the proxy to the contexts property of the context list view component. This is how to connect the view to the model without using Flex's binding framework—directly. In simple cases, any data added to the contexts collection will show up in any Flex components using the contexts property on the view as a data provider because they refer to the same object. In more complex cases, since the proxy contexts variable is an array collection (in this case), the view could listen for change events from the collection and respond accordingly.

We looked at the event flow of loading all contexts in the Cairngorm example, so let's look at the same flow here (see Listing 8.25).

Listing 8.25   **flexonrails/examples/stuff/controller/StartupCommand.as, #27**

```
sendNotification(ApplicationFacade.LOAD_CONTEXTS);
```

Back at the end of the execute method of the startup command, a notification to load all contexts is sent. A quick look at the `ApplicationFacade` shows that that key corresponds to the `LoadAllContextsCommand` (see Listing 8.26).

Listing 8.26   **flexonrails/examples/stuff/controller/LoadAllContextsCommand.as, #17–26**

```
override public function execute(notification:INotification):void {
    var delegate:ContextsDelegate = new ContextsDelegate(this);
    delegate.loadAll();
}


public function result(data:Object):void {
    var result:ResultEvent = data as ResultEvent;
    var contextProxy:ContextProxy =
facade.retrieveProxy(ContextProxy.NAME) as ContextProxy;
    contextProxy.reload(result.result as Array);
}
```

As we mentioned, we're using the same delegate code from Cairngorm, so that's what is happening in the `execute`. On the result, the work we do is on the `ContextProxy`, where we call a method called `reload`, responsible for setting up the model with a new list of contexts. Note that, as in the mediators, by virtue of extending `SimpleCommand` provided by the framework, we have access to a facade property through which we can look up the proxy (see Listing 8.27).

Listing 8.27   **flexonrails/examples/stuff/model/ContextProxy.as, #28–38**

```
public function reload(newContexts:Array):void {
    contexts.disableAutoUpdate();
    contexts.removeAll();
    contextIdMap = new Dictionary(true);
    for each (var context:Context in newContexts) {
        contexts.addItem(context);
        contextIdMap[context.id] = context;
    }
    contexts.enableAutoUpdate();
    sendNotification(ApplicationFacade.CONTEXTS_LOADED);
}
```

The `reload` method has to step lightly over the contexts array collection, since we can't just create a new one when we reload. Views might be tied directly to that variable, and without binding to update them, we'd have to manually reset view references. First, the proxy disables automatic updates on the array collection, which means that any components listening for collection change messages from the array collection (which all data-aware Flex components do) will not get a message for each item we add. Enabling the auto update again will send one change message.

Next, the proxy removes all the old contexts and initializes a dictionary to allow easy lookup of contexts by ID (see the `findById` method). It then loops through the incoming array of contexts and adds them to the contexts array and places a reference by ID into the dictionary. It enables automatic updates again, and then fires a notification with the key CONTEXTS_LOADED. Now any views that are using the contexts in the proxy's list should have access to the new contexts.

What does the notification at the end of the execute method do? If you scan through the ApplicationFacade again, you'll see that there are no commands registered to that notification type. This brings to light another feature of PureMVC. Mediators can register to receive notifications as well. In this application, only one mediator is registered to that notification, but any mediator can register to receive any notification. Listing 8.28 shows how mediators register to receive notifications:

Listing 8.28   flexonrails/examples/stuff/view/ContextListMediator.as, #54–68

```
        override public function listNotificationInterests():Array {
            return [ApplicationFacade.CONTEXTS_LOADED];
        }


        override public function
handleNotification(note:INotification):void {
            switch (note.getName()) {
                case ApplicationFacade.CONTEXTS_LOADED:
                    if (contextProxy.contexts.length > 0) {
                        contextList.contextList.selectedIndex = 0;
                        sendNotification(
                            ApplicationFacade.CONTEXT_SELECTED,
                            contextList.selectedContext
                        );
                    }
                break;


            }
        }
```

There are two overridden methods in the ContextListMediator: listNotificationInterests and handleNotification. When a mediator is initialized, the framework will call the listNotificationInterests method, and for each item in the array of strings it gets back, it will register the mediator to listen for these types of notifications.

When any of those notifications are received, handleNotification will be called. In that method, the mediator can decide what notification is incoming, and then decide what to do in that case. ContextListMediator listens for the "contexts loaded" notification, and if, when it gets that message, the new list of contexts is not empty, it selects the first one in the list and calls the contextSelected method, which sends a notification that that context has been selected.

The contextSelected method is set up to receive a flash event, so you can tell that we're just using it to avoid code duplication when we call from handleNotification. If you look further into the mediator, you'll see what is shown in Listing 8.29.

Listing 8.29   **flexonrails/examples/stuff/view/ContextListMediator.as, #24**

```
contextList.addEventListener(ContextList.SELECT, contextSelected);
```

You can see that the `contextSelected` method is designed to be called when the mediator receives an event from the view keyed by `ContextList.SELECT`. Let's look at the view (see Listing 8.30).

Listing 8.30   **flexonrails/examples/stuff/view/ContextList.mxml, #67**

```
<mx:List id="contextList" ... dataProvider="{model.contexts}"
itemClick="contextSelected()" />
```

The list is set up to call `contextSelected` when an item is clicked, as we saw seen in the previous example. This time, however, the method dispatches a regular Flash event (see Listing 8.31).

Listing 8.31   **flexonrails/examples/stuff/view/ContextList.mxml, #25–27**

```
private function contextSelected():void {
    dispatchEvent(new Event(SELECT, true));
}
```

This is the pattern promoted by PureMVC: views dispatch Flash Events, not PureMVC notifications, except in rare cases such as on the application for startup. It could be argued, though, that the code in the application root file will never be reused, so that doesn't matter as much. The mediator listens for these events and then does whatever it needs to do, like send off a notification that could be registered to a command, change something on a proxy, or perform an action on another part of the view it mediates.

Again, have a look around the PureMVC implementation and notice the patterns we've talked about. If you'd like, think up some other functionality for the application and try to implement it in both examples comparing the styles of each framework firsthand.

Summary

As you've seen, there are a lot of similarities and some key differences between these frameworks. Cairngorm doesn't have much to say about how you architect your application's view, but both frameworks support a decoupled architecture by using event listeners and the command pattern. PureMVC doesn't have much to say about how you access a back-end service, but both frameworks require some registration of the bits of the controller to string keys.

Both frameworks have a separate model concern, but where Cairngorm favors a "monolithic" model that easily supports the use of Flex's binding features, PureMVC likes to separate the model into sections focused around the parts of the domain.

The benefits of following a popular, public framework's way of building an application are probably clear to you. It's probably one of the reasons you like Rails. The choice of which framework you'd like to use for Flex is up to you, and now you have a better idea of which one you'd choose for your next application.

## 9

Performance and Optimization

Now it's time to talk about a topic that inevitably comes up: performance. What should you do when things aren't running as fast as you'd like? What's causing the slowdown? Is the client slow? Is the server not fulfilling requests fast enough? Is the database too much of a bottleneck?

These questions aren't easy to answer, and specifics as they apply to your situation are, for the most part, beyond the scope of this book. We can, however, arm you with knowledge of how to start to track down problem areas on either the Flex or the Rails side.

Flex Performance

As you've no doubt heard multiple times, Flex applications run in Flash. Understanding Flex performance well means understanding Flash performance well. It's definitely valuable to understand how Flex does things so that you can work with the framework instead of against it, but ultimately, understanding what happens in the Flash Player predicates understanding of how to make performant Flex applications.

The following two blog posts, one from Ted Patrick of Adobe and the other a response from Sean Christmann of EffectiveUI, provide valuable insight and a mental model for understanding how Flash breaks down and accomplishes tasks:

- www.onflex.org/ted/2005/07/flash-player-mental-model-elastic.php
- www.craftymind.com/2008/04/18/updated-elastic-racetrack-for-flash-9-and-avm2/

The basic mental model is that of an elastic racetrack. On one side of the track, there is ActionScript execution, and when the race gets to the other side of the track, there is rendering, which is the phase where the screen is updated.

The course of this track is a frame. If you're familiar with Flash in its traditional incarnation as a keyframe animation program, this is what's going on inside each keyframe of a running Flash movie.

The important thing to note is the track's elasticity. As Ted says, the Flash Player will always try to accomplish everything you ask it to do in a frame—there's no built-in way to defer code execution, and deferring rendering doesn't make any sense. If you have long-running ActionScript code, then rendering will be slow, which makes the application choppy and slow from the user's perspective. Making a performant Flex application means never doing more ActionScript than needed in each frame.

That's a very wide-ranging blanket statement and not completely helpful right up front, but it's at least better than simply saying "write faster code." Basically, when your application is sluggish, you need to find out what code is running at that time and do one of two things:

- Make it run faster.
- Make it run later.

Making code run faster may involve doing something smarter than you're currently doing it. For instance, instead of looping over an array and finding an object in another array by looping over that one, too, or making Flash look it up by calling `Array.indexOf`, change to looking up objects in a dictionary, which has a much faster lookup time.

Making the code run later is a little trickier. If you have a long-running task, for instance, calculating the value of a property on a long list of objects or, more likely, changing a property of several visual components that will cause Flash to redraw them, it's best to break up those actions into frame-sized bites and do a certain number of them in one frame, then a certain number in the next frame, and so on. In this way, the task actually takes longer to execute, but the app doesn't seem slow because nothing's getting in the way of rendering. Your friends here are the `callLater` method and the `ENTER_FRAME` event type.

This deferred execution is an advanced topic, though, and you can get a lot of mileage out of the "make it run faster" tactic. The important thing to know is what code is running slowly, and that's one thing that profiling helps you find. The other thing, which we haven't really touched on yet, is how much memory your application is using.

Simple Profiling Techniques

If you don't have Flex Builder Professional, you can still do a few things to track down long-running methods and memory usage.

To see how long it takes to run some code, use the global `getTimer` method. That works like this:

```
import flash.utils.getTimer;
...
var t1:Number = getTimer();
callAMethod();
// run some more code here...
var t2:Number = getTimer();
trace("Time:" + t2 - t1);
```

The `getTimer` method returns in milliseconds the amount of time elapsed since the application started. Use this technique with the command line debugger to start to drill down on long-running code.

To get an idea of how much memory your application is taking up, use the `flash.system.System's` `totalMemory` property, measured in bytes. For instance, you could try to prove a memory leak in a certain bit of code by doing this:

```
var memBefore:Number = System.totalMemory;
suspectMethod();
var memAfter:Number = System.totalMemory;
trace("Memory change:" + memAfter - memBefore);
```

If you continually run this part of the code and the change is near zero, or it at least peaks after a few calls, you know that part of the code is OK. If it keeps going up with no peak, you have a memory leak.

Flex Builder's Profiler

Those methods are all you need to track down slow-running code or memory leaks, but they're not as easy to use or as powerful as Flex Builder Professional's profiler. If at all possible, get this version of Flex Builder if you want to really get a handle on performance in your application.

Flex Builder's profiler enables you to profile your application to learn about both performance and memory usage. Let's look at performance first.

Performance Profiling

Performance Profiling is an exercise in finding code that runs too long and may degrade performance.

The Flash Content Debugger, or debugger player, has special functionality in it to do very intensive reporting on a running Flash application. One thing it can report is every time an object is created, and that comes into play in the next section on memory profiling.

For performance tuning, what you want to know is how often methods are called, which methods are called the most, and which method calls take up the most time in a running application. The Flex Profiler can report all of this information, which can help you to make informed decisions about where to hunt down and kill performance bottlenecks.

To learn about how performance profiling works, we're going to look at a very simple example that has one long-running method. Remember that a long-running method is bad because it not only takes up processing, but it also gets in the way of a render pass, which makes Flash *seem* to run slowly because all animation seems to stop.

First, let's look at the code (see Listing 9.1).

Listing 9.1   **flex/src/performance_examples.mxml**

```
<?xml version="1.0" encoding="utf-8"?>
<mx:Application
    xmlns:mx="http://www.adobe.com/2006/mxml"
    layout="vertical"
    creationComplete="boxRotator.play()">

    <mx:Script>
    <![CDATA[
```

Listing 9.1   *Continued*

```
        public function shortMethod():void {
              var a:int
              for (var i:int = 0; i < 1000; i++) {
                    a++;
              }
        }

        public function longRunningMethod():void {
              var a:int
              for (var i:int = 0; i < 10000000; i++) {
                    a++;
              }
        }

]]>
</mx:Script>
<mx:Rotate
      id="boxRotator"
      duration="2000"
      repeatCount="0"
      target="{coloredBox}"
/>

<mx:Canvas
      id="coloredBox"
      width="100"
      height="100"
      backgroundColor="0xFF0000"
/>

<mx:Spacer height="40" />

<mx:Button
      id="shortMethodButton"
      click="shortMethod()"
      label="run short method"
/>
<mx:Button
      id="longRunningMethodButton"
      click="longRunningMethod()"
      label="run long running method"
/>

</mx:Application>
```

Not too much is happening here. When the application starts to run, the red box continuously rotates in a circle. If you click the "run short method" button, a call to the shortMethod increments a variable 1,000 times, which is really not that much. This causes no degradation in performance at all.

If you click the "run long running method" button, the animation hangs for a second or so on a 2.4GHz Dual Core machine, because we're incrementing a variable 10 million times, and that's a little less trivial than 1,000 times. During the ActionScript execution pass, the Flash Virtual Machine finds that that many calculations are enough to offset a few render cycles, so any animation in the application stops and gives the impression that the app has "frozen," even though it's still running and doing work.

Think of this simple example in these terms: we have a Flex application, and we know that performing some action is causing the application to run slowly. To pinpoint the cause of this problem, we need to profile the application and study what's taking so long. To do that, we need to look at any statistics Flash can gather about methods run from a period directly before the action starts to after the action is complete.

To do this, we run our application using Flex Builder's profiler. First, click the Profile button, as shown in Figure 9.1; next, move on to the Run and Debug buttons and select your application (or choose Profile As if you haven't run your application yet).

Figure 9.1   First click the Profile button.

The application will start, but you'll first be presented with the dialog shown in Figure 9.2.

For this example, we're just going to profile performance, so make sure the Enable memory profiling option is unchecked. Next, click the Resume button.

Once you resume, Flex Builder will change perspective to the Performance perspective, the application will start running in your browser, and the red box will start rotating. Let it rotate a little bit, and then, back in Flex Builder, click the Capture Performance Profile button, as shown in Figure 9.3.

Capturing a profile prints a report of all the methods run up to that point and the time spent in each from a few different perspectives. Look at Figure 9.4 to see the type of data that Flex Builder has been collecting so far.

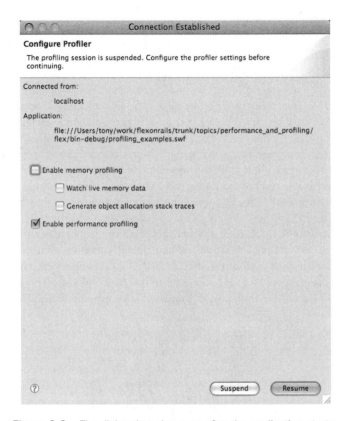

Figure 9.2   The dialog that shows up after the application starts.

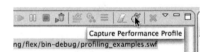

Figure 9.3   Click the Capture Performance Profile button.

From left to right, the columns are Method, Cumulative Time, Self Time, Average Cumulative Time, and Average Self Time. A few more columns (Calls and Packages) were moved for this screen shot, so your screen may look a little different. Table 9.1 describes each of these statistics.

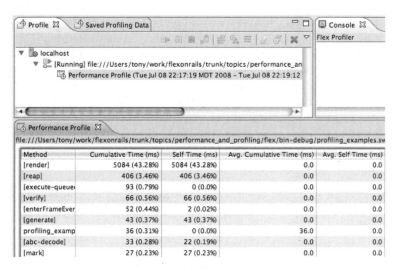

Figure 9.4   Flex Builder presents all sorts of data.

Table 9.1   **Descriptions of Profile Data by Column**

Column	Description
Method	The method name or Flash Player internal action.
Package	The name of the package that the method is in, if it has one.
Cumulative Time	The total amount of time spent running this method, including time spent in methods called from this method (methods deeper in the call stack).
Self Time	The total amount of time spent running this method alone, not counting time spent in methods called by this method.
Average Cumulative Time	The average amount of time for the period spent in this method or methods called by this method.
Average Self Time	The average amount of time for the period spent in this method not counting methods called by this method.
Calls	Number of times a method was called. May be 0 for some internal methods.

Now, you'll notice that the most time spent so far was in a method called [render], and the second most time spent was in a method called [reap]. You'll see a lot of methods named with a square bracket around them, such as [enterFrameEvent], or my personal favorite [tincan]. (What the heck is a tin can?) In any case, these square bracket methods are internal to the Flash Player and can't be directly invoked by our code. But they can show us what may be taking a lot of time, and in this case, [render] is taking a lot of execution time.

Of course, this is because we have the rotation effect playing on the red box canvas. Just because a method is called a lot doesn't mean it's a bad thing. In this case, we've got an application that is relatively render-intensive, and it causes Flash to spend time rendering to keep spinning that box. The fact that [render] is called so often is just an indication that we have some effects happening, not a symptom of a problem.

So now we've gotten our first taste of the Flex Profiler, and it has shown us a bit about what's going on in the application, but not really much we can act on. We need to look at what happens when we interact with the application in a way that users report causes the app to slow down.

The first step is to get rid of all the data we don't need that's been accumulating since the application started. We're going to clear the data we have so far, interact with the application to cause it to slow down, and then capture another performance profile. That will give us a better indication of what's happening when our app slows down.

Figure 9.5 shows how to reset the performance data we have gathered so far.

Figure 9.5   Click the reset performance data button to reset the data.

Click the Reset Performance Data eraser icon, click the run long-running method button, and then come back and click the Capture Performance Profile icon again. Now we have some more performance data, which we can see by double-clicking that new profile, as shown in Figure 9.6.

Method	Cumulat...ime (ms)	Self Time (ms)	Av...(ms)	Av...ms)	Calls
[mouseEvent]	1121 (71.36%)	28 (1.78%)	0.0	0.0	0 (0.0%)
profiling_examples.longRunningMethod	1084 (69.0%)	1084 (69.0%)	1084.0	1084.0	1 (0.0%)
profiling_examples.__longRunningMethodButton_click	1084 (69.0%)	0 (0.0%)	1084.0	0.0	1 (0.0%)
[render]	205 (13.05%)	205 (13.05%)	0.0	0.0	0 (0.0%)
[span]	13 (0.82%)	13 (0.82%)	0.0	0.0	0 (0.0%)

Figure 9.6   New performance data.

The columns shown here are Method, Cumulative Time, Self Time, Average Cumulative Time, Average Self Time, and Calls.

So what are we looking at? The top-running method is an internal method, [mouseEvent]. Whatever is slowing down our application started with a mouse event; that seems to be clear, because it's taking 71% of the time during this interaction, which is about 1 second. For an application with any sort of animation, that slowdown can really ruin the effect and cause users to lose trust that the application can handle any sort of interaction.

A mouse click can't be the source of that much pain though, and anyway, if we look at the Self Time column, it is way less time than the Cumulative Time column, so a method called by this method must be the source of the problem. Let's drill into that call stack by double-clicking the [mouseEvent] row. Figure 9.7 shows what we should see next.

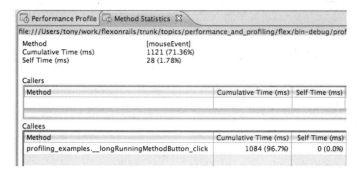

Figure 9.7   Statistics for the [mouseEvent] method.

The Method Statistics view shows the statistics for the method, and in two tables below, Callers and Callees, or, in other words, "who called this method?" and "who did this method call?" In this case, nothing called this method; it's an internal method, which happened to be kicked off by our mouse click on the button.

However, one method was called by this method, longRunningMethodButton_click, and it belongs to the profiling_examples object. That means it's also on the one Flex application that we have running here, profiling_examples.mxml. We don't have a method called by that name, though, so what's happening here? Well, since we have a click event on the longRunningMethodButton on line 49, that gives us a clue about what's happening. This method is one that's actually generated by Flex during the compile phase. It's the method that gets called by the button click mouse event, which calls the method we wanted to execute on the button click. Luckily, it's named well enough to give us a clue about what it is. You may run into a lot of indirection like this that you don't expect as you start to dig into your application, so be on the lookout.

A clue that we're not yet to the source of the problem is that the self time of this method is zero, while the cumulative time is very high. Double-click the row in the Callees table to see what's going on in this method. Figure 9.8 shows us that view.

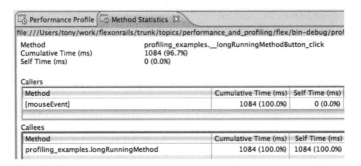

Figure 9.8   Callees for the method.

The caller for this method is the [mouseEvent] method but the callee is our longRunningMethod—code we actually wrote. Sure enough, the self time and cumulative time are equal, which means that any time spent running this method was spent in this method alone. The time spent running this method also about equals the full amount of the time spent running [mouseEvent], so it looks as if we found our slow-running method.

This is a simple example, of course, but it shows the pattern you'll use to track down any performance bottlenecks you have anywhere in your Flex applications. Profiling for performance is an exercise in diligence, intuition, and employing the scientific method liberally. Having a tool like the Flex Builder can mean the difference between testing some hunches and simply examining the raw numbers to track down the methods that caused them to be so high.

Memory Profiling

Now let's have a little fun exploring memory profiling in Flex. When profiling the memory of an application, the goal is to figure out what's taking up memory, where that stuff is getting created, and whether or not you think the objects taking up memory should still be hanging around the running application.

What does "hanging around" mean? Well, most of you have probably been introduced to the concept of garbage collection. Flex is no different from most platforms, such as Java, Windows, or MacOS. They all have some way for objects to be created, and they all have some way to get rid of those objects and free up memory when those objects are no longer useful.

Flex's method of doing this cleanup of useless objects is similar to Java's method. The VM, in this case, the one inside the Flash Player, has something called a garbage collector, which runs periodically through the objects in memory, decides if they still need to be there, and if not, **deallocates** them, or removes them from memory.

How does it decide whether objects are no longer used? The short story is that it keeps track of references. If an object no longer has any references to it, or, no variables pointing to it, then it can be safely discarded. It also watches for situations where two objects refer to each other but no other objects refer to either of them.

In case you're wondering, Flex does also have a concept of weak references, which are basically references that the garbage collector doesn't count as real references. You can use weak references when setting up event listeners, as an argument to `addEventListener`, or when setting up a dictionary, as an argument to the constructor—pass `true` to use weak references.

> **Note**
>
> When should you use weak references with event listeners? Since an event listener's targets are very hard to get a handle on to dereference variables once they're out of scope, it's generally the case that your event listeners should be added as weak references. Keep in mind, though, that using the profiler to find memory leaks is relatively easy compared to tracking down weird bugs where you're expecting an event to fire, but the garbage collector has already dereferenced the event listener's target. Make sure some other object is referring to the object containing the function that will be called by the event listener—if there is one, then it's probably OK to use a weak reference. If the only reference to that callee object is in a method that will soon be out of scope, you should either use a regular reference or figure out a different way to do what you're doing.

Just as in Java, developers don't have too much control over when this garbage collection process happens, but give it every chance to do the right thing when it does, and clean up references to objects that the application is no longer using.

Let's look at a fun application that will help us track down a gaping (and obvious) memory leak by taking a tour of the memory profiling capabilities of Flex Builder.

The application is a visualization of a Fibonacci sequence. If you're not familiar with the Fibonacci sequence, it's a formula for a sequence of numbers that follows this rule: Starting with 0 and 1, the next number in the sequence is the sum of the previous two numbers, which gives a sequence like this (to 20 members):

0, 1, 1, 2, 3, 5, 8, 13, 21, 34, 55, 89, 144, 233, 377, 610, 987, 1597, 2584, 4181, 6765

And so on. As you can see, the next number in the sequence gets big fairly quickly. Our visualization draws nested squares on the view given the number of positions to calculate the sequence to, as shown in Figure 9.9.

Of course, this isn't scalable past the 15th number or so, so we leave a note to that point. We're looking out for the user.

How is this data visualization feat accomplished? First, we have a simple application, as shown in Listing 9.2.

Listing 9.2   **memory_example.mxml #40-43**

```
<mx:Label id="sequenceLabel" text="How many Fibonacci Squares?
    (between 8-15 reccomended)" styleName="whiteLabel" />
<mx:TextInput id="sequenceLimit" width="50"
    enter="createSequence(Number(sequenceLimit.text))" />

<fibonacci:FibonacciVisual194194izer id="visualizer" />
```

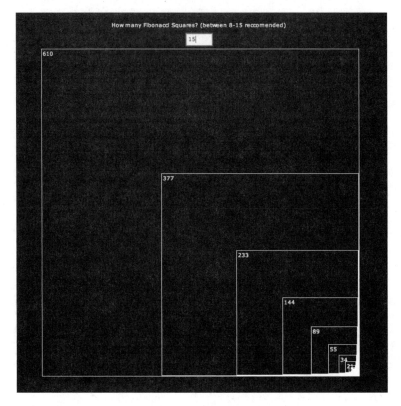

Figure 9.9   Fibonacci squares.

The application takes the position in the sequence to draw up to in a text input. Underneath that is the actual component that draws the squares.

When enter is pressed in the sequenceLimit text input, the function in Listing 9.3 runs.

Listing 9.3   **memory_example.mxml #22–35**

```
private function createSequence(n:Number):void {
    var currentSequence:Array = [0,1];
    var position:int = 1;
    var subOne:Number;
    var subTwo:Number;
    while (position < n) {
        subOne = currentSequence[position];
        subTwo = currentSequence[position - 1];
        currentSequence.push(subOne + subTwo);
        position++
    }

    visualizer.showForSequence(currentSequence);
}
```

This method creates an array containing the sequence to the given limit and passes it into the visualizer, which contains the method shown in Listing 9.4.

Listing 9.4   **fibonacci/FibonacciVisualizer #8–29**

```
public function showForSequence(sequence:Array):void {
    var highestFirst:Array = sequence.reverse();
    var i:String;
    var index:int;
    var num:Number;
    var s:FibonacciSquare;
    var parentContainer:Container = this;

    for (i in highestFirst) {
        index = int(i);
        if (index != highestFirst.length) {
            num = highestFirst[index];
            s = new FibonacciSquare();
            s.width = s.height = num
            parentContainer.addChild(s);
            parentContainer = s;
        }
    }
}
```

This method takes the sequence and creates FibonacciSquares for each number in the sequence, ignoring 0, and nests them inside the previous square. A FibonacciSquare is just a Canvas with a label inside (see Listing 9.5).

Listing 9.5   **fibonacci/FibonacciSquare**

```
<?xml version="1.0" encoding="utf-8"?>
<mx:Canvas xmlns:mx="http://www.adobe.com/2006/mxml">
    <mx:Label id="sizeLabel" top="0" left="0" text="{width}"
styleName="whiteLabel" />
</mx:Canvas>
```

Very simple, and if you study it for a few minutes, you may find the memory leak if the showForSequence method is called multiple times.

Let's see what happens when we profile for memory. Open the application for profiling, just like in the last section, but this time, choose Enable memory profiling, Watch live memory data, and Generate object allocation stack traces, as shown in Figure 9.10.

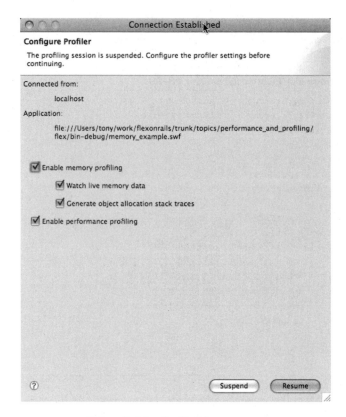

Figure 9.10   Profiling for memory.

Once the application starts, you'll be taken to the profiler again. This time, a few more views are shown; for instance, as shown in Figure 9.11, see the memory usage graph.

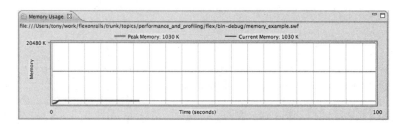

Figure 9.11   The memory usage graph.

This shows the memory in the application over time, live. This helps with one simple method of looking for memory leaks—running a certain sequence of actions over and over again until memory hits a peak. If you never hit a peak, you probably have a leak!

The other view you should see, shown in Figure 9.12, is the Live Objects view. This is a list of all the objects in memory in the running application, also continuously refreshed.

Class	Package (Filtered)	Cumulative Instances	Instances	Cumulative Memory	Memory
MethodClosure	builtin.as$0	75 (68.81%)	0 (0.0%)	2400 (33.67%)	0 (0.0%)
memory_example		1 (0.92%)	1 (9.09%)	1564 (21.94%)	1564 (37.96%)
FibonacciVisualizer	fibonacci	1 (0.92%)	1 (9.09%)	1308 (18.35%)	1308 (31.75%)
_memory_example_mx_managers_Systen		1 (0.92%)	1 (9.09%)	632 (8.87%)	632 (15.34%)
ModuleManagerImpl	ModuleManager.as$26	16 (14.68%)	1 (9.09%)	532 (7.46%)	52 (1.26%)
_fibonacci_FibonacciSquareWatcherSetup		1 (0.92%)	1 (9.09%)	444 (6.23%)	444 (10.78%)
MethodQueueElement	UIComponent.as$140	8 (7.34%)	0 (0.0%)	128 (1.8%)	0 (0.0%)
en_US$styles_properties		1 (0.92%)	1 (9.09%)	20 (0.28%)	20 (0.49%)
en_US$skins_properties		1 (0.92%)	1 (9.09%)	20 (0.28%)	20 (0.49%)
en_US$effects_properties		1 (0.92%)	1 (9.09%)	20 (0.28%)	20 (0.49%)
en_US$core_properties		1 (0.92%)	1 (9.09%)	20 (0.28%)	20 (0.49%)
en_US$controls_properties		1 (0.92%)	1 (9.09%)	20 (0.28%)	20 (0.49%)
en_US$containers_properties		1 (0.92%)	1 (9.09%)	20 (0.28%)	20 (0.49%)

Figure 9.12   The live objects view.

This view shows a count of the number of instances that have ever been created and how many there are now in Cumulative Instances and Instances, and also Cumulative Memory and Memory for each class.

So, let's enter 8 for the length of the sequence we want to see, as shown in Figure 9.13.

Figure 9.13   Put in 8.

Not very big eh? Maybe we need some way to scale the members of the visualization. Let's call that version 2. For now, let's do a sanity check on how many squares were created, as shown in Figure 9.14.

It looks like there are nine instances of the Fibonacci square. Since when we create the sequence, we start out with zero and one, but ignore zero later when creating the squares, that sounds like the right number of squares for a sequence out to the eighth position.

Class	Package (Filtered)	Cumulative Instances	Instances	Cumulative Memory	Memory
FibonacciSquare	fibonacci	9 (2.1%)	9 (23.68%)	12492 (37.98%)	2492 (68.11%)
MethodClosure	builtin.as$0	223 (52.1%)	0 (0.0%)	7136 (21.7%)	0 (0.0%)
ModuleManagerImpl	ModuleManager.as$26	87 (20.33%)	1 (2.63%)	2804 (8.52%)	52 (0.28%)
ContentRowChild	CanvasLayout.as$447	19 (4.44%)	0 (0.0%)	1976 (6.01%)	0 (0.0%)
ChildConstraintInfo	CanvasLayout.as$447	19 (4.44%)	8 (47.37%)	1824 (5.55%)	1728 (9.42%)
memory_example		1 (0.23%)	1 (2.63%)	1564 (4.75%)	1564 (8.53%)
ContentColumnChild	CanvasLayout.as$447	19 (4.44%)	0 (0.0%)	1520 (4.62%)	0 (0.0%)
FibonacciVisualizer	fibonacci	1 (0.23%)	1 (2.63%)	1308 (3.98%)	1308 (7.13%)
LayoutConstraints	CanvasLayout.as$447	20 (4.67%)	0 (0.0%)	720 (2.19%)	0 (0.0%)
_memory_example_mx_managers_System		1 (0.23%)	1 (2.63%)	632 (1.92%)	632 (3.45%)
_fibonacci_FibonacciSquareWatcherSetup		1 (0.23%)	1 (2.63%)	444 (1.35%)	444 (2.42%)
MethodQueueElement	UIComponent.as$140	22 (5.14%)	0 (0.0%)	352 (1.07%)	0 (0.0%)
en_US$styles_properties		1 (0.23%)	1 (2.63%)	20 (0.06%)	20 (0.11%)
en_US$skins_properties		1 (0.23%)	1 (2.63%)	20 (0.06%)	20 (0.11%)
en_US$effects_properties		1 (0.23%)	1 (2.63%)	20 (0.06%)	20 (0.11%)
en_US$core_properties		1 (0.23%)	1 (2.63%)	20 (0.06%)	20 (0.11%)
en_US$controls_properties		1 (0.23%)	1 (2.63%)	20 (0.06%)	20 (0.11%)
en_US$containers_properties		1 (0.23%)	1 (2.63%)	20 (0.06%)	20 (0.11%)

Figure 9.14   The sanity check.

Now let's try it with 15 positions and see what we get. Figure 9.15 is the Live Objects view for 15.

Hmmm . . . 25 instances?

Class	Package (Filtered)	Cumulative Instances	Instances	Cumulative Memory	Memory
FibonacciSquare	fibonacci	25 (2.5%)	5 (29.07%)	34700 (43.62%)	4700 (79.55%)
MethodClosure	builtin.as$0	480 (48.0%)	0 (0.0%)	15360 (19.31%)	0 (0.0%)
ModuleManagerImpl	ModuleManager.as$26	214 (21.4%)	1 (1.16%)	6868 (8.63%)	52 (0.12%)
ContentRowChild	CanvasLayout.as$447	56 (5.6%)	0 (0.0%)	5824 (7.32%)	0 (0.0%)
ChildConstraintInfo	CanvasLayout.as$447	56 (5.6%)	0 (58.14%)	5376 (6.76%)	4800 (11.0%)
ContentColumnChild	CanvasLayout.as$447	56 (5.6%)	0 (0.0%)	4480 (5.63%)	0 (0.0%)
LayoutConstraints	CanvasLayout.as$447	61 (6.1%)	0 (0.0%)	2196 (2.76%)	0 (0.0%)
memory_example		1 (0.1%)	1 (1.16%)	1564 (1.97%)	1564 (3.59%)
FibonacciVisualizer	fibonacci	1 (0.1%)	1 (1.16%)	1308 (1.64%)	1308 (3.0%)
MethodQueueElement	UIComponent.as$140	42 (4.2%)	0 (0.0%)	672 (0.84%)	0 (0.0%)
_memory_example_mx_managers_System		1 (0.1%)	1 (1.16%)	632 (0.79%)	632 (1.45%)
_fibonacci_FibonacciSquareWatcherSetup		1 (0.1%)	1 (1.16%)	444 (0.56%)	444 (1.02%)
en_US$styles_properties		1 (0.1%)	1 (1.16%)	20 (0.03%)	20 (0.05%)
en_US$skins_properties		1 (0.1%)	1 (1.16%)	20 (0.03%)	20 (0.05%)
en_US$effects_properties		1 (0.1%)	1 (1.16%)	20 (0.03%)	20 (0.05%)
en_US$core_properties		1 (0.1%)	1 (1.16%)	20 (0.03%)	20 (0.05%)
en_US$controls_properties		1 (0.1%)	1 (1.16%)	20 (0.03%)	20 (0.05%)
en_US$containers_properties		1 (0.1%)	1 (1.16%)	20 (0.03%)	20 (0.05%)

Figure 9.15   The Live Objects view for 15.

We were expecting 16, so something must be wrong. In fact, if our expectations were right, we're off by nine, which by a strange coincidence is the number of squares created the first time. Maybe the old ones just haven't been garbage collected . . . let's try that.

As shown in Figure 9.16, we're actually able to force a gc, or garbage collection. Of course we can try it, but that's not going to help us here . . . those objects are stuck in memory because something is holding the reference to them.

Figure 9.16   You can force garbage collection.

Let's try this again. Quit the application and profile it again, making sure to select the memory options. After the application starts, click the Take Memory Snapshot button, as shown in Figure 9.17.

Figure 9.17   Click the take memory snapshot button.

A memory snapshot enables us to dig deeper into what happened concerning object allocation at a certain point in the running application. After we have one snapshot for the fresh running application, enter 8 into the application, and then come back to the profiler and grab another snapshot. Figure 9.18 shows what we should get when we double-click on that new snapshot.

Class	Package (Filtered)	Instances	Memory
FibonacciSquare	fibonacci	9 (23.68%)	12492 (68.11%)
ChildConstraintInfo	CanvasLayout.as$447	18 (47.37%)	1728 (9.42%)
memory_example		1 (2.63%)	1564 (8.53%)
FibonacciVisualizer	fibonacci	1 (2.63%)	1308 (7.13%)
_memory_example_mx_managers_SystemManage		1 (2.63%)	632 (3.45%)
_fibonacci_FibonacciSquareWatcherSetupUtil		1 (2.63%)	444 (2.42%)
ModuleManagerImpl	ModuleManager.as$26	1 (2.63%)	52 (0.28%)
en_US$styles_properties		1 (2.63%)	20 (0.11%)
en_US$skins_properties		1 (2.63%)	20 (0.11%)
en_US$effects_properties		1 (2.63%)	20 (0.11%)
en_US$core_properties		1 (2.63%)	20 (0.11%)
en_US$controls_properties		1 (2.63%)	20 (0.11%)
en_US$containers_properties		1 (2.63%)	20 (0.11%)

Live Objects   Memory Snapshot ✕   Object References

file:///Users/tony/work/flexonrails/trunk/topics/performance_and_profiling/flex/bin-debug/memory_exam

Figure 9.18   The new memory snapshot.

It looks something like the Live Objects view, but if we double-click the FibonacciSquare row, we'll see something like what is shown in Figure 9.19.

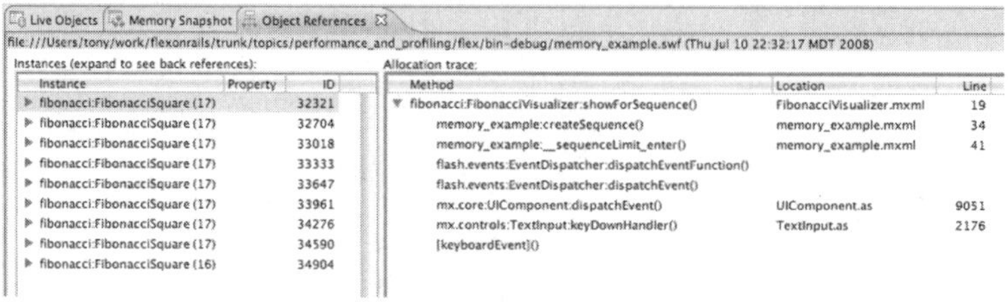

Figure 9.19   Clicking the FibonacciSquare row presents you with this view.

This view shows all instances of that class in memory. If you click an instance, it shows the stack trace of where that object was created. If you expand the instance list item, you'll see which objects are holding a reference to each instance. Very powerful!

Nothing is strange at this point, so let's try entering 15 for the sequence. When you've done that, come back and create another memory snapshot, and you should see what's in Figure 9.20. You should now have three memory snapshots.

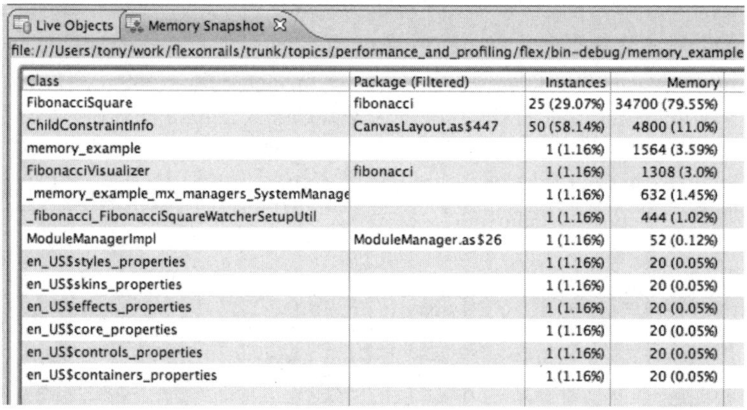

Figure 9.20   Take another memory snapshot.

Double-click the FibonacciSquare row to see Figure 9.21.

Sure enough, 25 squares are all being referenced by FibonacciVisualizer, which is why they won't go anywhere during garbage collection. Another view into the issue is to look at an allocation trace.

First, select the second and third memory snapshots, and then click the button shown in Figure 9.22, and you should see something like what is shown in Figure 9.23.

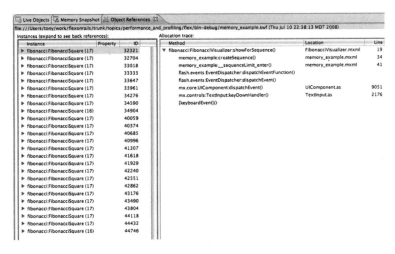

Figure 9.21   Double-clicking the FibonacciSquare row again gives you this view.

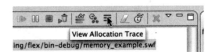

Figure 9.22   Click the View Allocation Trace button.

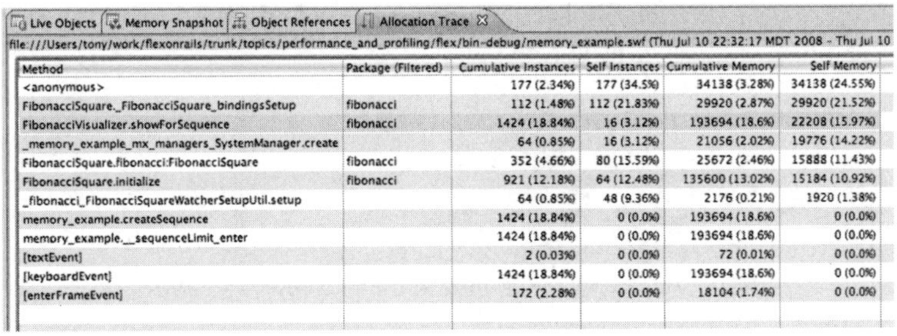

Figure 9.23   The Allocation Trace view.

This view shows all the times objects were created between the two snapshots. The Cumulative Instances column shows all objects allocated as a result of a method call, and Self Instances shows how many objects were allocated inside just that method call, not any subsequent methods called from that call or objects created by objects created in that call. This proves that nothing untoward happened when we entered 15 just now—between these two snapshot instances, 16 of the squares were created. To hone this point even further, double-click the showForSequence method to see something like Figure 9.24.

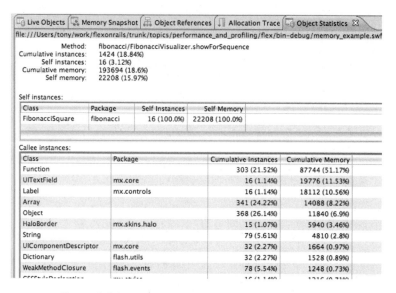

Figure 9.24   Double-clicking the `showForSequence`.

This Object Statistics view shows us that, indeed, 16 FibonacciSquares were created in this method between these two snapshots. Anything listed in the Callee instances table was created as a result of anything created solely in this method.

Another technique we can use to see how many objects of a certain type are hanging around is to look for Loitering Objects. Select the second and third memory snapshots and click the button, as shown in Figure 9.25.

Figure 9.25   Click the Find Loitering Objects button.

Now you should see something like Figure 9.26.

Class	Package	Instances	Memory
TypeError		1 (0.06%)	40 (0.02%)
FibonacciSquare	fibonacci	16 (1.0%)	22208 (10.35%)
Graphics	flash.display	16 (1.0%)	192 (0.09%)
TextFormat	flash.text	16 (1.0%)	1600 (0.75%)
Binding	mx.binding	16 (1.0%)	896 (0.42%)
PropertyWatcher	mx.binding	16 (1.0%)	704 (0.33%)

Figure 9.26   The Loitering Objects view.

This shows that between the second and third memory snapshots, after we put in 8 and then 15 for the sequence limit, 16 squares were created and were still in memory, and this is what we expect. Now if we select the *first* and third memory snapshots and look for Loitering Objects, we'll see what is shown in Figure 9.27.

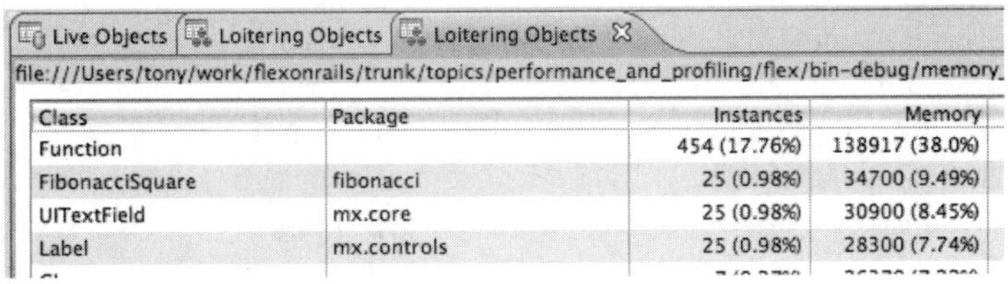

Class	Package	Instances	Memory
Function		454 (17.76%)	138917 (38.0%)
FibonacciSquare	fibonacci	25 (0.98%)	34700 (9.49%)
UITextField	mx.core	25 (0.98%)	30900 (8.45%)
Label	mx.controls	25 (0.98%)	28300 (7.74%)

Figure 9.27 Loitering objects from first and third memory snapshots.

This shows that 25 of the squares created between the first and third snapshots are still in memory, but we only want 16 of those.

In case you haven't figured it out yet, what we need to do is make sure we remove all the old squares from the FibonacciVisualizer before we add the new ones. That's as simple as putting a call to `removeAllChildren()` on line 17 in that class, which will dereference all the previously drawn squares each time we go to draw new ones.

If you run the profiler and follow the steps we've done so far, after entering 15, you should see something like Figure 9.28 for the Live Object view.

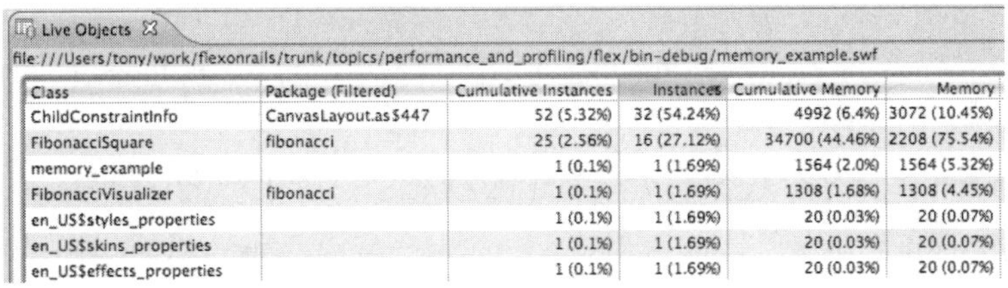

Class	Package (Filtered)	Cumulative Instances	Instances	Cumulative Memory	Memory
ChildConstraintInfo	CanvasLayout.as$447	52 (5.32%)	32 (54.24%)	4992 (6.4%)	3072 (10.45%)
FibonacciSquare	fibonacci	25 (2.56%)	16 (27.12%)	34700 (44.46%)	2208 (75.54%)
memory_example		1 (0.1%)	1 (1.69%)	1564 (2.0%)	1564 (5.32%)
FibonacciVisualizer	fibonacci	1 (0.1%)	1 (1.69%)	1308 (1.68%)	1308 (4.45%)
en_US$styles_properties		1 (0.1%)	1 (1.69%)	20 (0.03%)	20 (0.07%)
en_US$skins_properties		1 (0.1%)	1 (1.69%)	20 (0.03%)	20 (0.07%)
en_US$effects_properties		1 (0.1%)	1 (1.69%)	20 (0.03%)	20 (0.07%)

Figure 9.28 The new profiler view.

Now the profiler reports that FibonacciSquare has been created 25 times, but only 16 are still in memory, which is exactly what we want. If you were to compare the third snapshot to either the second or first snapshot, you'd see 16 loitering FibonacciSquares, which would be another way to show we'd gotten the results we wanted.

That's a tour through the profiler looking at memory, which lets us see why our application is taking up as much memory as it is.

Rails Performance

Rails performance, while just as important as Flex performance, is a different beast than Flex performance. Although each has its own quirks and interesting nooks and crannies to explore, making sure Rails performs efficiently is a bit tougher. This is because much more that isn't quite Rails perse affects the performance of a Rails application.

You may have a simple Rails application but a lot of data to move around. Rails can't make up for a poorly designed database. You have to understand or have someone around who understands how to index and maintain the database to get the most out of it.

There has been a lot of talk, good and bad, about Rails performance. You may have heard triumphant blog posts about how terribly Rails performs or scales and comeback blog posts about how, of course, it scales! Scaling Rails applications has received a lot of attention, and at some point, as your application starts to get popular, you'll need to consider getting your app on multiple servers and possibly using multiple databases.

These topics are out of scope for this chapter—luckily, there's good information out there and more is released all the time. You can take just a few steps that involve profiling to get a handle on what's happening in your application, so let's look at those.

Reading the Logs

The first and easiest thing you can do is look at your log files. There's a wealth of information about everything from incoming parameters to database time right there in the development log, and if you really need to, you can change your production log level to debug from its default info with a line like this in config/production.rb:

```
config.log_level = :debug
```

You've probably already seen the logs several times, but it's worth looking at the output once more:

```
Processing WidgetsController#index (for 127.0.0.1 at 2008-07-13 21:28:22) [GET]
  Session ID:
BAh7BiIKZmxhc2hJQzonQWN0aW9uOaW9uQ29udHJvbGxlcjo6Rmxhc2g6OkZsYXNo%0ASGFzaHsABjoKQH
VzZWR7AA%3D%3D--e92c5e3864793375b8c8e69ecd1eb28a0e03d07b
  Parameters: {"action"=>"index", "controller"=>"widgets"}
  Widget Load (0.000456) SELECT * FROM widgets
Rendering template within layouts/widgets
Rendering widgets/index

Completed in 0.01937 (51 reqs/sec)
Rendering: 0.00500 (25%)
DB: 0.00046 (2%)
200 OK [http://localhost/widgets]
```

Those last four lines (formatted a little differently here for readability) tell you a lot; for instance, rendering took 25% of the time, while the database query took 2% of the time. What you want to do to get an idea of how long people are spending in certain actions is find a way to get aggregate information from the logs.

One of these two projects is a good place to start:

- http://rails-analyzer.rubyforge.org/—A set of tools to analyze different aspects of the Rails logs to help track down slow spots.

- http://www.myspyder.net/tools/railslogvisualizer—An AIR app that visually breaks down the Rails logs by controller and action to give an idea of the cumulative time spent in controller actions. This was created by Daniel!

Looking at the logs is the right place to start.

Simple Benchmarking

When you want to get a more fine-grained look at how long something takes to run, use one of the `ActiveRecord::Base`, `ActionController`, or `ActionView` benchmark class methods. These act similarly to logging from inside your application. They're a way to print a log message and the time it takes to execute a block of code into the logs, provided that the log level for the current environment is above the level specified. Here's an example:

```
WidgetsController.benchmark("finding all widgets >>>>>>>>") do
  @widgets = Widget.find(:all)
end
```

In the `WidgetsController`, this would produce a log message like this (benchmark output bolded):

```
Processing WidgetsController#index (for 127.0.0.1 at 2008-07-13 21:51:20) [GET]
  Session ID:
BAh7BiIKZmxhc2hJQzonQWN0aW9uQ29udHJvbGxlcjo6Rmxhc2g6OkZsYXNoASGFzaHsABjoKQH
VzZWR7AA%3D%3D--e92c5e3864793375b8c8e69ecd1eb28a0e03d07b
  Parameters: {"format"=>"xml", "action"=>"index", "controller"=>"widgets"}
finding all widgets >>>>>>>> (0.00672)
Completed in 0.01488 (67 reqs/sec) | Rendering: 0.00104 (7%) | DB: 0.00000 (0%) |
200 OK [http://localhost/widgets.xml]
```

You could do the same thing around a block of code in any active record model as well. This approach gives you a fine-grained look at a very specific chunk of code. Since it follows the same rules as a logger, it's safe to leave benchmarking code in your app, too.

The Rails Performance Scripts

Rails also ships with some helpful scripts inside script/performance. Let's take a look at these. Note that most of these require the ruby-prof gem, which you can install with `gem install ruby-prof` from the command line.

> **Note**
>
> At the time of writing, Rails is at version 2.1 and ruby-prof is at version 0.6.0. However, the
> script/performance/request script requires ruby-prof 0.6.1. This is a bug. If you'd like to try
> the request profiler, do one of two things: use Rails < 2.1 or get Jeremy Kemper's updated
> ruby-prof here: http://github.com/jeremy/ruby-prof/tree/master.
>
> Of course, this may have changed, so you may want to try seeing which version of
> ruby-prof you get from gem install or check to see if the request profiler works with a later
> version of Rails.

script/performance/profiler

The profiler script is the most basic performance script. It takes a snippet of Ruby code and
uses the standard or ruby-prof profiler to profile the full stack of whatever happens in that
code. For instance, here's a call to find all widgets (Rails 2.0.2 style instead of 2.1 Widget.all).

```
$ ./script/performance/profiler 'Widget.find(:all)'
Loading Rails...
Using the standard Ruby profiler.
  %        cumulative    self              self     total
 time       seconds     seconds   calls   ms/call  ms/call  name
 48.09      1.26        1.26      76      16.58    23.42    Array#select
 19.08      1.76        0.50      7956    0.06     0.06     Hash#key?
  5.34      1.90        0.14      215     0.65     2.79     Array#each
  3.82      2.00        0.10      20      5.00     265.00
Kernel.gem_original_require
  2.67  2.07           0.07      105     0.67     19.90    Array#collect
  1.91  2.12           0.05      157     0.32     0.32
Module#blank_slate_method_added
...
```

You can see how this call would be useful and easy to profile a method you have on a
model that does a lot of work. Get your database set up the way you need and run this
call, and right from the command line, you have a profile. This method is of limited use
when you want to test web interaction, though.

script/performance/benchmarker

The Benchmarker script is there to help you get an idea of simply how long it takes to
run some code. Optionally, you can do a comparison of two blocks of code, perhaps to
check if a proposed optimization is actually faster.

Here's a benchmark of a finder method:

```
$ ./script/performance/benchmarker 'Widget.find(:all)'
      user     system    total       real
#1  0.000000  0.000000  0.000000  ( 0.001813)
```

Of course, with little data, this process takes almost no time. Here's a more rigorous test where we pit a simple find against a find and order by, then run them 100 times to get some sense of how long things actually take:

```
$ ./script/performance/benchmarker 100 'Widget.find(:all)' 'Widget.find(:all,
:order => "name")'
              user        system        total          real
#1        0.130000      0.040000      0.170000      ( 0.187982)
#2        0.140000      0.050000      0.190000      ( 0.193949)
```

We can see by this method that the order by clause costs slightly more than leaving it out.

script/performance/request

The request script is a relatively recent addition, and it's pretty powerful. This one relies on the ruby-prof gem.

It takes a little more set up to get the request script up and running. First of all, although you run it from the command line, you need to write the scripts to test into a separate file, passed as an argument to the script. The instruction set inside that script is the same that's available in an integration test (c.f., http://api.rubyonrails.org/classes/ActionController/Integration/Session.html). For instance, here's a very simple test:

```
get '/widgets.xml'
```

This makes a HTTP GET request to /widgets.xml, which, as you know, loads all widgets in an XML structure. To run this script, we'd put it somewhere convenient, perhaps the lib directory, and then enter this command:

```
$ ./script/performance/request lib/profile_widgets.rb
Warming up once
0.14 sec, 1 requests, 7 req/sec

Profiling 100x
 x.........x.........x.........x.........x.........x.........x.........x......
...x.........x.........

19.09 sec, 100 requests, 5 req/sec
```

You'll see that 100 requests is the default, to get a statistically valid sample. Also, it "warms up" one time to get a majority of caching done to give you an idea of what really happens.

Figure 9.29 shows the resulting HTML, which lets you explore from the top down into the profiling stacks created by the test. At the top level is the profiler script itself, which has a total of 100%, but 0% of that time was spent in self. Just as in the Flex Builder Profiler, this data indicates that something deeper in is taking all the time.

On a Mac, which the Rails core team tends to prefer, this HTML opens right up at the end of the profiling session. If you're not blessed with a Mac, you can find the HTML in the tmp directory, alongside a text-based version of the same profiling data.

One thing to note: if you're using RubyAMF, there's no good way (yet) to submit an AMF request through this profiler (or integration tests, for that matter). Read the next section for another option.

Profile Report

Thread ID	Total Time
213420	18.837325

Thread 213420

%Total	%Self	Total	Self	Wait	Child	Calls	Name	Line
100.00%	0.00%	18.84	0.00	0.00	18.84	0	**ActionController::RequestProfiler#profile**	75
		18.84	0.00	0.00	18.84	1/1	ActionController::RequestProfiler#benchmark	75
		18.84	0.00	0.00	18.84	1/1	ActionController::RequestProfiler#profile	75
100.00%	0.00%	18.84	0.00	0.00	18.84	1	**ActionController::RequestProfiler#benchmark**	81
		0.00	0.00	0.00	0.00	1/2	Kernel#puts	85
		0.00	0.00	0.00	0.00	1/106401	Hash#[]	83
		0.00	0.00	0.00	0.00	1/1	Float#to_f	83
		0.00	0.00	0.00	0.00	1/1001	Fixnum#/	85
		0.00	0.00	0.00	0.00	2/2	ActionController::Integration::Runner#method_missing	84
		0.00	0.00	0.00	0.00	1/1	Integer#to_i	84
		0.00	0.00	0.00	0.00	1/301	String#%	85
		18.84	0.00	0.00	18.84	1/1	ActionController::RequestProfiler::Sandbox#benchmark	83
		18.84	0.00	0.00	18.84	1/1	ActionController::RequestProfiler#benchmark	83

Figure 9.29   The profile report.

New Relic RPM

Now that you have a good survey of a majority of methods of tracking performance available out of the box, another good option is one offered by New Relic, called RPM or Rails Perfomance Management. It's a product that many high-profile Rails applications use, including apps by 37Signals. New Relic offers a development mode profiler free to anyone to use without limits. Once in production, you have to pay, but it keeps tracking performance data over time, allowing you to keep tabs on performance once your application is actually in front of customers.

One good thing about at least the development mode, if you don't choose to use the production version yet, is that RubyAMF gets profiled just like any other requests.

RPM is installed as a plug-in, like this:

```
$ script/plugin install http://svn.newrelic.com/rpm/agent/newrelic_rpm
```

Once the plug-in is installed, it profiles the last 100 requests in memory for you to use or throw away. First, fire up a server, and then make a few web requests. Then go to http://localhost:3000/newrelic, and you'll see something like what's shown in Figure 9.30.

It even tracks the SQL called during the request, as shown in Figure 9.31.

Even in development mode, that's very powerful, useful data for tracking down hotspots in your application.

[Summary] [Details] [SQL]

Performance Summary

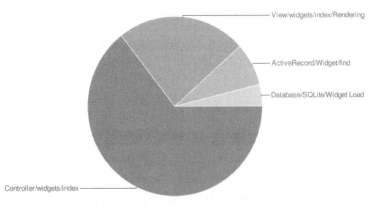

Metric	Count	Exclusive		Total	
Controller/widgets/index ?	1	16 ms	63%	25 ms	100%
View/widgets/index/Rendering ?	1	6 ms	26%	6 ms	26%
ActiveRecord/Widget/find ?	1	2 ms	6%	3 ms	11%
Database/SQLite/Widget Load ?	1	1 ms	5%	1 ms	5%

Figure 9.30   The RPM report.

[Summary] [Details] [SQL]

Timestamp	Duration	SQL
0.015	1 ms	📄 SELECT * FROM "widgets"

Figure 9.31   The SQL portion of the report.

Summary

Performance is a very big, wide-ranging subject, and it's easy to get scared into optimizing too early. Some people call this premature optimization, by which they mean that you spend too much time too early with code that is not ready for optimization. First, you probably have an app to build, which you're getting distracted from doing, and second, that code may not yet be in the context it will be in later, which may render all your hard tinkering with performance moot.

Optimizing is an exercise in finding the most slow or leaky code, fixing it, and then repeating the process. It's never actually finished, and sometimes the code may not be the real culprit. At least now, though, you're familiar with some tools you can use to make the case for what to fix next.

Cookbook Recipes

10

Source Control Flex and Rails Projects

Goal

Keep your Flex and Rails project under a source control management system to protect your source and manage your team's changes to the code-base.

Solution

Use your source control system's ignore features to make sure only the right files are managed. If you're not sure what we mean by source control, read the discussion at the end of the recipe first.

Ignoring Files in Subversion

A few files and directories shouldn't be stored in your source control system. In general, these include any files derived from a compilation process, such as the SWF file generated from your Flex project. It's also a great help to developers to exclude from source control the configuration files like database.yml, but provide them with example files that contain sample settings.

Figure 10.1 shows the standard structure of a Flex project generated by Flex Builder. One directory we probably don't want to version is the bin-debug directory. This directory contains the generated SWF and some other assets that are copied from other parts of the project.

Figure 10.1   You can ignore particular directories.

To ignore this directory from Subversion, sometimes called svn, either consult the Help files for whichever client you use or execute this command line from the root of the Flex project:

```
$ svn propset svn:ignore 'bin-debug' .
```

Subversion stores properties, such as which files to ignore, in metadata instead of in the directory as a file. This command tells svn to set the `svn:ignore` property to the text `bin-debug`, which will keep that directory and its contents untracked. To add other directories or files, just separate all the entries with a carriage return. To get a list of properties on a directory, just type:

```
$ svn proplist .
```

And to get a list of all the ignored files in a certain directory, type:

```
$ svn propget svn:ignore .
```

Sometimes, because of how developers are using libraries on their systems or because of system-dependent weirdness, it may be necessary to ignore the .actionSriptProperties file in the root of the Flex project. I've not often found this necessary, but once or twice have had to deal with this problem, on Windows especially. If you run into issues, provide an example file called something like .actionScriptProperties.example and ignore the .actionScriptProperties file, along with the bin-debug directory (note that [enter] means to press enter at that point in the command—remember that svn wants each item in an `ignore` property to appear on a new line):

```
$ svn propset svn:ignore 'bin-debug[enter]
> .actionScriptProperties' .
```

Rails has a few files we want to ignore, too. Figure 10.2 shows a standard Rails directory. What are some files that will change frequently but that we don't care to track in source control? Well, there are the logs to start with, as well as the contents of the tmp and pid child directories. If you go so far as to generate the Rails documentation for your application, you probably want to ignore some things in the doc directory too.

Figure 10.2   A standard Rails directory.

Ignore these files with these commands:

```
$ svn propset svn:ignore "*" log/
$ svn propset svn:ignore "*" tmp/sessions tmp/cache tmp/sockets tmp/pids
$ svn propset svn:ignore "api[enter]
> app" doc
```

One other file we should ignore is the database.yml file. Why? Because we want to let each developer configure local databases with whatever passwords they want. Use this same pattern for any other config files that make sense. First, move config/database.yml to config/database.example.yml and leave some friendly defaults there. Then ignore database.yml:

```
$ svn propset svn:ignore "database.yml" config/
```

Now your working copy will be changed, so be sure to commit.

Git

If you're working with Git instead, things work slightly differently. Git keeps a special file named .gitignore in any directory you choose in the working copy. This file pertains to all directories beneath it and contains patterns to match files to ignore. The .gitignore file is a lot like svn, except the ignore properties are kept in a file instead of metadata.

Here's a sample .gitignore file for the Flex project directory:

```
bin-debug
```

And for the Rails directory:

```
log/*
tmp/**/*
doc/api
doc/app
```

One slightly annoying aspect of Git is that it doesn't keep track of empty directories. Linus has his reasons for this peculiarity, but until this gotcha is solved more elegantly, developers that check out the project will probably be missing important directories like log and tmp.

Solve this problem in one of two ways: by telling other developers to simply create the directories the first time they check out the project or by putting an empty .gitignore in any empty directories you want to track, and then add this line to a parent gitignore: !.gitignore. That "reverses" the ignore on .gitignore files so that the following are not ignored:

```
log/.gitignore
tmp/cache/.gitignore
tmp/pids/.gitignore
tmp/sessions/.gitignore
tmp/sockets/.gitignore
```

Discussion

Source control is a very important part of maintaining the code for your application. Using a source control management system, or SCM, gives you a number of benefits:

- A history of all the changes made to your code over time.

- The capability to manage the integration of possibly conflicting changes from other members of your team into a central, official version of the code base.

- The capability to maintain separate but related paths of development, commonly called **branches**, to develop new features without affecting your ability to maintain the **main line** of development.

It's beyond the scope of this book to thoroughly cover the different SCM options available to you, but we will mention two popular options: Subversion and Git, and how to set them up to manage your project.

Subversion

Subversion is a very popular, fairly easy-to-use SCM that works on most popular operating systems. For information on how to get and install svn for your system, visit http://subversion.tigris.org.

Subversion comes with a command line client, which does everything you need to do. Not everyone likes to work on the command line, though, so there are some other clients available: For Mac, try svnX, found at www.lachoseinteractive.net/en/community/subversion/svnx/features/. For Windows, try TortoiseSVN from http://tortoisesvn.tigris.org/. A cross-platform eclipse plug-in called Subclipse is available at http://subclipse.tigris.org/ and works great alongside Flex Builder.

Consult the sites above for more information on how to work with those tools. All the examples here will use the command line, which is good to learn no matter which client you use.

Git

Git (http://git.or.cz/) is generating a lot of buzz in the software development world and is starting to be a competitor to Subversion for the hearts and minds of many popular open source projects, for instance, Rails itself. On April 11, 2008, the Rails source was moved to http://github.com/rails from its old Subversion servers.

Git was developed by Linus Torvalds, the creator of Linux, and is currently used to manage the Linux kernel code base, which lends it a lot of "geek cred." It's a distributed source code management tool, which means that it doesn't rely on a central server. It offers several powerful methods of working with other developers on the same project.

Git also works very differently from Subversion and its predecessor, CVS, although the commands and most workflow steps are similar. Git makes it incredibly easy to branch development and share code patches, and offers some very interesting tools to work with your code. For instance, the git-bisect command lets you move your source code back in version history steps at a time to find out when bugs were introduced.

All that said, Git is a not currently a tool for the faint of heart. No graphical client that does everything you need to do is available for either Mac or Windows, and most operations are better executed from the command line. Speaking of Windows, that platform isn't even supported by Git, and must be run on a *nix emulator like Cygwin (www.cygwin.com/), although another project called msysgit (http://msysgit.googlecode.com) is attempting to make running Git a little easier.

One last note on Git: there is a tool called git-svn, best installed from your favorite package manager like MacPorts or through the Cygwin configuration utility. Git-svn works to add knowledge of an svn server to a local Git working copy. Git-svn will help in the transition from svn to Git if you decide to take that plunge.

Summary

Source control is an essential part of any team development effort, so it's helpful to have a good idea of what works with your particular SCM.

11

Building Flex with Rake

Goal

You'd like to compile your Flex applications with a few simple commands. You may want to simply build from the command line, or you may want to make this build part of a continuous integration build.

Solution

Make a simple build file using Rake to help automate this task.

Rake Is Your Friend

You can't get very far working with Rails before you run into Rake, the Ruby build tool (http://rake.rubyforge.org/). Use Rake to run tests, migrate the database, and do several other useful tasks.

Rake certainly isn't Rails-specific, though you can use it to do just about anything you want on your system. Here we're going to look at making a Rake build file that will provide a simple wrapper around mxmlc and do a few other neat tricks, as well as build some Flex applications.

> **Note**
>
> For this Rakefile to work, you need to have mxmlc in your path. Read the Flex SDK documentation if you're not sure how to do this.

First, in the sample code for this topic, you'll find a very simple Flex application, Main.mxml, and another more complex one called MainWithCoverflow.mxml. You may notice that the example code was written in Flex Builder, suggested by the presence of some Flex Builder files present in the directory. Even if you use Flex Builder, you can still get use out of making a Rake task to build from the command line, though, because you need something besides Flex Builder to build in a continuous integration environment.

Let's look at the Coverflow application in a second; for now, here's the basic one:

```
<?xml version="1.0" encoding="utf-8"?>
<mx:Application xmlns:mx="http://www.adobe.com/2006/mxml" layout="absolute">
    <mx:Text id="flexText" text="Flex Meet Rails!" fontSize="18"
verticalCenter="0" horizontalCenter="0" />
</mx:Application>
```

The Rakefile

In the src directory, along with Main.mxml, is a file called Rakefile. When you run
Rake, it will look for a file called either rakefile, Rakefile, rakefile.rb, or Rakefile.rb (in
that order). Rakefile seems to be the conventional name, so we've used that one here.

Let's look at a few things in the Rakefile. First, we define some constants on the first
three lines:

```
FLEX_SRC='src'
FLEX_LIB='libs'
FLEX_BIN='bin-debug'
```

They will point to the source directory, library directory, and bin-debug, which is the
name Flex Builder usually uses for a build directory. Remember that anything that
begins with a capital letter is a constant in Ruby and that nonclass constants are in all
caps by convention. That's your first lesson about Rake: a Rakefile is just a Ruby program, so any valid Ruby code can go into a Rakefile.

Next, you'll see this line:

```
task :default => :compile_main
```

Tasks in Rake are similar to functions, but slightly different (they are actually *blocks*).
They define a task that Rake will run *once* per invocation and contain Ruby code in the
block. Each task has a name, which you can use to call it from the command line. The
task named :default is special and will be run if no task is specified.

In this case, we're defining a task named :default that depends on another task
named :compile_main—so there you see another Rake capability, the capability to
define task dependencies.

Here's the :compile_main task:

```
desc 'Compile Main.mxml'
task :compile_main do
  Dir.chdir(FLEX_SRC) do
    puts "Compiling Main.mxml"
    sh %{ mxmlc -locale=en_US Main.mxml }
    FileUtils.move 'Main.swf', "../#{FLEX_BIN}/", :verbose => true
  end
end
```

First, using desc, we describe the task so that when you run rake -T, you'll get a help-ful description of the tasks that can be run:

```
$ rake -T
(in /Users/tony/work/flexonrails/trunk/topics/cookbook/build_flex_with_rake/flex)
rake compile_main  # Compile Main.mxml
```

When rake is invoked, since :compile_main is the default task, the Ruby code inside will be executed. First, it changes directories into the Flex source directory we defined as src because mxmlc wants you to be in the same directory as the mxml it's compiling. Then it outputs a helpful message to the console. Next is a call to sh, which is a feature of Rake that executes a shell command taking a set of commands. The text in the curly braces is what you'd probably call from the command line yourself, so we've only got a fairly simple wrapper around mxmlc at this point. Next, though, since mxmlc generates the SWF file to the current directory, we use Rake's move command to move the SWF up to the bin directory and be verbose about it so we can have a little feedback on the console.

This is fairly simple and not too far away from the command line. Now we don't need to memorize the mxmlc syntax; we can simply call Rake:

```
$ rake
(in /Users/tony/work/flexonrails/trunk/topics/cookbook/build_flex_with_rake/flex)
Compiling Main.mxml
 mxmlc -locale=en_US Main.mxml
Loading configuration file /Applications/fb_3/sdks/3.0.0/frameworks/flex-
config.xml
/Users/tony/work/flexonrails/trunk/topics/cookbook/build_flex_with_rake/flex/src/M
ain.swf (153167 bytes)
mv Main.swf ../bin-debug/
```

Let's look at a slightly more complex situation. What if we have a few different mxml files to compile and we have a few SWC dependencies, too? That's what the next task you may have already seen in the Rakefile is for.

Now we have two application files in our Flex project. One was the simple one, and the other is a more complex version that looks like this:

```
<?xml version="1.0" encoding="utf-8"?>
<mx:Application xmlns:mx="http://www.adobe.com/2006/mxml" layout="vertical"
xmlns:containers="com.dougmccune.containers.*" backgroundColor="0x000000">
    <containers:CoverFlowContainer id="coverFlowContainer" width="500"
height="600">
        <mx:Panel width="200" height="200">
            <mx:Text id="flexText" text="Flex" fontSize="18" />
        </mx:Panel>
        <mx:Panel width="200" height="200">
            <mx:Text id="meetText"text="Meet" fontSize=""8"" />
        </mx:Panel>
        <mx:Panel width="200" height="200">
            <mx:Text id="railsText" text="Rails!" fontSize="18" />
```

```
            </mx:Panel>
        </containers:CoverFlowContainer>
        <mx:HScrollBar
            id="coverFlowScroller"
            width="{coverFlowContainer.width}"
            pageSize="1"
            maxScrollPosition="{coverFlowContainer.numChildren - 1}"
            scrollPosition="{coverFlowContainer.selectedIndex}"
            scroll="coverFlowContainer.selectedIndex =
Math.round(coverFlowScroller.scrollPosition)" />
</mx:Application>
```

This says the same thing as the Main application but in a much more fun way using
Doug McCune's excellent Coverflow component (http://dougmccune.com/blog/
2007/11/19/flex-coverflow-performance-improvement-flex-carousel-component-and-
vertical-coverflow/), which comes in a SWC and depends on a few other SWCs as well.
   Here's the Rake task to compile both:

```
desc "Compile All Flex Applications in #{FLEX_SRC}"
task :compile_all do

  Dir.chdir(FLEX_SRC) do
    Dir["*.mxml"].each do |flex_file|
      swf_file = flex_file.gsub /mxml/, 'swf'
      puts "Compiling #{flex_file} => #{swf_file}"
      sh %{ mxmlc -locale=en_US -library-path+=../#{FLEX_LIB} #{flex_file}}
      move swf_file, "../#{FLEX_BIN}/", :verbose => true
    end
  end

end
```

   The :compile_all task takes one extra step from the :compile_main task, which is
to do a glob of all the files matching *.mxml in the source directory, and then loop over
those and compile them. Now when we run rake :compile_all, we get this output:

```
$ rake compile_all
(in /Users/tony/work/flexonrails/trunk/topics/cookbook/build_flex_with_rake/flex)
Compiling Main.mxml => Main.swf
 mxmlc -locale=en_US -library-path+=../libs Main.mxml
Loading configuration file /Applications/fb_3/sdks/3.0.0/frameworks/flex-
config.xml
/Users/tony/work/flexonrails/trunk/topics/cookbook/build_flex_with_rake/flex/src/
Main.swf (153168 bytes)
mv Main.mxml ../bin-debug/
Compiling MainWithCoverflow.mxml => MainWithCoverflow.swf
mxmlc -locale=en_US -library-path+=../libs MainWithCoverflow.mxml
```

```
Loading configuration file /Applications/fb_3/sdks/3.0.0/frameworks/flex-
config.xml
/Users/tony/work/flexonrails/trunk/topics/cookbook/build_flex_with_rake/flex/src/
MainWithCoverflow.swf (212909 bytes)
mv MainWithCoverflow.mxml ../bin-debug/
```

This tells us we're getting all the mxml files in src compiled and copied to the build directory. A lot simpler than doing it by hand!

And now for a gratuitous look at the Coverflow version of the sample app we just built from Rake! Take a look at Figure 11.1.

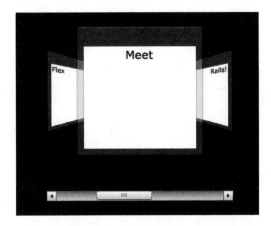

Figure 11.1   Coverflow version of the sample application.

Summary

Rake is a great way to automate any number of system tasks using Ruby. It's a lot lighter weight than Ant, a Java-based, XML-driven build tool with the same goals as Rake, and using it gives you a chance to learn more about Ruby in a setting other than Rails. This recipe should give you a practical basis to start using Rake in your project.

## 12

Deploying Flex and Rails Applications

Goal

You'd like to automate the deployment of your Flex and Rails project, getting Flex built and deployed to an integration or production environment.

Solution

Use Capistrano, the remote automation tool by Jamis Buck (http://weblog.jamisbuck.org/) built with deploying Rails applications in mind. As part of a normal Capistrano deployment, it can find the compiled SWF assets and any other files that need to accompany them and upload them to the right places on the right servers. Find out more about Capistrano at www.capify.org.

Capistrano

Capistrano is the de facto tool used to deploy Rails applications, and for good reason. First, it's written in Ruby and feels a lot like Rake. In fact, one of the only complaints about Capistrano is that it's not just an extension to Rake, which is neither here nor there, really. It just shows that Cap (as most people call it) fits right into the Rails toolset and seems to do well what it professes to do.

Another credential for Cap is that it was written by Jamis Buck, one of the major contributors to Rails. Cap was written for Rails originally, and only lately has it become more general and less Rails-specific.

Capistrano is essentially a way to log in to a group of SSH-enabled servers and run commands in a certain order with an easy way to assign roles to machines and run specific tasks on certain roles. It doesn't matter how many servers are classified in each role; Cap works with clusters really well.

Let's consider a couple of requirements about Cap. Your servers must have a POSIX-compliant shell, with SSH installed. Linux, BSD, and Mac servers are in, but that most likely leaves Windows servers out of the question. However, just as on your development machines, it may be possible to accomplish this requirement using Cygwin. Your mileage may vary.

One more thing before we get started. This chapter isn't a comprehensive resource on Capistrano, merely a discussion of how to add Flex into the mix. Anything more is beyond the scope of this book. You should take the time to read about how Cap works if you plan to use it. The following samples are only fragments meant to fit into a Cap deploy script that works for your environment.

Deploying with Capistrano

Suppose we have a Rails application we want to deploy, but with the interface built in Flex, there's nothing in the documentation that talks about getting Flex-ready before deployment. How do we do that?

First, what do we really need from the Flex part of the application when it comes time to put things on a server? For a basic Flex application, that comes down to just the SWF. We don't need any of the mxml or ActionScript code on the server. If you have any assets that are loaded at runtime, such as Runtime Shared Libraries (RSLs), images you load at runtime, or other SWFs, you'll need those too, but for our simple example application, all we need are two SWFs.

If you read Chapter 11, Building Flex with Rake, you'll recognize the sample application for that topic as the starting point for this application. In fact, it's exactly the same except Cap was installed and one file was modified.

Installing Cap is easy. First, you need to install the capistrano gem:

```
$ gem install capistrano
```

Then you'll need to "capify" your application:

```
$ capify .
    [add] writing './Capfile'
    [add] writing './config/deploy.rb'
[done] capified!
```

This creates Cap's requisite Capfile (similar to rake's Rakefile) and a Rails-specific deployment configuration file in config/deploy.rb, as shown in Figure 12.1.

Figure 12.1   Capifying your application creates the Capfile and a
rails-specific deployment configuration file in config/deploy.rb.

Non-Rails Cap deployments work from the Capfile, but that behavior was backfilled,
and early Cap worked only with deploy.rb. In a Rails deployment, you'll be working
only in the deploy.rb file for most cases.

If all we need are the SWFs from this Flex/Rails app, let's think about how we want a
deploy to happen. Besides all the other stuff that Cap usually does, like stopping servers,
migrating, moving code into place, and keeping a history for easy rollbacks in case of an
emergency, what we want Cap to do in this case is get the built SWF assets onto the
servers that will serve web requests.

Why make that distinction? Because Cap does: out of the box, it makes a distinction
between database servers, application servers, and web servers. Even if for right now
everything is on the same server, we'll still choose to put the SWFs on the web server
explicitly because that will be the most scalable solution for the future.

Now that we know which types of servers we want our Flex resources on, where do
we want them? Well, for right now, unless we get more distributed, we just want to put
them in the Rails public folder. Why not check the SWFs into source control in the
public directory? Because we need them built fresh every time; we don't want to rely on
guessing that the SWFs are up to date with the Flex code.

Now the process looks like this: figure out where the SWFs are and upload them to the web server in the Rails public directory. Simple right? Here's the fragment of the deploy.rb to get that done:

```
flex_build_dir = '../flex/bin'
flex_build_files = ['Main.swf', 'MainWithCoverflow.swf']

namespace :deploy do

  after "deploy:update_code", "deploy:push_flex_build"

  desc "copies all the flex built swfs to the web server"
  task :push_flex_build, :roles => :web do
    flex_build_files.each do |f|
      build_file = "#{flex_build_dir}/#{f}"
      logger.trace("uploading flex build file #{build_file}...")
      put(File.read(build_file), "#{current_release}/public/#{f}")
    end
  end

end
```

A lot is going on here, so let's dig in. First, we keep a list in the first two lines of which files are deployed as part of the build and where they're located. Next we open the :deploy namespace. Once you get familiar with Cap, you'll find that the tasks in the deploy namespace do most of the heavy lifting in a typical Cap session. Here's a list of tasks:

```
$ cap -Tv
cap deploy                  # Deploys your project.
cap deploy:check            # Test deployment dependencies.
cap deploy:cleanup          # Clean up old releases.
cap deploy:cold             # Deploys and starts a 'cold' application.
cap deploy:finalize_update  # [internal] Touches up the released code.
cap deploy:migrate          # Run the migrate rake task.
cap deploy:migrations       # Deploy and run pending migrations.
cap deploy:pending          # Displays the commits since your last
                                deploy.
cap deploy:pending:diff     # Displays the 'diff' since your last
                                deploy.
cap deploy:push_flex_build  # copies all the flex built swfs to the web
                                server
cap deploy:restart          # Restarts your application.
cap deploy:rollback         # Rolls back to a previous version and
                                restarts.
cap deploy:rollback_code    # Rolls back to the previously deployed
                                version.
```

```
cap deploy:setup          # Prepares one or more servers for
                              deployment.
cap deploy:start          # Start the application servers.
cap deploy:stop           # Stop the application servers.
cap deploy:symlink        # Updates the symlink to the most recently
                              dep...
cap deploy:update         # Copies your project and updates the
                              symlink.
cap deploy:update_code    # Copies your project to the remote servers.
cap deploy:upload         # Copy files to the currently deployed
                              version.
cap deploy:web:disable    # Present a maintenance page to visitors.
cap deploy:web:enable     # Makes the application web-accessible
                              again.
cap invoke                # Invoke a single command on the remote
                              servers.
cap shell                 # Begin an interactive Capistrano session.
```

Since deploying our Flex-built assets is part of the deploy process, we use the deploy namespace and name our task `deploy:push_flex_build`.

The next line, using the `after` command, tells Cap where in the deploy to automatically run our task. Looking at the descriptions above, you'll see that `deploy:update_code` puts all of the other files on the servers, so that's an appropriate place in the deploy to upload the Flex assets.

Next, you'll notice that things start to look a bit like Rake, if you're familiar with that tool. There are `desc` and `task` commands, just like Rake. The task is named `:push_flex_build`. Right after the name, we tell Cap that we want this task to work only on the web servers, or any server that's placed in a role of web server. See the Cap documentation for more information.

The rest of the deploy script is simple. Inside the task block, we simply loop over the list of Flex assets to deploy, be verbose about what we're doing by logging the action, and then run the `put` command. Running that command uploads those files to a certain directory, in this case, the public directory in the current_release directory. The current_release directory is a Cap variable that points to where the current code base is being deployed.

Simple, yes? One extra caution: we ran into some problems getting this to work with a Capistrano deploy, and we had to use the `--synchronous_connect` command line option. Working with some systems, the file upload would hang unless this option was specified. It appears to be a problem with some SFTP implementations. More information on the bug can be found here: http://dev.rubyonrails.org/changeset/7201/tools/ capistrano. Your mileage may vary, but here's how the command looks with `cap`:

```
$ cap deploy --synchronous_connect
```

Summary

Once again, there's a lot more to Capistrano—we've only scratched the surface and mentioned how you may integrate a task to upload the current Flex-compiled assets, along with the rest of your Rails app, as part of a Capistrano deployment.

This task assumes that you have your Flex assets built and ready to go as well. It shouldn't be Cap's job to make that happen—see Chapter 11 to see how to get that part done. Then you'll want something automated to kick off the Flex build, followed by the Cap deploy. This will change based on the various possible ways you could decide to work an automated build and deploy into your development strategy.

Capistrano is a great tool, and you'll find it useful for a lot of things, not the least of which is getting your Flex application built and on the server, ready for your fans to enjoy!

13

Read the Source!

Goal

You want to figure out why something in Flex or Rails works the way it does. For instance, how does all this data binding and active record association magic work?

Solution

Look at the source!

The Beauty of Open Source

You're wary of magic. On the other hand, take an SQL-select statement: now there's something you can understand. It does what it says, and returns a result you can manage. Setting a variable to a new value; nothing magic there—you change the variable and it has a new value. Nothing else did it for you; you took action and manipulated it yourself, and now it has a new value.

Flex makes things easy and declarative. You have an XML tag that describes what you want to see, like a List or a Horizontal Slider. It gets a little jarring and surprising to see data binding start to work, though. It works, but how?

Similarly, ActiveRecord associations, like `has_many` or `belong_to`, are great, because you write code that says things the way you already talk. But, something's a little fishy about how easily that all works out, especially if you've come from a Java or PHP background. You say to yourself, "I've always had to manage these things myself—what's going on in there that makes all this so easy?"

Well, that's the beauty of both Flex and Rails: they're open source, so you can find out for yourself.

Let's look at a bit of magic in Rails first. To start, look at these classes from the sample code for this cookbook topic:

```
class Company < ActiveRecord::Base
  has_many :users
end

class User < ActiveRecord::Base
  belongs_to :company
end
```

Migrate and load fixtures for the sample code for this cookbook topic, and then open a console in the sample code directory and type the following lines (don't mind the :select key in the find if you haven't run across that one before—it just limits the columns to bring back from the database to make it easier to read here):

```
>> company = Company.find :first, :select => "name, id"
=> #<Company id: 1, name: "MegaCorp, Inc">
>> company.users.find(:all, :select => "full_name")
=> [#<User full_name: "J. Sterling Wiltshire III">, #<User full_name:
"Richard Hammilton, Esquire">]
>> company.users.count
=> 2
```

Rails 101, right? Calling the has_many association users find method brings back an array of users. Or, we can call count and get the number of users in that table. In fact, we don't have to call the find or any other method; we could just call users and we get the whole shooting match:

```
>> company.users
=> [#<User id: 182450999, full_name: "J. Sterling Wiltshire III", company_id:
1, created_at: "2008-06-08 22:36:48", updated_at: "2008-06-08 22:36:48">>,
#<User id: 598291949, full_name: "Richard Hamilton, Esquire", company_id: 1,
created_at: "2008-06-08 22:36:48", updated_at: "2008-06-08 22:36:48">]
```

So, when we call users, we get back an array. What kind of class is this useful little guy?

```
>> company.users.class
=> Array
```

Wait! What? It is an array? How can we call count on it, then, since there is no Array#count?

```
>> Array.new.respond_to? "count"
=> false
```

Something tricky's going on here. It's time to look at the source.

The Rails Source

Since Rails is installed as a gem (actually a set of gems), the source code is sitting with the rest of the gems. You'll need to know where Ruby is installed on your system. Here are some possible locations:

- Windows: C:\ruby
- Mac/Linux: /usr/local/lib/ruby
- Mac (via MacPorts): /opt/local/lib/ruby

To find out for sure, use the `gem environment` command. Here's the output on a Mac using MacPorts:

```
RubyGems Environment:
  - RUBYGEMS VERSION: 1.2.0
  - RUBY VERSION: 1.8.6 (2007-09-23 patchlevel 110) [i686-darwin9.2.0]
  - INSTALLATION DIRECTORY: /opt/local/lib/ruby/gems/1.8
  - RUBY EXECUTABLE: /opt/local/bin/ruby
  - EXECUTABLE DIRECTORY: /opt/local/bin
  - RUBYGEMS PLATFORMS:
    - ruby
    - x86-darwin-9
  - GEM PATHS:
    - /opt/local/lib/ruby/gems/1.8
  - GEM CONFIGURATION:
    - :update_sources => true
    - :verbose => true
    - :benchmark => false
    - :backtrace => false
    - :bulk_threshold => 1000
  - REMOTE SOURCES:
    - http://gems.rubyforge.org/
```

You can also use `gem which <gem name>` to find out where a specific gem is located, for instance:

```
$ gem which activerecord
(checking gem activerecord-2.1.0 for activerecord)
/opt/local/lib/ruby/gems/1.8/gems/activerecord-2.1.0/lib/activerecord.rb
```

From your Ruby library root, go to gems/1.8/gems (replacing 1.8 with whatever version you're using) and open it in your file manager. You may see something similar to Figure 13.1, especially if you've installed as many gems as are on this system.

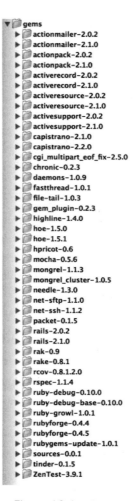

Figure 13.1   Gems.

This directory shows a directory for every version of every gem installed on the system. Rails itself is a gem, and so are ActiveRecord, ActiveResource, ActiveSupport, ActionMailer, and ActionPack—the full suite of Rails modules.

We're interested in figuring out what's going on inside an active record association, so let's look in that directory, as shown in Figure 13.2.

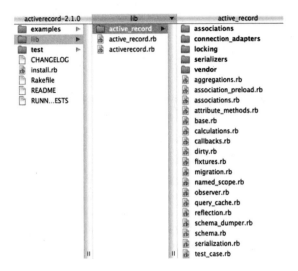

Figure 13.2   The active_record directory.

There are a lot of normal gem classes, and in lib, there are files that include a lot of other files. Inside the active_record directory is the meat of the gem, though. `ActiveRecord::Base` is defined in active_record/base.rb, along with a lot of exception classes.

What we're interested in, though, are the associations, stored in the directory of that name, as shown in Figure 13.3.

Figure 13.3   The associations.

To save a little digging around, the one we want to look at first is association_proxy.rb. Right off the bat, we find what we're looking for—a little documentation. Here are lines 33 through 40 of that class:

```
# This class has most of the basic instance methods removed, and delegates
# unknown methods to <tt>@target</tt> via <tt>method_missing</tt>. As a
# corner case, it even removes the +class+ method and that's why you get
```

```
#
#   blog.posts.class # => Array
#
# though the object behind <tt>blog.posts</tt> is not an Array, but an
# ActiveRecord::Associations::HasManyAssociation.
```

If you ignore the rdoc markup and read a little bit, you can see why the object acts like an array. Line 52 of the class shows where some of that happens:

```
instance_methods.each { |m| undef_method m unless
m =~ /(^__|^nil\?$|^send$|proxy_|^object_id$)/ }
```

Rails associations use a proxy pattern on associations like has_many and belongs_to. A proxy is a middleman that passes messages through to another object but may take some action in special cases. Magic? It seems like it, but the source tells you what's really going on. On this line, we can see that it loops through each instance method of an array and undefines them, unless they're certain important messages. Then, when these methods are called later, a method_missing can catch them and either proxy that message on or take the correct Array-like action.

Rails is fairly well documented, but even if you're unfamiliar with Ruby, you can learn a lot about Ruby and Rails just by looking at the actual code. Sometimes the embedded documentation makes it even easier than that, as in this case.

If you want to know what's really going on, keep a link or bookmark to the Rails source handy so you can open it in your favorite editor!

Flex Source

Now let's take a look at some Flex source. First, a little orientation. If you're using Flex Builder, you can remain happily ignorant of the next part because it's very easy to look at Flex source directly from your projects. All the same, someday you may want to know where the source is, so you may want to follow along.

You may have installed the Flex SDK in many different places, but once you find that directory, look at the frameworks directory from the Flex SDK root. Flex Builder users can find the SDK files in <FlexBuilder Root>/sdks/<version number>, as shown in Figure 13.4.

Inside the SDK root are a few things, but if you're looking for source, go to the **projects** directory. Inside the projects directory, you will find a lot of source roots. The rpc directory houses many of the networking classes, the airframework directory contains what you might expect (Adobe's AIR-specific classes), and the framework directory contains the classes that make up Flex and its components. Ignore the flex directory; it contains only some import statements in an ActionScript file to define some dependency starting points.

If you're not sure where classes are located in the package structure, it's best to check the online Flex API documentation (http://livedocs.adobe.com/flex/3/langref/index.html, at the time of writing).

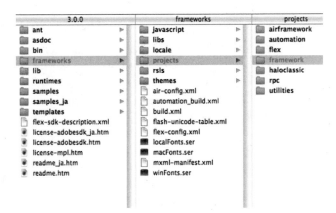

Figure 13.4   Flex SDK files.

Now, for FlexBuilder users, all you need to do is put your cursor on a class name or tag, such as Application, and press F3 (assuming you haven't changed key bindings), or right-click and choose Goto Definition from the context menu, as shown in Figure 13.5.

Figure 13.5   Choose Goto Definition.

Now you are in the Flex framework class! You can also use Ctrl (Windows) or Command (Mac)-Shift-T to open the Open Type dialog and start typing a framework class, as Figure 13.6 shows.

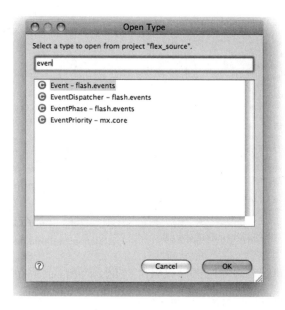

Figure 13.6   Just start typing a framework class.

It's great to be able to easily look inside Flex source classes to see how they work. There's one more interesting option you have, though, which is even more informative about how Flex works.

Generated Flex Source

The Flex compiler is the program you call from the command line or from Flex Builder that knows how to take MXML, ActionScript, and other assets, and compile them together into the bytecode that makes up an SWF file. But, during that compilation phase, a lot of things happen to the code you've written even before it's turned into bytecode. The compiler first creates some interim ActionScript out of all the MXML files you've made, and that's where we get to see the magic of things like binding become more clear. To see these files, just add the -keep option when you call the command line compiler. To do this in Flex Builder, go to the properties for your project, then the Flex Compiler section, and add the -keep option to Additional compiler arguments, as shown in Figure 13.7.

To see what happens when you do this, let's look at a small sample project that has only one MXML file:

```
<mx:Application xmlns:mx="http://www.adobe.com/2006/mxml" layout="absolute">
    <mx:Script>
    <![CDATA[
        [Bindable]
```

```
        private var theText:String = "Hello World!";
    ]]>
    </mx:Script>
    <mx:Text id="helloWorldText" text="{theText}" />
</mx:Application>
```

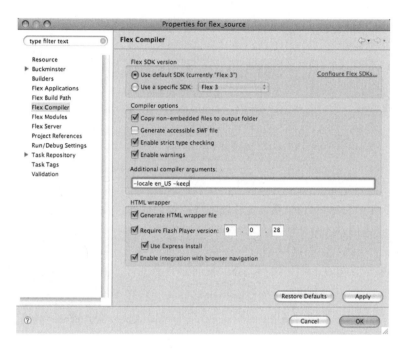

Figure 13.7   Add -keep to Additional compiler arguments.

Once the project is compiled again, all of a sudden there's a new directory called generated inside your source folder, looking something like Figure 13.8.

That's a lot of classes! There are 41 classes generated just to build that simple MXML application. One of the classes in that directory is called flex_source-generated.as, which corresponds to the name of the application file in this case, flex_source.mxml. The class isn't the simplest to read, but if you take the time, you'll see some interesting things. For instance, look at lines 70–84:

```
    //   Container document descriptor
private var _documentDescriptor_ : mx.core.UIComponentDescriptor =
new mx.core.UIComponentDescriptor({
  type: mx.core.Application

  propertiesFactory: function():Object { return {
    childDescriptors: [
      new mx.core.UIComponentDescriptor({
```

```
        type: mx.controls.Text
        ,
        id: "helloWorldText"
    })
  ]
 }}
})
```

Figure 13.8   The generated directory should look something like this.

Notice anything familiar? The the definition for the `<mx:Text>` tag that we had in the application is going into something called an `mx.core.UIComponentDescriptor`, which is going into an array in an object property called `childDescriptors`. This is how the Flex framework sees the MXML you write as a set of instructions for, creating ActionScript code that works with the framework.

The magic we're most interested in, though, is the binding. Simply putting the `Text` in the binding expression in the text property of `helloWorldText` was enough to tell Flex to generate all this:

```
//   binding mgmt
private function _flex_source_bindingsSetup():Array
{
    var result:Array = [];
    var binding:Binding;

    binding = new mx.binding.Binding(this,
        function():String
```

```
        {
            var result:* = (theText);
            var stringResult:String = (result == undefined ? null :
String(result));
            return stringResult;
        },
        function(_sourceFunctionReturnValue:String):void
        {

            helloWorldText.text = _sourceFunctionReturnValue;
        },
        "helloWorldText.text");
    result[0] = binding;

    return result;
}

private function _flex_source_bindingExprs():void
{
    var destination:*;
    [Binding(id='0')]
     destination = (theText);
}
```

This is what's actually doing the work of setting up something called an
mx.binding.Binding to watch for changes to that variable and make it update that
control. And now that you know where to find mx.binding.Binding, you know where
to look if you want to figure out what that class does.

Summary

One of the beauties of working with open source software is the capability to get into
the framework you're using and see what's really going on when you use some tools and
syntactic sugar that you may otherwise keep viewing as magic. There's also a great
opportunity to learn a lot by seeing how some of the problems addressed by the
framework are solved. Don't let that chance pass you up! Look at the source!

## 14

Using Observers to Clean Up Code

Goal

You'd like to decrease the dependency certain parts of your application have on other parts of it to keep things flexible and clean, especially when you need to take action in one part of your application when something in another part changes.

Solution

In Flex, use binding tags, `BindingUtils` and `ChangeWatchers`, to be notified when state changes occur in another part of the application.

In Rails, use the ActiveRecord lifecycle methods and observers to take action when certain events take place on your models.

BindingUtils and ChangeWatchers in Flex

As you've gone through this book and seen how powerful and useful Flex's binding syntax is for cleaning up your code, you may have noticed a few gaps in what it can do.

It's easy to say "keep the text in this text field updated when this variable changes."

```
[Bindable] public var sampleText:String;
...
<mx:Text text="{sampleText}" />
```

But what if you want to do the opposite? What if you want to keep the variable up to date when the text field changes? In many cases, you could use an event listener (with addEventListener) to listen for certain change type events, but then you have to write a function yourself to do the work.

To help keep your code simple, though, a few other options are available.

Figure 14.1 shows a simple blog tool example. It uses the Rich Text Editor component for the blog entry, and then keeps track of the Flash HTML formatting the text
editor defines. It also shows a word count and character count for the post.

Figure 14.1   A simple blog tool example.

The application code has a simple singleton model that holds both the raw text and
HTML text from the Rich Text Editor (see Listing 14.1).

Listing 14.1   **flex/model/BlogModel.as #8–9**

```
public var entryHTMLText:String;
public var entryRawText:String;
```

The Rich Text Editor exposes a change event, which we could use to trigger a function that updated the model, but instead, Flex's binding utilities can do that work for us.
Listing 14.2 shows the meat of the editor code.

Listing 14.2   **flex/src/view/Editor.mxml excerpt**

```
<mx:Script>
private var blogModel:BlogModel = BlogModel.getInstance();
</mx:Script>

<mx:Binding source="editor.text"
    destination="blogModel.entryRawText" />
```

Listing 14.2   *Continued*

```
<mx:Binding source="editor.htmlText"
    destination="blogModel.entryHTMLText" />


<mx:RichTextEditor id="editor" width="100%" height="100%" />
```

The Binding tag is a declarative way to set up a binding from one property to another. Now Flex will watch any changes to the HTMLText or text properties of the Rich Text Editor and change the model accordingly.

Listing 14.3 provides another way to do the same thing, but programmatically instead of declaratively:

Listing 14.3   **flex/src/view/Editor.mxml excerpt**

```
<mx:Script>
import mx.binding.utils.BindingUtils;
private function init():void {
    BindingUtils.bindProperty(blogModel, "entryRawText", editor, "text");
    BindingUtils.bindProperty(blogModel, "entryHTMLText", editor, "htmlText");
}
</mx:Script>


<mx:RichTextEditor id="editor" width="100%" height="100%" />
```

The BindingUtil.bindProperty method takes a destination object, a property chain, which could be a string or an array of strings that name nested properties on that object. It then takes a source object and another property chain to watch for changes. You get the same results: whenever the text or HTMLText property changes on the editor, the model will be changed.

Now, what about watching a property for a change and taking some action when a change occurs? What's actually doing the heavy lifting inside most of the Flex binding magic is something called a ChangeWatcher. Look at the code in Listing 14.4, which watches the model entryRawText property for any changes and updates the word and character counts.

Listing 14.4   **flex/src/view/Details.mxml excerpt**

```
private function init():void {
    var postingChangeWatcher:ChangeWatcher =
     ChangeWatcher.watch(blogModel, "entryRawText",
      calculateEntryText);
}


private function calculateEntryText(pce:PropertyChangeEvent):void {
    calculateWordCount(blogModel.entryRawText);
    calculateCharacterCount(blogModel.entryRawText);
}
```

When `init` is called, a change watcher is created using the static watch method on `ChangeWatcher`. This takes the same types of arguments that `BindingUtils.bindProperty` takes—a source object and property chain (string or array). The third argument is a callback function. Now whenever the `entryRawText` property of the `blogModel` changes, the `calculateEntryText` method will be called.

When that callback is called, it gets a `PropertyChangeEvent`, which contains information about what changed on which object and what the old value (if any) was. All we need to know to do in this case is to calculate the word count or character count.

Of course, all this magic isn't free, and you should clean up unneeded watchers. To do that, just call the `unwatch` method on the watcher object:

```
postingChangeWatcher.unwatch();
```

Taking Action on ActiveRecord Lifecycle Events

When Rails responds to a request, it's a fairly straightforward chain of events. Rails calls a controller action, which may take an action on a model, and then sends back some HTML, XML, or AMF if you're using RubyAMF. Wrangling together a lot of disparate pieces isn't necessary as far as your code is concerned.

One place where you may want to hook in and get callbacks on certain events is with ActiveRecord models.

Rails allows you to receive notification on what it calls lifecycle events and to register some methods to be run at those times. For instance, if you want to do a little work before validations are run on a model being created or updated, or if you want the chance to take action before a record is deleted, use a lifecycle callback.

As you may expect, registering for these callbacks is easy. Here's a model called BlogPost, where we want to do extra logging after a successful save is executed on any instance:

```
class BlogPost < ActiveRecord::Base

  def after_save
    log_save
  end

  def log_save
    logger.debug "Saving a blog post: #{self.inspect}"
  end

end
```

Simply defining a method with the lifecycle event name, `after_save` in this case, is enough for Rails to know to call that method at that point in the lifecycle.

Another way to do the same thing, in case you want to call more than one method, is to declare the callback instead of explicitly defining a method:

```
class BlogPost < ActiveRecord::Base

  after_save :log_save, :do_something_else_important

  def log_save
    logger.debug "Saving a blog post: #{self.inspect}"
  end

  def do_something_else_important
    #important code
  end

end
```

To give this a try, pull up the Rails console and type this at the prompt:

```
>> ActiveRecord::Base.logger = Logger.new(STDOUT)
```

That will redirect the logger to your console so you can watch log output. Then try creating a new BlogPost:

```
>> BlogPost.create
 <lots of sql here>
Saving a blog post: #<BlogPost id: 12, content: nil, created_at: "2008-06-08
00:28:35", updated_at: "2008-06-08 00:28:35">
```

You can see that your callback is called and running the logging method.

Now that you know about the callback methods, you'll notice that all these methods are implemented in the model, which may be good or bad depending on what you're trying to do. This is one of the benefits that observers provide—the capability to implement "cross-cutting concerns" somewhere that makes sense and doesn't pollute domain code or business logic with application-specific code, like logging for instance.

A BlogPost should know how to format itself or what its title is, but should it know about logging? Not necessarily, especially since logging is a cross-cutting concern or something that needs to be done to many things in your application no matter what they are.

That's where observers come in. Look at this class:

```
class BlogPostObserver < ActiveRecord::Observer
    def after_create(created_post)
    created_post.logger.debug "creating a new blog post
#{created_post.inspect}"
  end

end
```

Following the Rails naming convention, the BlogPostObserver class is an observer of BlogPosts and resides in the model's directory next to the blog post model. Generate an observer with the ./script/generate observer command from the command line, and it will place the observer in the directory. Once you generate an observer, you need to tell Rails in config/environment.rb to have it start observing, like this:

```
# file names of observer without.rb goes here
config.active_record.observers = :blog_post_observer
```

Any of the lifecycle methods you can define in a model can also be defined in an observer.

Models and observers don't need to have a one-to-one relationship either; you can put a line like this in an observer:

```
observe User, Blog, BlogPost
```

The observer will listen for callbacks on all those models.

Finally, let's take a look at all the lifecycle methods Rails defines. Table 14.1 presents the lifecycle methods by type of callback.

Table 14.1   **Lifecycle Methods Defined by Rails**

Find Callbacks	Create Callbacks	Update Callbacks	Destroy Callbacks
before_find	before_validation		before_destroy
after_find	after_validation		after_destroy
	before_save		
	after_save		
	before_validation_ on_create	before_validation_ on_update	
	after_validation_ on_create	after_validation_ on_update	
	before_create	before_update	
	after_create	after_update	

Summary

Using these methods of observing changes or events in one part of the application from another lets you find ways to clean up and better organize your code, or in some cases, do things you wouldn't have otherwise been able to do.

## 15

Authenticating

Goal

You need to build a system to restrict registered users' access to certain resources. In short, you need users to log in.

Solution

Use the `restful_authentication` Rails plug-in, with the default Rails cookie session storage, to make sure an authenticated user exists before allowing access to certain controllers.

Authenticating Users

Sooner or later, just about every web app needs to track users and restrict access to certain resources based on whether users are logged in or not. Luckily, a tried-and-true Rails plug-in called `restful_authentication` helps us with all those things with just a few commands and a bit of configuration.

Starting a few versions ago, the default session store for Rails became browser cookies, so anything stored in the session hash in Rails will be put in a cookie. What's good about that default for our needs is that since every request to Rails from Flash goes through the browser, cookies are sent along with every Flash request. All we need to do to log in is to set up the right cookies so Rails knows we're logged in, then we're off to the races. Accomplishing that involves nothing more than calling the same controller actions we would call if we weren't using Flex.

Installing restful_authentication

Rick Olson, one of the Rails core team members, wrote a plug-in called `acts_as_authenticated` in the early days of Rails. That plug-in was widely used for solving the authentication problem. When the Rails community, and then Rails itself, went more RESTful near the end of the version 1.x, Rick rewrote the plug-in to work well in a RESTful world and called it restful_authentication.

Install the plug-in by using the following command:

```
$ ./script/plugin install restful_authentication
```

Once installed, it should print some instructions, but here's the gist of what to do next. The plug-in introduces a few elements that you don't need to worry about elsewhere: a user, a user controller, and a controller to manage a user's session. If you already have any of these elements, let the plug-in generate them and then integrate your code into the plug-in-generated code.

What follows are instructions on how to install and configure the plug-in, but you can also see the working application in the example code for this cookbook recipe. The sample code uses RubyAMF, but the principles work the same as when the plug-in is used with Flex using XML.

To generate the code the way the plug-in wants it, run the following:

```
$ ./script/generate authenticated user sessions
      ...
      create  app/models/user.rb
      create  app/controllers/sessions_controller.rb
      create  app/controllers/users_controller.rb
      create  lib/authenticated_system.rb
      create  lib/authenticated_test_helper.rb
      create  test/functional/sessions_controller_test.rb
      create  test/functional/users_controller_test.rb
      create  test/unit/user_test.rb
      create  test/fixtures/users.yml
      create  app/helpers/sessions_helper.rb
      create  app/helpers/users_helper.rb
      create  app/views/sessions/new.html.erb
      create  app/views/users/new.html.erb
      create  db/migrate
      create  db/migrate/20080618025859_create_users.rb
       route  map.resource :session
       route  map.resources :users
```

If you read the readme text the plug-in generates after installation, you'll notice a few other options that are outside the scope of this book but that you might want to look into down the road. To find those instructions again, look at vendor/plugins/restful_authentication/README from the Rails root or find out more at http://github.com/technoweenie/restful_authentication.

Now you have a user model, UserController, and a SessionsController, the normal generated tests, views, and a migration. Run the migration next:

```
$ rake db:migrate
(in/Users/tony/work/flexonrails/trunk/topics/cookbook/authentication/rails)
== 20080616014553 CreateUsers: migrating
=======================================
-- create_table("users" , {:force=>true}) -> 0.0177s
== 20080616014553 CreateUsers: migrated (0.0178s)
=============================
```

The user controller is a standard controller; not too much interesting there, so make any necessary changes. Let's look at SessionsController.rb though, because that's where we'll be doing our work.

First thing, on lines three and four, you'll see this code:

```
# Be sure to include AuthenticationSystem in Application Controller instead
include AuthenticatedSystem
```

That code mixes in the AuthenticatedSystem module with this controller, which adds the authentication logic code as callable methods. Follow the instructions in the comment, and move that include statement to the ApplicationController (application.rb). You'll find the same code in users_controller.rb, too—if you already moved it to the ApplicationController you can delete it from the UsersController. Since all controllers extend ApplicationController, they all have the added functionality.

Now let's study the meat of the code in the SessionsController (See Listing 15.1). Remember that this code is modified slightly to work with RubyAMF, but everything except the render code is the same as the plug-in-generated code. Compare it against the generated code if you're unsure of anything.

Listing 15.1   **rails/app/controllers/sessions_controller.rb #9–19**

```
def create
  self.current_user = User.authenticate(params[:login], params[:password])
  if logged_in?
    if params[:remember_me] == "1" self.current_user.remember_me
      cookies[:auth_token] = {
            :value => self.current_user.remember_token,
            :expires => self.current_user.remember_token_expires_at }
    end
    flash[:notice] = "Logged in successfully"
    success = true
  else
    success = false
  end
# ...
```

In the create method of the SessionsController, you'll see two things right away that were added to the controller by the AuthenticatedSystem module: `current_user` and a `logged_in?` method. The `current_user` property is always available to controllers that include that module, which lets any controller get access to the user currently logged in. The `logged_in?` method, of course, checks to see that a current user is logged in successfully.

User now supports a method called authenticate, which takes a login and a password and returns a user if those keys are valid. Also, the plug-in will track whether the user wants to be remembered for a time period, which is how long to keep the user logged in.

That's the code to create a session, or in other words, to log in a user. Listing 15.2 presents deleting a session, or logging out.

Listing 15.2   **rails/app/controllers/sessions_controller.rb #41–54**

```
def destroy
  self.current_user.forget_me if logged_in?
  cookies.delete :auth_token
  reset_session
  flash[:notice] = "You have been logged out."

  respond_to do |format|
    format.html do
      redirect_back_or_default('/')
    end
    format.amf { render :amf => nil }
  end

end
```

It "forgets" the user, or gets rid of remembered authentication information, and then removes the authentication token from the cookies and resets the session, which is a Rails method. We've again modified this code slightly to work with RubyAMF, so it returns nil if we're calling from Flex.

Pretty straightforward. Let's look at the Flex side. First, we have a simple `User` object to match the RubyAMF-returned version of the Rails `User` object. If you were using XML instead, you may have something similar that knew how to decode itself from XML.

```
package vo {
    [Bindable]
    [RemoteClass(alias="User")]
    public class User {
        public var login:String;
        public var email:String;
    }
}
```

Next we're going to have a simple application with two states that represent the logged in and logged out states, shown in Figures 15.1 and 15.2.

Figure 15.1   Logged out state.

Figure 15.2   Logged in state.

We also have a button, labeled Test Authenticated Service Call, that makes a simple call to another Rails controller, called `TestServiceController`, to see if we're logged in or not. Here's that code:

```
class TestServiceController < ApplicationController
  before_filter :login_required
  def test
    respond_to do |format|
      format.amf { render :amf => true }
    end
  end
end
```

The magic happens in before_filter, which calls the login_required method mixed in by the AuthenticatedSystem module in ApplicationController. That returns false and breaks the chain of execution if the user isn't logged in, which comes back to the Flex request as a false. A little simplistic, and you may need more complex logic for more complex cases, but for now, that should work for most cases.

Back to Flex, in authentication_example.mxml. Since we're using RubyAMF, we have two RemoteObject tags:

```
    <mx:RemoteObject id="sessionService" destination="rubyamf"
source="SessionsController"
endpoint="http://localhost:3000/rubyamf_gateway" result="loginResult(event)"
fault="loginFault(event)" />
    <mx:RemoteObject id="testService" destination="rubyamf"
source="TestServiceController"
endpoint="http://localhost:3000/rubyamf_gateway" result="testResult(event)"
fault="testFault(event)" />
```

Each service has one remote object. If you run the example code, try clicking the test service button first to verify that you can't call the authenticated service. Here's the code for that:

```
private function testResult(re:ResultEvent):void {
    var success:Boolean = re.result as Boolean;
    if (success) {
        Alert.show("Authenticated Test Call Successful!");
    } else {
        Alert.show("Authenticated Test Call Failed!");
    }
}
```

Then try to log in with the username of quentin and a password of test. That simply calls the create method on the session controller:

```
private function login():void {
    sessionService.create({login:usernameText.text,
password:passwordText.text});
    usernameText.text = passwordText.text = '';
}
```

If you snuck ahead and loaded the test fixtures into the development database with the following, then that may have worked for you.

```
$ rake db:fixtures:load
```

If not, then you got to see an example of a login failure, which in our controller modified for RubyAMF just returns a FaultObject to call the fault callback of the session controller remote object, which is:

```
private function loginFault(fe:FaultEvent):void {
    Alert.show(fe.fault.message);
}
```

To actually log in, you could create a new user from the console or load the test fixtures and log in as quentin/test. See the screen in Figure 15.2. The button to call the test service should also return a successful result.

Logging out works just as simply; it calls the `destroy` method on the sessions controller, and that clears the cookie. Try the test service call again; it should fail.

```
private function logout():void {
    sessionService.destroy();
}
```

Summary

Using the `restful_authentication` plug-in makes it easy to get going quickly with any kind of authentication you need through the browser. No matter whether you're calling the service from HTML or Flex using XML or AMF, if the call goes through the browser, then logging in is out of the way.

## 16

Reusing Commands with Prana Sequences

Goal

You're using Cairngorm, and you want to describe sequences of events that take place on certain user actions. These sequences of events involve different commands that you'd like to keep separate from each other, so that each remains reusable in the maximum number of scenarios.

Solution

Use Prana (http://pranaframework.org) and its EventSequence class to describe a sequence of CairngormEvents, the properties of which, when changed, should trigger them.

Sequences

Keep your Cairngorm commands reusable by keeping them from knowing too much about other commands. Commands should be as atomic as possible; to use a time-honored phrase, they should do one thing and do it well. If you have a command that deals with logging in a user, it shouldn't also have to deal with loading other data, like unread messages or products, the user wants after logging in.

That's not to say your commands should avoid working with large sets of data or doing a lot of heavy lifting; the important point is that your commands should be *focused*.

One technique to use to enforce this kind of focus is to think about the task you want to accomplish and name your command very specifically to reflect that task. For instance, naming a command GetCurrentStockPrice seems like you know clearly what this one important step in the application is supposed to do. LoginAndShowCurrentSpecials indicates you're thinking about what you want the application to do, but in one big chunk rather than discrete steps.

One of the things that often gets in the way when trying to keep commands atomic is dealing with events that clearly need to follow a sequence. When a user checks out, you need to create the order, empty the shopping cart, and show the order statement. Even if you're disciplined and keep those three tasks in three separate commands, the easiest thing to do is to have the `CheckOutCommand` dispatch `EmptyShoppingCartEvent` on result, and have `EmptyShoppingCartCommand` dispatch `ShowOrderStatementEvent` after it's done with its execute method.

That may be the way things work most of the time, but now that you have those commands tied so tightly together, you can't fit `EmptyShoppingCartEvent` into the event flow for canceling an order, even though one of the steps for canceling an order is to empty the shopping cart. That's a recipe for duplicating logic.

A better alternative would be if we had another way to knit a few event/command combinations into a sequence, and that's what we have with Prana's EventSequence. If you read the recipe in Chapter 19, Runtime Flex Configuration with Prana, you'll be familiar with Prana and how it works as an Inversion of Control container for Flex. Prana also ships with some helper classes for Cairngorm. Think of EventSequences as meta-events, or events that describe events.

Instead of the list of events and commands described above, you may have a `CheckoutSequence` sequence, which lists `CreateOrderEvent`, `EmptyShoppingCartEvent`, and `ShowOrderStatementEvent` as the events that need to happen in that specific sequence.

Order is important since the command calls a sequence of events. If you have few events that need to happen all at once, triggered by a single user gesture, it's fine to have a separate command that kicks off those events, since that's very clearly that command's job. The problem comes when you have commands that know about their own jobs *and* the next event that needs to take place.

How does an EventSequence work? First, you add a list of events into it, probably in the constructor, and when the user gesture takes place, you dispatch the EventSequence, just like a regular CairngormEvent. Here's a look at the `addSequenceEvent` statement, which places an event into a sequence:

```
addSequenceEvent(eventClass:Class, parameters:Array=null, triggers:Array=null)
```

For each event you put into place in the sequence of an EventSequence, you need to know the name of the class and two more things: (1) what are the arguments to the CairngormEvent? and (2) what are the properties that the preceding commands will change to let the EventSequence know it's time to dispatch the event?

Let's set aside the trigger for the moment. The parameters the event needs on construction are clear enough, right? One problem, though, is what happens when an event takes a constructor argument that's not yet available because the command that precedes it in the sequence is responsible for setting that variable? For instance, if you have two events, `LoginEvent` and `GetMessagesForUserEvent`, the login event is probably the one getting the user set up. If both events are added to the sequence at the same time, we need some way to **lazily load** the user, meaning define the fact that we want to use the user property from somewhere, but defer looking that property up until later.

Prana gives us that with a class called `Property`. A `Property` defines an object and a chain of properties on that object that point down to a specific property. With that definition in hand, the EventSequence can choose to look up the value of a property at any time, even if the `Property` class was defined before the variable was set.

Triggers, the third argument to the `addSequenceEvent` method, are an array of `Property` objects that point to variables the EventSequence should watch for change to know when to dispatch a certain event. Again, if we had `LoginEvent` and `GetMessagesForUserEvent`, we may have a user property on the model that `LoginEvent` will set to be the newly authenticated user object. That's as good a trigger as any to tell the next event, `GetMessagesForUserEvent` to dispatch, so we can define that property as a trigger property and Prana will watch it, and when it changes, it will dispatch the next event. Now let's look at some code.

Prana's EventSequence

The example application for this topic is a very simple online notes application. Once a user logs in, the next task is to get all the notes for that user. We're using Cairngorm on the Flex side and RubyAMF with the `restful_authentication` plugin on the Rails side. To learn more about authenticating with Flex using the `restful_authentication` plugin, read the cookbook recipe in Chapter 15, Authenticating.

The Rails side is made up of a simple `NotesController` generated by RubyAMF's scaffold and then set to require a login. The `find_all` action returns all notes for the current user. The code is presented in Listing 16.1.

Listing 16.1   **rails/app/controllers/notes_controller.rb #1–10**

```
class NotesController < ApplicationController

  before_filter :login_required

  # return all Notes
  def find_all
    respond_to do |format|
      format.amf  { render :amf => self.current_user.notes }
    end
  end
```

The sequence is to authenticate with a username and password supplied by the user, and if the authentication works, return a user object and put that on the model. After putting the user object on the model, we need to get the user's notes, so we send a request to the notes controller to get all notes for the authenticated user.

Of course, there are many ways to skin this cat. We could send the notes back with the authenticated user, for instance, which would require fewer requests to the server. But, let's just keep things this way so we can look at what Prana does for us.

Listing 16.2 shows the model where things are stored.

Listing 16.2   **flex/src/com/flexonrails/pranaSequences/model/ModelLocator.as #9–20**

```
[Bindable]
public final class ModelLocator {

    public static const LOGGED_OUT:int  = 0;
    public static const LOGGED_IN:int    = 1;

    // bindable state
    public var appState:int = LOGGED_OUT;

    // application state
    public var user:User;
    public var selectedNote:Note;
```

The model is bindable, of course, and we use an `appState` variable to bind a ViewStack on the application to the child that corresponds to the `LOGGED_OUT` or `LOGGED_IN` constants defined on the model, which is a common Cairngorm pattern. Then there are two variables: the user and the selected note.

`LoginEvent` and `LoginCommand` are responsible for taking the user-supplied username and password, sending these to the SessionController on the back end for authentication, and, if successful, putting the returned user on the model and changing the model's state to the logged-in state so the view moves away from the login screen (see Listing 16.3 and Listing 16.4).

Listing 16.3   **flex/src/com/flexonrails/pranaSequences/events/LoginEvent.as #15–36**

```
public class LoginEvent extends CairngormEvent {

    public static const Login_Event:String = "(LoginEvent)";
    public var username:String;
    public var password:String;

    public function LoginEvent(username:String, password:String) {
        super(Login_Event);
        this.username = username;
        this.password = password;
    }
}
```

Listing 16.4   **flex/src/com/flexonrails/pranaSequences/commands/LoginCommand.as**
                #15-36

```
public class LoginCommand implements ICommand, IResponder {

    private var model:ModelLocator = ModelLocator.getInstance();

    public function execute(event:CairngormEvent):void {
        var evt:LoginEvent = event as LoginEvent;
        var delegate:SessionDelegate = new SessionDelegate(this);
        delegate.login(evt.username, evt.password);
    }

    public function result(data:Object):void {
        var result:ResultEvent = data as ResultEvent;
        var user:User = result.result as User;
        model.user = user;
        model.appState = ModelLocator.LOGGED_IN;
    }

    public function fault(info:Object):void {
        var fault:FaultEvent = info as FaultEvent;
        Alert.show(fault.fault.message, "Error Logging In");
    }
}
```

Next, `LoadUserNotesEvent` and `LoadUserNotesCommand` need to get the notes for the current user from the NotesController on the Rails side (see Listing 16.5).

Listing 16.5   **flex/src/com/flexonrails/pranaSequences/commands/LoadUserNotes**
                Comand.as #16-37

```
public class LoadUserNotesCommand implements ICommand, IResponder {

    private var model:ModelLocator = ModelLocator.getInstance();

    public function execute(event:CairngormEvent):void {
        var evt:LoadUserNotesEvent = event as LoadUserNotesEvent;
        var delegate:NotesDelegate = new NotesDelegate(this);
        delegate.findAllForCurrentUser();
    }
    public function result(data:Object):void {
        var result:ResultEvent = data as ResultEvent;
        var notes:ArrayCollection = result.result as ArrayCollection;
        model.user.notes = notes;
    }
```

Listing 16.5 *Continued*

```
    public function fault(info:Object):void {
        var fault:FaultEvent = info as FaultEvent;
        Alert.show(fault.fault.message, "Error Loading Notes");
    }

}
```

Now, since both of these tasks need to happen, we could either have `LoginCommand` kick off `LoadUserNotesEvent` or have something else control dispatching both events in sequence. In the discussion above, we talked about the problems with tying the sequences together, so now let's look at Prana's solution to the problem, `LoginSequence`, as shown in Listing 16.6.

Listing 16.6 **flex/src/com/flexonrails/pranaSequences/sequences/LoginSequence.as #9–21**

```
public class LoginSequence extends EventSequence {

    private var model:ModelLocator = ModelLocator.getInstance();

    public function LoginSequence(username:String, password:String) {
        super();

        addSequenceEvent(LoginEvent, [username, password]);
        addSequenceEvent(LoadUserNotesEvent,
            null,
            [new Property(model, "user")]);

    }

}
```

Now `LoginSequence`, instead of `LoginEvent`, takes the username and password. Then two events are added to the sequence: `LoginEvent` and `LoadUserNotesEvent`.

```
addSequenceEvent(LoginEvent, [username, password]);
```

`LoginEvent` is the first event added to the sequence, so it will be the first event dispatched when the sequence is dispatched. That means we don't need a trigger property, so the third argument to `addSequenceEvent` is left to be the default null. We do need to get the username and password arguments to `LoginEvent`, however, so those are placed in an array and passed to the method and stored to be passed into the event when it's constructed and dispatched.

```
addSequenceEvent(LoadUserNotesEvent,
    null,
    [new Property(model, "user")]);
```

LoadUserNotesEvent doesn't take any arguments, so null goes to that argument because we do need to specify a trigger property. When LoginCommand is complete, it sets the model.user property to be the newly authenticated user, and that will be the indication that Prana should call dispatch on LoaduserNotesEvent.

Why do we need to use the Property object again? Well, if you were to debug the application and look at the model.user property when the addSequenceEvent method is being called, you'd see that it was null. Once again, the Property object points to a property or chain of properties on another object, in this case the model, that Prana can look back to and evaluate when it's needed. We need this option in the trigger argument because we want to tell Prana to watch that property chain for changes. As it so happens, the way a Property object is set up, it contains exactly the same type of arguments, an object and a single string or array of strings as a chain of properties to watch, that a ChangeWatcher contains, and that's exactly what Prana uses to watch the trigger property.

It's worth noting that you can use a Property object for the second argument to the addSequenceEvent method too, in case the argument you need to pass to the corresponding event needs to be evaluated at dispatch time.

Summary

Now you know a great way to build sequences of events using Prana and to help keep commands from knowing too much about the rest of the application. Once again, there's more to Prana than just this ability, so check out the cookbook recipe in Chapter 19 or at http://pranaframework.org.

## 17

Hierarchical Data with RubyAMF

Goal

You want to get some structured, hierarchical data from Rails to Flex using RubyAMF.

Solution

Use a nested set Rails plug-in, such as `awesome_nested_set` (http://github.com/collectiveidea/awesome_nested_set), and RubyAMF's method class mapping option to return an object graph to Flex with one call.

Nested Sets

Rails has a few options for storing hierarchical data, and one of them is called "Awesome Nested Set," which is, you must admit, an awesome name. A Nested Set is a way to store data that maps into a hierarchical, tree-like structure in a database table, which does not natively support hierarchical relationships.

Basically, the idea is to store information about sets that contain other sets. To do that in SQL, you could have a column on a parent that stores the "left boundary" and one that stores the "right boundary," each as numbers. If you selected all the rows where the left and right boundary column are both between the parent node's left and right boundary columns, then you'd have a list of children for a given node. When adding a child anywhere in the tree, you'd need to traverse up all the parent records and fix the sizing of the left and right boundaries, but that's pretty much all you'd need to do to easily and quickly select hierarchical data from a flat database table. Of course, this is a bit of a glossing-over, and you can read more at www.dbmsmag.com/9603d06.html.

Luckily, this work is done for you by the `awesome_nested_set` Rails plug-in. All you need to do is generate your nested set models with a left and right boundary column.

The example code for this recipe is a fairly simple example that just stores a textual outline that could be an outline for a paper or a presentation. We're merely interested in bringing this data back to Flex from Rails using RubyAMF and putting it in Flex's tree control. We'll call the class of the object in the tree an `OutlinePoint`.

First, install the RubyAMF and Awesome Nested Set plug-ins:

```
$ ruby script/plugin install
git://github.com/collectiveidea/awesome_nested_set.git


$ ruby script/plugin install
http://rubyamf.googlecode.com/svn/tags/current/rubyamf
```

Then you generate a RubyAMF scaffold for the outline point model:

```
$ script/generate rubyamf_scaffold outline_point label:string lft:integer
rgt:integer parent_id:integer
```

Next you do the migration:

```
$ rake db:migrate
```

We used some weird column names for the left and right boundary columns, `lft` and `rgt`. We can't use "left" or "right" because those are reserved keywords in most databases, so Awesome Nested Set uses the abbreviated forms you see there. You can redefine the column names, but since you won't often be referring to these columns, you may as well leave these defaults. Convention over configuration, right?

Now, inside the `OutlinePoint` class we need to do a little set up:

```
class OutlinePoint < ActiveRecord::Base
  belongs_to :parent, :class_name => "OutlinePoint"
  acts_as_nested_set
end
```

The `acts_as_nested_set` macro registers the class as a nested set and adds lots of convenient methods, some of which we'll see later.

The plug-in adds a parent method, which finds the parent of an object by using the awesome_nested_set api, in case the conventional `parent_id` wasn't used for the parent ID column. If you did use `parent_id`, you may as well define the relationship using `belongs_to` and `class_name` to let Rails know what kind of class it is, which is more Rails-like.

Awesome Nested Set can store many trees in one table. Each root node contains all the child nodes by having the lowest left boundary and the highest right boundary of all nodes from that tree, regardless of depth. If any node falls outside the left or right boundaries of a node, it is no longer a child of that node. Therefore, if a node is outside the boundaries of a root node, it must belong to another tree. In that way, the root records all provide a starting place for a tree. To find the roots, you'd look for any records where `parent_id` was null. Or, Awesome Nested Set provides a helper method called `roots` you can use on any class defined with acts_as_nested_set:

```
>> OutlinePoint.roots
=> [#<OutlinePoint id: 1, label: "An Outline", lft: 1, rgt: 24, parent_id: nil,
created_at: "2008-06-22 22:40:24", updated_at: "2008-06-22 22:40:24">]
```

One method added by the AwesomeNestedSet plug-in is the `children` method:

```
>> root = OutlinePoint.roots.first
 => #<OutlinePoint id: 1, label: "An Outline", lft: 1, rgt: 24, parent_id: nil,
created_at: "2008-06-22 22:40:24", updated_at: "2008-06-22 22:40:24">
>> root.children
 => [#<OutlinePoint id: 4, label: "3", lft: 2, rgt: 19, parent_id: 1, created_at:
"2008-06-22 22:48:09", updated_at: "2008-06-22 22:48:09">, #<OutlinePoint id: 3,
label: "2", lft: 20, rgt: 21, parent_id: 1, created_at: "2008-06-22 22:47:50",
updated_at: "2008-06-22 22:47:50">, #<OutlinePoint id: 2, label: "1", lft: 22,
rgt: 23, parent_id: 1, created_at: "2008-06-22 22:45:52", updated_at: "2008-06-22
22:45:52">]
```

That method returns an array of that node's immediate children.

Next, let's look at the controller. OutlinePointsController is a standard RubyAMF-generated controller, but as shown in Listing 17.1, we've added one action to get the root (not very flexible since it finds the first root only, but it's good enough to get started).

Listing 17.1   **rails/app/controllers/OutlinePointsController.rb #3–7**

```
def find_root
  respond_to do |format|
    format.amf { render :amf => OutlinePoint.roots.first }
  end
end
```

And the RubyAMF configuration:

rails/config/rubyamf_config.rb #9-16
```
ClassMappings.register(
  :actionscript  => 'OutlinePoint',
  :ruby          => 'OutlinePoint',
  :type          => 'active_record',
  :associations  => ["parent"],
  :attributes    => ["id", "label", "created_at", "updated_at"],
  :methods       => ["children"]
 )
```

This means that we're going to use the methods option of RubyAMF to load children for an OutlinePoint every time we see one. Since the controller starts by rendering the root, the root's children will be rendered into the AMF, and the children's children, and so on down the line.

Listing 17.2 presents the ActionScript class that will be constructed on the Flex side.

Listing 17.2   **flex/src/com/flexonrails/outliner/vo**

```
package com.flexonrails.outliner.vo {

    import mx.collections.ArrayCollection;

    [Bindable]
    [RemoteClass(alias="OutlinePoint")]
    public class OutlinePoint {

        public var id:Number;
        public var label:String;
        public var parent:OutlinePoint;
        public var createdAt:Date;
        public var updatedAt:Date;

        public var children:ArrayCollection;

    }
}
```

This simple application uses Cairngorm. For more information on Cairngorm, see Chapter 8, Flex MVC Frameworks. Listing 17.3 presents the command that does the loading.

Listing 17.3   **flex/src/com/flexonrails/outliner/commands/**
LoadOutlinePointsCommand.as #16–37

```
public class LoadOutlinePointsCommand
    implements ICommand, IResponder {

    private var model:ModelLocator = ModelLocator.getInstance();

    public function execute(event:CairngormEvent):void {
        var evt:LoadOutlinePointsEvent = event
                as LoadOutlinePointsEvent;
        var delegate:OutlinePointsDelegate =
                new OutlinePointsDelegate(this);
        delegate.findRootOutlinePoint();
    }

    public function result(data:Object):void {
        var result:ResultEvent = data as ResultEvent;
        var rootPoint:OutlinePoint = result.result as OutlinePoint;
        model.outlinePoints = new ArrayCollection([rootPoint]);
    }
```

Listing 17.3   *Continued*

```
public function fault(info:Object):void {
    var fault:FaultEvent = info as FaultEvent;
    Alert.show(fault.fault.message, "Error Loading Notes");
}

}
```

So, when the root is returned, it's simply set into an `ArrayCollection`, since the Flex tree prefers that if it is not displaying XML.

Let's have a look at the object graph we get back when the call returns (see Figure 17.1).

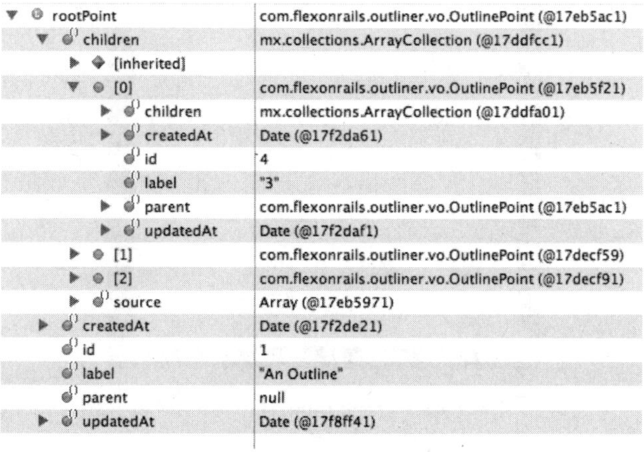

Figure 17.1   The object graph returned, as seen from the Flex Debugger.

There's the root, and there's the children array collection with three `OutlinePoint` children, each with children, and so on.

The Flex tree control only needs to bind to that property on the model (see Listing 17.4).

Listing 17.4   **flex/src/com/flexonrails/outliner/hierachical_data_w_rubyamf #40–47**

```
<mx:Tree id="outlineTree"
    width="300"
    height="500"
    verticalCenter="0"
    horizontalCenter="0"
    dataProvider="{model.outlinePoints}"
    dataDescriptor="{new OutlinePointTreeDataDescriptor()}"
/>
```

Now it's ready to display the object graph, shown in Figure 17.2.

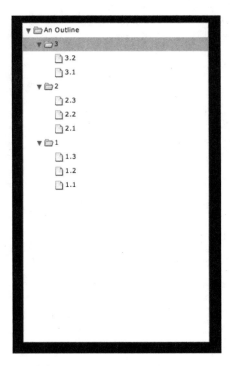

Figure 17.2   The object graph returned from the Flex tree control.

You'll notice that the tree also defines a `dataDescriptor`. What's that? Flex's tree is
pretty well prepared to take data in the way we've described it and display it with few, if
any, issues. One thing you may notice is that it gets a little confusing with the branch
nodes and leaf nodes, or the nodes that have children compared to those that don't. The
data descriptor helps sort out things like that. Listing 17.5 shows the data descriptor for
our example.

Listing 17.5   **flex/src/com/flexonrails/outliner/model/**
                OutlinePointTreeDataDescriptor.as #9–25

```
public class OutlinePointTreeDataDescriptor
                        extends DefaultDataDescriptor {

    override public function hasChildren(
            node:Object, model:Object=null):Boolean {
        var point:OutlinePoint = node as OutlinePoint;
        return (point.children && point.children.length > 0);
    }
```

Listing 17.5   *Continued*

```
    override public function isBranch(node:Object,
                    collection:Object=null):Boolean {
        return hasChildren(node);
    }

    override public function getChildren(node:Object,
                    model:Object=null):ICollectionView {
        var point:OutlinePoint = node as OutlinePoint;
        return point.children;
    }

}
```

Note that it extends a `DefaultDataDescriptor`, which is what the tree uses by default. All we're doing here is providing some hints about whether a node has children or not, based on whether the child ArrayCollection is empty.

Summary

There you have the starting point for working with hierarchical data in Flex sent from Rails and RubyAMF, using the power of Awesome Nested Set.

## 18

Advanced DataGrid and Awesome Nested Set

Goal

You want to read and manipulate structured, hierarchical data exposed by a RESTful Rails application using the Flex Advanced DataGrid component.

Solution

Expose the nested set as a RESTful resource providing the `create`, `update`, and `delete` verbs, as well as a custom `move` verb, to support manipulating hierarchical data from the Flex application using the standard HTTPService component.

Overview

Flex Builder Professional provides the advanced data grid component, which can display hierarchical data and provides advanced features, such a multicolumn sorting, data grouping, and summaries. Rails supports nested sets, which can easily be displayed and manipulated with the advanced data grid. Awesome Nested Set is a Rails plug-in that enables you to easily create and manipulate hierarchical data, such as categories of items that are sold on an auction site. To show you some capabilities of the Flex Advanced DataGrid, we will create a simple Rails application that will use the Awesome Nested Set plug-in and create a Flex application that will use the Advanced DataGrid to display this data.

Create the Rails Application and Database

As usual, a few simple steps are followed to create a working Rails application. First, install the plug-in before using the application.

```
$ rails rails; cd rails
$ ./script/plugin install
git://github.com/collectiveidea/awesome_nested_set.git
```

We are adding the categories table, which will keep track of a hierarchy of items and simply list the number of items in that category. So, let's just generate a migration:

```
$ ./script/generate migration AddCategories
```

Next we define the categories table (see Listing 18.1).

Listing 18.1   **db/migrate/20080818142019_add_categories.rb**

```
class AddCategories < ActiveRecord::Migration
  def self.up
    create_table :table do |t|
      t.string   :name
      t.text     :description
      t.integer :parent_id, :lft, :rgt, :qty_in_stock
      t.timestamps
    end
  end

  def self.down
    drop_table :categories
  end
end
```

Note that the `parent_id`, `lft`, and `rgt` columns are required for the nested set. Now we can create the Category active record that acts as a nested set. This will provide additional functionality to our active record. Now we can manipulate a hierarchy of categories. The nested set also provides the `children` method to find all the children of a Category. Also, categories can be moved in the hierarchy using the `move_to_child_of`, `move_to_right_of`, and `move_to_left_of` methods.

```
app/models/category.rb
  class Category < ActiveRecord::Base
    acts_as_nested_set
end
```

Creating a Script to Load the Data

Since we don't have a user interface yet, we can just write a Rails script to load some test data (see Listing 18.2). We use the `move_to_child_of` method to assemble the hierarchy of categories.

Listing 18.2   **db/load_categories.rb**

```ruby
Category.transaction do
  root = Category.create(:name => "Main Category")

  cameras = Category.create(:name => "Cameras & Photo")
  cameras.move_to_child_of(root)
  Category.create(:name => "Bags",
                  :qty_in_stock => 2).move_to_child_of(cameras)
  Category.create(:name => "Accessories",
                  :qty_in_stock => 12).move_to_child_of(cameras)
  Category.create(:name => "Analog Cameras",
                  :qty_in_stock => 0).move_to_child_of(cameras)
  Category.create(:name => "Digital Cameras",
                  :qty_in_stock => 5).move_to_child_of(cameras)

  phones = Category.create(:name => "Cell Phones")
  phones.move_to_child_of(root)
  Category.create(:name => "Accessories",
                  :qty_in_stock => 8).move_to_child_of(phones)
  Category.create(:name => "Phones",
                  :qty_in_stock => 20).move_to_child_of(phones)
  Category.create(:name => "Prepaid Cards",
                  :qty_in_stock => 3).move_to_child_of(phones)

  dvds = Category.create(:name => "Dvds")
  dvds.move_to_child_of(root)
  Category.create(:name => "Blueray",
                  :qty_in_stock => 10).move_to_child_of(dvds)
  Category.create(:name => "HD DVD",
                  :qty_in_stock => 0).move_to_child_of(dvds)
  Category.create(:name => "DVD",
                  :qty_in_stock => 100).move_to_child_of(dvds)

end
```

Use `script/runner` to run the script and preload the hierarchy we will use from Flex.

```
$ ./script/runner db/load_categories.rb
```

We also need a method that returns the whole nested set in XML format. So, let's implement a method named `full_xml` that recursively builds the XML. The default Rails implementation of the `to_xml` method does allow you to specify associations to include in the XML using the `:include` option, but this method isn't recursive and doesn't return the full tree of categories. Additionally, we want the XML formatted using attributes such as `<category name="Dvds" qty_in_stock="" id="11">` and not nested XML nodes, because attributes will map to the advanced data set more easily.

Luckily, creating XML using the `Builder::XMLMarkup` class provided by Rails is pretty easy. Let's look at our new method:

```
class Category < ActiveRecord::Base
  acts_as_nested_set
  def full_xml(builder=nil)
    xml = builder ||= Builder::XmlMarkup.new(:indent => 2)
    xml.category(:id => id,
                 :name => name,
                 :description => description,
                 :qty_in_stock => qty_in_stock) do
      children.each { |child| child.full_xml(xml) }
    end
  end
end
```

First we create an instance of the `XmlMarkup` class, which we pass down recursively to all the children of the category. We then specify the `id`, `name`, and `qty_in_stock` to be used as attributes to a node named "category." The category node will contain the nodes of all its children. Let's now invoke this method on our root category.

```
Category.root.full_xml
```

It returns this XML:

```
<category name="Main Category" qty_in_stock="" id="1">
  <category name="Dvds" qty_in_stock="" id="11">
    <category name="DVD" qty_in_stock="100" id="14">
    </category>
    <category name="HD DVD" qty_in_stock="0" id="13">
    </category>
    <category name="Blueray" qty_in_stock="10" id="12">
    </category>
  </category>

  <category name="Cell Phones" qty_in_stock="" id="7">
    <category name="Prepaid Cards" qty_in_stock="3" id="10">
    </category>
    <category name="Phones" qty_in_stock="20" id="9">
    </category>
    <category name="Accessories" qty_in_stock="8" id="8">
    </category>
  </category>
  <category name="Cameras &amp; Photo" qty_in_stock="" id="2">

    <category name="Digital Cameras" qty_in_stock="5" id="6">
    </category>
    <category name="Analog Cameras" qty_in_stock="0" id="5">
```

```
    </category>
    <category name="Accessories" qty_in_stock="12" id="4">
    </category>
    <category name="Bags" qty_in_stock="2" id="3">
    </category>
  </category>
</category>
```

Let's create the Rails `CategoriesController` to serve this XML. Take a look at Listing 18.3.

Listing 18.3   **app/controllers/categories_controller.rb**

```
class CategoriesController < ApplicationController
  def index
    render :xml => Category.root.full_xml
  end
end
```

And, of course, we need to define the new resource in the routes configuration file, config/routes.rb.

```
    map.resources :categories
```

Flex Application

Now that we have a Rails server that can return a hierarchy of categories, we will create a Flex application to display and manipulate the categories. So let's go ahead and build the application step by step.

Create an empty Flex application and add the following `HTTPService` component used to query the categories.

```
<mx:HTTPService id="categories" url="http://localhost:3000/categories"
 resultFormat="e4x" />
```

We will invoke this server when the application is starting by adding the `applicationComplete` event listener and invoking the `send` method of the categories service.

```
<mx:Application xmlns:mx="http://www.adobe.com/2006/mxml" layout="horizontal"
        applicationComplete="categories.send()">
```

We are using the horizontal layout, because we will create three ways to display the data returned by the server just to show different usages. First, we are going to use a tree view, which can be used to show hierarchical data. Then we will use the `AdvancedDataGrid`, since this component provides some really useful features to show hierarchical data that go beyond what the tree component supports. And, just to get a better feel for the data returned by the server, we are going to display the XML in a text area component.

First let's add the tree:

```
<mx:Tree dataProvider="{categories.lastResult}"
    labelField="@name"
    width="33%" height="100%" />
```

As you know, the HTTPService component has a lastResult attribute that provides a convenient way to bind directly visual component to the data returned by the service. In our case, we want to display the @name attribute of each of the elements in the hierarchical data returned. The tree looks like what is shown in Figure 18.1.

Figure 18.1   The resulting tree.

To give yourself a good idea of the data returned by the server, add the following TextArea tag to display the resulting XML:

```
<mx:TextArea width="33%" height="100%"
text="{categories.lastResult.toXMLString()}" />
```

To display hierarchical data in the AdvancedDataGrid, the Flex framework provides the mx.collections.HierarchicalData class, which allows a consistent way to navigate hierarchical data whether it is an object hierarchy or XML data. So, we are creating the following function that creates a HierarchicalData instance from the XML the server provides. As you can see, we don't do any manipulation because the HierarchicalData instance just wraps our XML.

```
<mx:Script>
  <![CDATA[
    import mx.collections.HierarchicalData;

    private function createHierarchicalData(root:XML):HierarchicalData {
      return new HierarchicalData(root);
    }


  ]]>
</mx:Script>
```

Then we just pass the created HierarchicalData to the AdvancedDataGrid and define the Name column, which maps to the @name attribute, and the Qty In Stock column, which in turn maps to the @qty_in_stock attribute.

```
<mx:AdvancedDataGrid id="grid" width="33%" height="100%"
        dataProvider="{createHierarchicalData(categories.lastResult as XML)}">
    <mx:columns>
            <mx:AdvancedDataGridColumn headerText="Name" dataField="@name"/>
            <mx:AdvancedDataGridColumn headerText="Qty In Stock"
dataField="@qty_in_stock"/>
    </mx:columns>
</mx:AdvancedDataGrid>
```

Now you can start to see some of the advantages of the advanced data grid. Look at Figure 18.2. The first column displays the name attribute in a tree view form, and the grid can display additional columns.

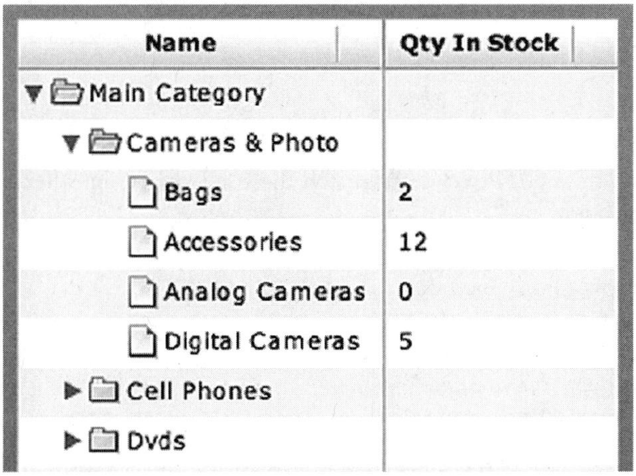

Figure 18.2   The grid can display additional columns beyond the tree view.

The Advanced DataGrid has more to offer than just a tree view with multiple columns. It provides multiple-column sort capabilities, cell renderers that can span multiple columns, data grouping, and summary rows.

Adding CRUD

We are going to extend the Categories controller to allow adding, deleting, updating, and moving categories. To simplify our Flex code, we will also return the new list of categories after each of the `create`, `update`, and `delete` operations. Doing so will refresh the grid automatically without an additional server call to reload the data.

Let's now add support for these operations to our Flex and Rails application.

Create (Rails)

Because we want to update the tree after each remote call, we are changing the `create`, `update`, `move`, and `destroy` methods of the Rails `CategoriesController` to return the new list of categories in case of success and an XML-formatted error message when something goes wrong.

```
def create
  parent = Category.find_by_id(params[:category][:parent_id])
  @category = Category.new(params[:category])
  if @category.save
    @category.move_to_child_of(parent) if parent
    render :xml => Category.root.full_xml, :status => :created
  else
    render :xml => @category.errors
  end
end
```

Create (Flex)

We will now add the HTTP service to match the Categories controller `create` method to our Flex application:

```
<mx:HTTPService id="categoriesCreate"
    url="http://localhost:3000/categories.xml"
    method="POST"
    resultFormat="e4x"
    contentType="application/xml"
    result="resultHandler(event)" />
```

As the controller returns the update list of categories, we will assign the result to a bindable variable named categories. This variable will be bound to the Advanced DataGrid and tree. We also invoke a function to expand the tree and grid.

```
[Bindable]
private var categories:XML;
private function resultHandler(result:ResultEvent):void {
  categories = result.result as XML;
  callLater(expandTreeAndGrid);
}
private function expandTreeAndGrid():void{
  tree.expandChildrenOf(categories, true);
  grid.expandAll();
}
```

Of course, we need a form to enter the new category information. We will create a form that we can use for all the operations.

```
<mx:Label text="Parent id:{grid.selectedItem.parent() != null ?
grid.selectedItem.parent().@id : 'root' }" />
<mx:Form>
  <mx:FormItem label="id">
    <mx:Label text="{grid.selectedItem==null? 'New record' :
grid.selectedItem.@id}"  />
  </mx:FormItem>
  <mx:FormItem label="name">
    <mx:TextInput id="nameField" text="{grid.selectedItem.@name}" />
  </mx:FormItem>
  <mx:FormItem label="description">
    <mx:TextInput id="descriptionField" text="{grid.selectedItem.@description}"
'/>
  </mx:FormItem>
</mx:Form>
```

So now we can use the data entered in the nameField and the descriptionField to create the XML to be sent to the categories create service. Additionally, we use the currently selected category as the parent of the category.

```
private function createCategory():void {
  var newCategory:XML =
      <category name={nameField.text}
              description={descriptionField.text} />;
  if (grid.selectedItem != null)
        newCategory.@parent_id = grid.selectedItem.@id
  categoriesCreate.send(newCategory);
}
```

Update (Rails)

Adding the update category method is even simpler since we don't need to find the parent category and awesome nested set ensures that when the parent_id is moved, the category parent is effectively changed.

```
def update
  @category = Category.find(params[:id])
  if @category.update_attributes(params[:category])
    render :xml => Category.root.full_xml
  else
    render :xml => @category.errors
  end
end
```

Update (Flex)

The update service will use the same result handler as the create service.

```
<mx:HTTPService id="categoriesUpdate"
 url="http://localhost:3000/categories/{grid.selectedItem.@id}.xml?_method=put"
    method="POST"
    resultFormat="e4x"
    contentType="application/xml"
    result="resultHandler(event)" />
```

And the updateCategory method is also simpler than it's create counterpart since we just update the selected item of the grid and send this object to the category update service.

```
private function updateCategory():void {
  var updateCategory:XML = grid.selectedItem as XML;
  updateCategory.@name = nameField.text;
  updateCategory.@description = descriptionField.text;
  categoriesUpdate.send(updateCategory)
}
```

Destroy (Rails)

The destroy method is also straightforward because we just need to find the category and ask it to destroy itself.

```
def destroy
  @category = Category.find(params[:id])
  @category.destroy
  render :xml => Category.root.full_xml
end
```

Destroy (Flex)

As usual for the destroy service, we need to ensure that the POST method is set, and we pass the additional _method parameter so Rails understands our intent to destroy this category.

```
<mx:HTTPService id="categoriesDelete"
    url="http://localhost:3000/categories/{grid.selectedItem.@id}.xml"
    method="POST"
    resultFormat="e4x"
    result="resultHandler(event)">
    <mx:request xmlns="">
      <_method>delete</_method>
    </mx:request>
</mx:HTTPService>
```

As the service `url` is bound to the grid selected item, we can just invoke the service as follows:

```
categoriesDelete.send()
```

Let's add a couple of buttons just under the grid to drive this functionality

```
<mx:HBox>
  <mx:Button label="Clear"    click="clearFields();" />
  <mx:Button label="Create"   click="createCategory();" />
  <mx:Button label="Update"   click="updateCategory()" />
  <mx:Button label="Delete"   click="categoriesDelete.send()" />
</mx:HBox>
```

Now we have a functional UI that supports editing of the categories (see Figure 18.3). But wait . . . there is more. We still would like to move categories around.

Move (Rails)

In our controller, we move the category identified by `params[:category][:id]` to `params[:category][:parent_id]` using the Awesome Nested Set `move_to_child_of` method.

```
def move
   parent = Category.find_by_id(params[:category][:parent_id])
   @category = Category.find(params[:category][:id])
   @category.move_to_child_of(parent)
   render :xml => Category.root.full_xml
 end
```

Before going back to our Flex application, let's not forget to add support for the move operation to our routes configuration file:

```
map.resources :categories, :member => { :move => :post }
```

Move (Flex)

For the move functionality, we are using the Flex built-in drag-and-drop functionality to enable us to drag a category on top of another to change the parent of that category. For simplicity, we simply decide that if you drop a category before another one, that other one becomes the parent.

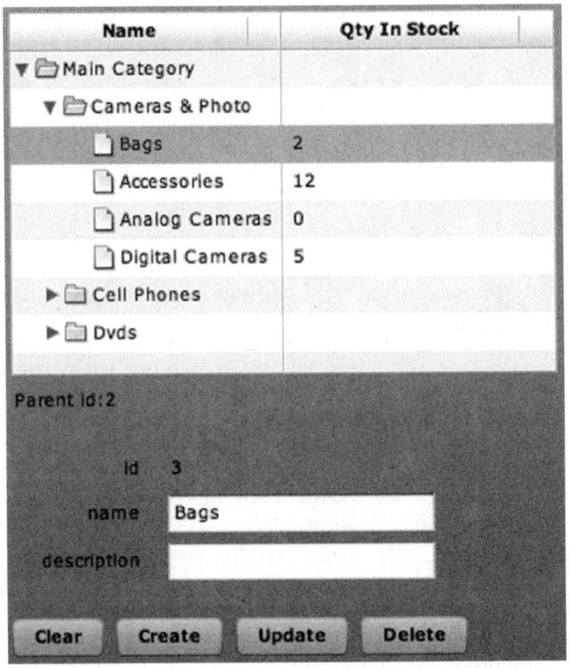

Figure 18.3   Editing functions are now available.

To drag-and-drop-enable the grid, we set the `dragEnabled` and `dropEnabled` properties of the grid to true. We also set the `dragMoveEnabled` property to true to ensure that Flex doesn't display the default copy icon while dragging the category. Finally, set the `dragDrop` handler to invoke our `dropCategory` function, which will then determine the category to move and call Rails to actually perform the move.

```
<mx:AdvancedDataGrid id="grid" width="100%" height="100%"
  dataProvider="{createHierarchicalData(categories)}"
  dragEnabled="true"
  dropEnabled="true"
  dragMoveEnabled="true"
  dragDrop="droppedCategory(event)"
  >
  <mx:columns>
    <mx:AdvancedDataGridColumn headerText="Name" dataField="@name"/>
    <mx:AdvancedDataGridColumn headerText="Qty In Stock"
dataField="@qty_in_stock"/>
  </mx:columns>
</mx:AdvancedDataGrid>
```

As usual, we need to declare the HTTP service to invoke the move method of the controller.

```
<mx:HTTPService id="categoriesMove"
   url="http://localhost:3000/categories/{grid.selectedItem.@id}/move"
   method="POST"
   resultFormat="e4x"
   contentType="application/xml"
   result="resultHandler(event)" />
```

Our `droppedCategory` event handler is triggered when a category is dropped onto another one. The first thing this method does is to cancel the event, because we will refresh the tree only after calling the server. Otherwise, you would see the result of the drop before it was performed by the server. That could be an issue in case of a server error. The current `selectedItem` is the item that will be moved. The grid provides the `calculateDropIndex` as a convenience method to find out where the category was dropped. We use this method to identify the new parent category.

```
private function droppedCategory(event:DragEvent):void {
  event.preventDefault();
  event.currentTarget.hideDropFeedback(event);
  var movedCategory:XML = grid.selectedItem as XML;
  grid.selectedIndex = grid.calculateDropIndex(event);
  var dropOnCategory:XML = grid.selectedItem as XML;
  movedCategory.@parent_id = grid.selectedItem.@id;
  categoriesMove.send(movedCategory)
}
```

Summary

We created a simple Flex application showing how we used the `AdvancedDataGrid` to manipulate a hierarchical data structure implemented using the Awesome Nested Set Rails plug-in. Give this plug-in a try!

## 19

Runtime Flex Configuration with Prana

Goal

You have some configuration that you want your Flex application to load when it first starts.

Solution

Use Prana, an IoC Library for ActionScript, to configure and set variables on your Flex application at runtime.

IoC, Eh?

Inversion of Control, or IoC, is a method of programming that seeks to simplify the code developers must write to access application resources or do something based on input or an event that comes from another part of the application. For instance, the normal way of accessing a logger may be to get a reference to a singleton. The IoC way would be to declare a variable with some metadata that tells the container to "inject" a reference to the correct logger at runtime. That way, the logger is available, but the code didn't need to know anything about the logger's implementation. This way makes the code cleaner and more focused.

If you've ever used Spring and IoC container for Java, you're familiar with the type of container Prana emulates. You can find more information about Prana at http://pranaframework.org. We're going to review one of the things Prana does well, which is runtime configuration for Flex using Dependency Injection, an IoC concept that keeps the complexity of searching for dependencies out of your code and lets you wire up these dependencies to be set when you need them.

What are some common scenarios for which you may want runtime configuration? Well, a big part of Flex and Rails development, or Flex with any service access for that matter, is pointing to the service at the right location. When you're working in

development, you're probably pointing at your local server at http://localhost:3000/.
When you're in production or staging, that's not likely to be the case. One of the things
that Prana can help with is configuring the URL for your services.

Look at the source code for this cookbook topic. It consists of a very simple
application that will show us some Prana basics. But first, notice that in the libs
directory there's an SWC file called prana-main.swc. That's the Prana library, and
it needs to be included in the classpath. Now, in the code, let's look at the model:

```
package {
    [Bindable]
    public class AppModel {
        private static var instance:AppModel;
        public var serviceURL:String;

        public static function getInstance():AppModel {
            if (!instance) {
                instance = new AppModel();
            }
            return instance;
        }

    }

}
```

This model looks a lot like a singleton Cairngorm model. Even if you're not interested
in using this type of pattern in your application, look at how Prana works anyway; you'll
probably get an idea of how it could work for your situation.

First, the model has an instance of itself and an accessor for that instance called
getInstance. That will be important soon, so keep that in mind.

Next, here's an application:

```
<?xml version="1.0" encoding="utf-8"?>
<mx:Application xmlns:mx="http://www.adobe.com/2006/mxml" layout="vertical"
applicationComplete="init()">
    <mx:Script>
    <![CDATA[
    import mx.controls.Alert;
    import
        org.pranaframework.context.support.XMLApplicationContext;

    private var applicationContext:XMLApplicationContext;

    [Bindable] public var model:AppModel = AppModel.getInstance();

    private function init():void {
        applicationContext =
            new XMLApplicationContext("applicationContext.xml");
```

```
            applicationContext.addEventListener(Event.COMPLETE,
onApplicationContextLoad);
            applicationContext.load();
    }

    private function onApplicationContextLoad(event:Event):void {
    }


    ]]>
    </mx:Script>

    <mx:HTTPService id="service" url="{model.serviceURL}"
    contentType="application/xml" resultFormat="e4x" />
    <mx:Button id="callServiceButton" label="Check Service URL"
    click="Alert.show('service url is ' + service.url)" />

</mx:Application>
```

First, for components, there's an `HTTPService` tag to access some service, it doesn't matter what at this point. Next, there's a button that simply reports the URL configured on `HTTPService`.

The `init` method, which is called on `creationComplete`, is a little more out of the ordinary. It creates an `XMLApplicationContext` object, which you'll see comes from the Prana library. That object is told to load a file called applicationContext.xml (which is what this file is usually called in the Spring framework). An event gets dispatched when that file is loaded.

Let's have a look at that file:

```
<objects>
    <object id="productionServiceURL" class="String">
        <constructor-arg value="http://foocorp.com"/>
    </object>

    <object id="localServiceURL" class="String">
        <constructor-arg value="http://localhost:3000"/>
    </object>

    <object class="AppModel" factory-method="getInstance">
        <property name="serviceURL">
            <ref>localServiceURL</ref>
        </property>
    </object>
</objects>
```

You'll see three object tags of type `String` that have values for different URLs, one for each of the environments: production and local development. Next, there's an object of type AppModel—which you'll notice is the name of the model we already saw above. Then there's another attribute, factory-method, which is set to getInstance, the singleton accessor method on our model. On that object is a property that corresponds to the serviceURL variable on the model. The ref tag is a reference to localServiceURL right now.

What happens is this: when Prana loads this file, it creates objects of the type defined in any object tag's class property; so, for the URLs, it creates three strings and assigns them to local variables named the same as the id property.

When it encounters the object that points to AppModel, it sees a factory-method attribute, so it expects a static method with the name getInstance on the AppModel class. Now it knows how to create an object of type AppModel—it calls the getInstance method. Once it has that object, it sets the value of serviceURL to the value of the string referenced by localServiceURL (that's where the ref tag comes in).

If we run this application now and click the Check Service URL button, we get what we see in Figure 19.1.

Figure 19.1   The result of clicking on the Check Service URL button.

Great! Now we can send any service requests to a known service name by just appending the request onto the URL property of the HTTPService.

Now, what if we change lines 15–19 of the applicationConfiguration.xml file to look like this?

```
<object class="AppModel" factory-method="getInstance">
    <property name="serviceURL">
        <ref>stageServiceURL</ref>
    </property>
</object>
```

If we point to the stage URL, we'll see what's in Figure 19.2.

Figure 19.2   The result of pointing to the stage URL.

Now we have a way of controlling the URL of HTTPService at runtime. Anytime the Flex-generated SWF runs, it looks in the applicationContext.xml file first.

Of course, this application is simple, but I'm sure you can see how to take it to the next level for a more real-world application.

One other thing. Best practice is to not check any configuration files into source control, but to check in an example file instead. That way, everyone can configure the application the way their system requires.

Also, now that you don't have the actual configuration checked in, when you pull a build out of your source control system during a deployment, you can use the search-and-replace features of your build tool, Ant or Rake for instance, to set the value of HTTPService to what it needs to be.

Summary

Prana is a valuable tool for doing things like runtime configuration, and we've only scratched the surface of what it can do for you. Make sure you check it out further at http://pranaframework.org. For another example of how to use Prana, look at the Chapter 16 cookbook recipe, Reusing Commands with Prana Sequences.

## 20

Server Push with Juggernaut

Goal

You need your Rails server to send, in real time, a notification to one specific user, a group of users, or to all connected users.

Solution

Use the Juggernaut Rails plug-in together with the XMLSocket provided by Flex framework to allow the Rails server to send a notification to your Flex application.

Push Technology

For a brief definition of the concept of push technology, consider this one from Wikipedia:

> Push technology on the Internet refers to a style of communication protocol where the request for a given transaction originates with the publisher, or central server. It is contrasted with pull technology, where the request for the transmission of information originates with the receiver, or client.
>
> Server push or webcasting is specifically related to the HTTP protocol, used on the World Wide Web. Typical World Wide Web usage is a pull operation—the end-user requests a web page using a web browser. Wikipedia (01/07/2008)

Juggernaut

With the Juggernaut push technology, a Rails server can send messages to your Flex application in real time. For example, you can build an Instant Messaging (IM) application, a message alert system right in your Flex application, or a help desk support application that lets you remotely control your application. Push technology opens quite a few doors. In this cookbook recipe, we will build a small IM application with a Flex front end enabling us to send messages to a Rails server, which in turn will broadcast the message to the other Flex front ends listening. This simple application will show you everything you need to get started with push trechnology.

Since a picture is worth a thousand words, let's begin by visualizing the message flow we will implement (see Figure 20.1).

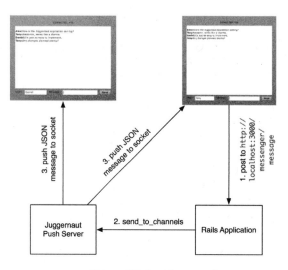

Figure 20.1   Message flow.

This diagram shows two chat users, Daniel and Tony, talking to each other. When Daniel says "Hi," a simple post using HTTPService is sent to the MessengerController message method, and this Rails controller then forwards the posted data to the Juggernaut Push Server, which in turn, broadcasts the message to all the listening sockets. All the Flex IM applications then receive the message via a Socket and display the message in their text area. "Socket" is the key to making the push technology work. When our Flex IM application starts, it creates an XMLSocket connected to the Juggernaut push server, which enables the server to send data to the Flex application.

It is also important to understand both the limitations and advantages of using sockets. Using a Socket, the Flex application can connect to the Juggernaut push server, which creates a direct communication line between the server and the Flex application. When the client application terminates, this connection is closed. The server keeps a unique communication channel (socket) to each of the clients and keeps the list of all connected clients. This could pose a scalability issue; however, Juggernaut uses the EventMachine plug-in, which is designed with performance in mind to be highly scalable. This performance is achieved, as its name indicates, by using events to handle incoming client requests rather than using a dedicate thread per client. Read more on EventMachine at http://rubyeventmachine.com.

Now, if you look at the diagram, you will notice that the Rails server is also a client to the push server, more precisely the MessengerController, which uses the Juggernaut class provided by the Juggernaut plug-in to send messages to the push server by using a socket.

Juggernaut supports the notion of clients and channels. A channel, for example, could represent a specific discussion topic out of a larger list of topics. The client can decide to listen only to messages on a specific channel, then when a discussion for that specific topic occurs, the server can dispatch messages to that channel and only the users listening to the channel would receive the message. Juggernaut supports a relevant mix of `send` methods that can target a combination of specific channels and clients. For example, these methods enable a Rails application to send messages to all the connected clients, to specific channels, to specific clients, or to specific clients on specific channels. The methods include the following:

- `send_to_all`
- `send_to_channels`   `channels`
- `send_to_channel`   `channel`
- `send_to_client`   `client_id`
- `send_to_clients`   `client_ids`
- `send_to_client_on_channel`   `client_id,  channel`
- `send_to_clients_on_channel`   `client_ids, channel`
- `send_to_client_on_channels`   `client_id,  channels`
- `send_to_clients_on_channels`   `client_ids, channels`

In these method, `client_ids` represent an array of client IDs, `client_id` is the client ID, `channels` is an array of channel names, and `channel` is the name of one channel. Juggernaut doesn't use XML or AMF to pass data between the client and the server, it uses JSON (JavaScript Object Notation, www.json.org/). In our example, we will broadcast a message to a specific channel. We could just as well have used `send_to_all` to send the message to all listening clients, or we could have used `send_to_client` to establish a private communication. In the context of a messaging client, these different levels of destination could, for example, enable you to create a private chat room, a group chat room, and a public message board.

Juggernaut was written by Alex McCaw and can be found at http://juggernaut.rubyforge.org/. The push server is built on top of the excellent EventMachine library (http://rubyforge.org/projects/eventmachine).

In the first part of this recipe, we will create the Rails application, and in the second part, we will create the Flex application.

Creating the Rails Messaging Application

First, let's create a fresh Rails application and install the JSON and event machine gems.

```
$ rails rails; cd rails
$ sudo gem install json
$ sudo gem install eventmachine
```

You can also install the Juggernaut push server via a gem, so let's install it.

```
$ sudo gem install juggernaut
```

Next, let's generate the default juggernaut.yml configuration file, which sets the default port of the push server to 5001. You need to create this file once, and it's needed when starting the Juggernaut server. Make sure you are in the root folder of your Rails project.

```
$ juggernaut -g config/juggernaut.yml
```

Start the push server with the following command:

```
$ juggernaut -c config/juggernaut.yml
```

We now could use this push server without even having a Rails application, but for our example, we want to have our Rails application communicate with the push server. That's where the Juggernaut Rails plug-in comes into play, so let's install this plug-in into our Rails application:

```
$ ./script/plugin install http://juggernaut.rubyforge.org/svn/trunk/juggernaut
```

And let's define in the config/environment.rb file that our Rails application depends on the three gems we just installed.

```
Rails::Initializer.run do |config|
  config.gem "juggernaut", :version => "0.5.7"
  config.gem "eventmachine", :version => "0.12"
  config.gem "json", :version => "1.1.3"
end
```

Our Rails application will accept a message from the Flex client applications via a standard HTTP request, and the controller will notify the **push server** to dispatch the message to all clients. This may not be the most typical approach, as we could implement this same application by just using the push server, but it demonstrates how a Rails application can communicate with currently connected clients. So let's generate an empty Rails messenger controller using script/generate:

```
$ ./script/generate controller messenger
```

As you know, this command creates the controller in app/controllers/messenger_controller.rb. You can now add an action called message that transmits the username and a text message using Juggernaut to a channel named `im_channel`.

```
class MessengerController < ApplicationController
  def message
    data = {:user => params[:user], :message => params[:message]}
    Juggernaut.send_to_channel(data, :im_channel)
    render :nothing => true
  end
end
```

We already started the push server before, so now let's start the Rails application before coding the Flex part of our application:

```
$ ./script/server
```

Creating the Flex Messaging Client Application

The Flex application is quite simple, and it just shows a text area with all the messages the server pushes to the client. These messages are sent by the server via a socket that the Flex application creates upon startup using the `flash.net.XMLSocket` class. Despite its name, the `XMLSocket` class enables you to send different types of data, such as a string in our case. The client application also has a text input field where you can enter a message to be sent to the Rails application with a standard HTTP request using the `mx:HTTPService` component. So, let's declare the socket using MXML and assign the various relevant event handlers:

```
<net:XMLSocket id="socket"
     connect="connectHandler(event)"
     data="dataHandler(event)"
     close="closeHandler(event)"
     ioError="ioErrorHandler(event)"
     securityError="securityErrorHandler(event)" />
```

Communicating using the XMLSocket is similar to using the `HTTPService` component, and sending data is also an asynchronous operation. One difference is that the socket keeps a connection to the server, and therefore, **connect** and **close** event handlers are notified upon being connected to and disconnected from the server. But, more importantly, the **data** event handler is triggered when the server pushes data to the client. Also, error event handlers notify the application when something went wrong receiving or sending data.

When declaring the socket, we used the `net` namespace, as defined in the following `Application` declaration.

```
<mx:Application
     xmlns:mx="http://www.adobe.com/2006/mxml"
     xmlns:net="flash.net.*"
     layout="vertical"
     applicationComplete="setup()"
     defaultButton="{send}" >
```

Now let's create the method named `setup` that the application invokes in its `applicationComplete` handler, thus connecting to the push server upon startup:

```
private var hostName:String = "9127.0.0.1";
private var port:uint = 5001;
public function setup():void {
  socket.connect(hostName, port);
}
```

We define the `hostName` and `port` variables to set on the address and port the socket will connect to the push server. The port 5001 is the default port number set up by the Juggernaut gem. You can override it in the juggernaut.yml configuration file, and of course, your Rails application could also pass this port number to your Flex application without hardcoding the value.

Now, upon a successful connection to the push server, the connection handler is invoked. Note that at this point, just a socket connection has been established; the server doesn't know what the client wants to listen to, so we use `connectHandler` to send a command to the server notifying it that we want to listen to any message pushed to the `:im_channel`. The Juggernaut push server expects the commands as a JSON encoded string, as shown hereafter:

```
private function connectHandler(event:Event):void {
  connected = true;
  var request:String = '{"command":"subscribe", "body":"", "type":"to_channels",
"channels":["im_channel"]}';
  socket.send(request);
}
```

Now the Flex application is subscribed to the `:im_channel`, and when the Rails application sends data to this channel via the Juggernaut push server, each connected client receives the data via the socket via the `data` event handler. The data is passed as a JSON encoded string. Let's look at the data handler:

```
private function dataHandler(event:DataEvent):void {
    var data:Object = JSON.decode(event.data);
    messages += "<br/><b>"+data.body.user+":</b>"+data.body.message;
}
```

To decode a JSON string to an ActionScript object, we can just use as3corelib (download it from http://code.google.com/p/as3corelib/), and then in our Flex application, import the `com.adobe.serialization.json.JSON` class and use the `decode` method passing the JSON string as shown above. Note our Rails messenger controller class pushes only the user and message parameters to the client, but your application could pass any data that can be encoded in JSON format. Upon receiving these parameters, the Flex application simply adds the user name in bold and the message to the text area of the application.

So far, our application can listen to messages; we now also need to send messages. To demonstrate how Rails can interact with the Juggernaut push server, we simply send a text message to the Rails messenger controller we created in the first part of this chapter using a standard HTTP request, not using the socket, and then have our Rails controller class use the `Juggernaut` class provided by the Juggernaut plug-in to dispatch the message. Behind the scenes, the `Juggernaut` class also does a socket connection to the push server and passes a `:broadcast` command, along with the channel name to broadcast to and the message to broadcast. So let's create the Flex user interface to send a text message. It consists simply of a `TextInput` field for the username and one for the message to send along.

```
<mx:HBox>
    <mx:Label text="User:" />
    <mx:TextInput id="user" text="me"  width="100"/>
    <mx:Label text="Message:" />
  <mx:TextInput id="msg" />
  <mx:Button id="send" label="Send"  click="sendMessage.send()" />
</mx:HBox>
```

We also add a Send button that triggers the following `HTTPService`. We bind the parameters of the request directly to the user and message input field declared above.

```
<mx:HTTPService id="sendMessage" url="http://localhost:3000/messenger/message"
        method="POST" result="msg.text=''"
fault="mx.controls.Alert.show(event.fault.faultString);">
  <mx:request xmlns="">
    <user>{user.text}</user>
    <message>{msg.text}</message>
  </mx:request>
</mx:HTTPService>
```

Upon clicking the send button, the `message` method of the MessengerController is invoked with the following parameters:

```
Parameters: {"user"=>"me", "message"=>"How are you?", "action"=>"message",
"controller"=>"messenger"}
```

And again, all connected clients receive this message.

Summary

In this chapter, we created a basic IM client that demonstrates some of the basics of push technology, and we showed how easily push technology can be added to your Flex with Rails application thanks to the Juggernaut push server gem and its companion Rails plug-in. We also only scratched the surface of what can be achieved using channels, and we hope you will start exploring the new possibilities now offered to you.

21

Communicating between Flex and JavaScript

Goal

You'd like to integrate Flex with an existing JavaScript-powered HTML application.

Solution

Use either Flex's `ExternalInterface` or the Flex-Ajax Bridge to enable two-way communication between Flex and JavaScript.

Communication between Flex and JavaScript

What does it mean that we can communicate between Flex and JavaScript? Pretty much anything you'd like to tell Flex to do from JavaScript, and vice versa. The communication can either be in terms of calling methods with `ExternalInterface` or setting properties in Flex via the Flex-Ajax bridge.

Even though we haven't mentioned it much so far, since it's not something that requires extra work to accomplish, Flex works great alongside JavaScript-powered HTML applications. A lot of debate goes on around whether Flex or Ajax (HTML applications that use JavaScript to dynamically change the HTML or access services) are the best technologies for rich Internet applications (RIAs). It doesn't have to be one over the other. In fact, your app will probably benefit from your thinking about what makes each technology the best choice in a given situation and using each for whatever makes sense to solve your problem.

Security

Flash has a very tight security model, which is usually called the Security Sandbox. It would be beneficial to dig a little deeper than we have time for here, but the upshot for these two methods of accessing JavaScript is that you're unable to do so when loading the web page locally; JavaScript is only accessible through a web server from which both the HTML and Flash are loaded.

If you use Flex Builder, it takes care of this restriction when loading the application locally. For everyone else, luckily, we have a convenient web server with Rails. Accessing the SWF through the Rails server makes sure that the Flash player's security model doesn't have a problem, which it would if the app were running from the file system.

For the sample code for this topic, we used Rake to compile a simple Flex app inside the public directory of a Rails project. If you're using Flex Builder, you'll need to modify the generated HTML in the html-template directory with the JavaScript you need.

Building the Samples

There's a simple Rake task in the public directory of the example application that builds the Flex files. It depends on mxmlc being in your local path. It also has a reference to the source path for the FlexAjax bridge relative to the path of your Flex SDK. Change the path to your Flex SDK to make both MXML files compile (see Listing 21.1).

Listing 21.1   **public/Rakefile**

```
require 'rake/clean'

#change these paths to match the location of the Flex SDK files
FLEX_SDK="/Applications/fb_3/sdks/3.0.0"
FA_BRIDGE_SRC="/frameworks/javascript/fabridge/src"

# invoke rake:clean to clean up derived files
CLEAN.include '*.swf'

task :default => [ :index, :fabridge ]

file "index" do
  sh %{ mxmlc -locale=en_US index.mxml }
end

file "fabridge" do
  sh %{ mxmlc -locale=en_US -sp+=#{FLEX_SDK}#{FA_BRIDGE_SRC} fabridge.mxml }
end
```

ExternalInterface

`ExternalInterface` is the most straightforward way to communicate between JavaScript and a Flex application embedded on the same page. Inside Flex are two methods to keep track of: `ExternalInterface.call` and `ExternalInterface.addCallback`.

`ExternalInterface.call` calls a JavaScript function and passes optional parameters. If the method doesn't exist, you'll get a null response, which can make debugging a little weird; be careful to get the names right. The arguments you pass are cast as JavaScript types, with objects getting turned into basic JavaScript Objects. Any returned values are returned by the call method.

`ExternalInterface.addCallback` takes a string, which is the method name you want JavaScript to call, and the second is a method you want Flex to call when JavaScript calls the method named in the first argument.

On the JavaScript side, first we need to get a handle to the object in the DOM that holds the Flex application and then call methods on it.

SWFObject and Prototype

For our example HTML, we're going to use a helper JavaScript library called SWFObject, which takes care of loading Flash in the right way for whatever myriad browsers are out there. Download and learn more about SWFObject at http://swfobject.googlecode.com/.

For a little extra help on the HTML side, we're also using the Prototype JavaScript library, which, as you probably already know, ships with Rails. Find out more at http://prototypejs.org/. The main thing we're using is Prototype's $ function, which makes it easy to find DOM elements in a cross-browser-compatible way. We'll see more in a bit.

ExternalInterface in Action

To test out `ExternalInterface`, we'll use this simple application that chats back and forth from Flex to JavaScript. To view the application, fire up the Rails script/server and go to http://localhost:3000. You will see something like what is shown in Figure 21.1.

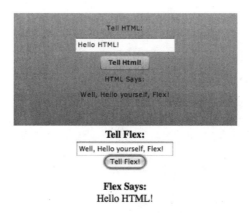

Figure 21.1   The sample applications.

When you enter some text into the Flex text input and click Tell Html!, it sends the string to a JavaScript function that prints to the screen in the HTML section. Also, when you enter some text into the HTML text input and click Tell Flex!, it sends the text to a JavaScript function that the Flex application has registered as a callback function.

First, let's look at the HTML view code (see Listing 21.2).

Listing 21.2   **public/index.html #40–60**

```
<body onLoad="init()">
    <div id="flashContent">
        <a href="http://www.adobe.com/go/getflashplayer">
          <img
            src=http://www.adobe.com/images/shared/
            download_buttons/get_flash_player.gif
            alt="Get Adobe Flash player" />
        </a>
    </div>
    <div id="htmlContent" align="center">
        <strong>Tell Flex:</strong>
        <div id="tellFlex">
          <input id="tellFlexString" type="text" />
            <br/>
          <input id="tellFlexButton" type="button"
            value="Tell Flex!" onClick="tellFlex()">
        </div>
        <br/>
        <strong>Flex Says:</strong>
        <br/>
        <div id="flexSays">

        </div>
    </div>
</body>
```

The HTML part of the application is easy enough to understand; it lives in the div with the ID htmlContent. The div with the ID flexSays is empty, and we'll put the text of whatever Flex says inside there.

The Flex part may be a bit more confusing. It lives in the flashContent div, but what's currently in there is an image and a link directing users to get Flash. This content gets displayed only if SWFObject can't replace the contents of the div with the Flex-generated SWF, which should only happen when Flash is not installed on the browser. Otherwise, the contents of this div are replaced with the correct HTML to embed the Flash Player pointing at the Flex-generated SWF.

Listing 21.3 shows the JavaScript functions.

Listing 21.3   **public/index.html #15–38**

```
<script type="text/javascript" src="javascripts/swfobject.js"></script>
<script type="text/javascript" src="javascripts/prototype.js"></script>
<script type="text/javascript">

    function init() {
        var flashvars = {};
        var params = {};
        params.quality = "high";
        params.bgcolor = "#ffffff";
        params.allowfullscreen = "true";
        params.allowscriptaccess = "sameDomain";
        var attributes = {};
        attributes.id = "flexApplication";
        swfobject.embedSWF("index.swf", "flashContent", "100%", "50%",
  "9.0.115", false, flashvars, params, attributes);
    }

    function flexSays(something) {
        $('flexSays').update(something);
    }

    function tellFlex() {
        $('flexApplication').htmlSays( $('tellFlexString').getValue() )
    }
</script>
```

First, the SWFObject and Prototype libraries are included, then the `init` function, which is run when the page is loaded (check the body tag), does all the setup for SWFObject. Note the last two lines of that function. The `embedSWF` function takes the name of the SWF and the name of the div to embed it in, along with some other attributes, such as size, version, and attributes, to pass along into the SWF. The second-to-last line gives the embedded SWF an ID, which we'll later use to address the SWF from JavaScript.

When the `flexSays` function is called, it uses Prototype to look up the `flexSays` div by ID. The $ function means "find a DOM element with this ID," and works across browsers. It then uses Prototype's update function to change the HTML contents of that div with the incoming text from Flex. To prove this function, try sending some HTML with the text, wrapping it in H1 tags.

Then when the Tell Flex! button is pressed to send some text from JavaScript to Flex, the `tellFlex` function is called. It looks up the Flash app by the ID we gave SWFObject and calls the `htmlSays` function, passing in the contents of the text input, which is called `tellFlexString`. That function wasn't defined in the HTML, but by Flex, which we'll see in Listing 21.4.

Listing 21.4   public/index.mxml #31–36

```
<mx:Label id="tellHtmlLabel" text="Tell HTML:" />
<mx:TextInput id="tellHtmlText" enter="tellHtml()" />
<mx:Button id="tellHtmlButton" label="Tell Html!" click="tellHtml()" />

<mx:Label id="htmlSaysLabel" text="HTML Says:" />
<mx:Label id="htmlSaysContent" text="{htmlSaysText}" />
```

This is the view part of the Flex app. It has the analogous controls to the HTML side.
Also notice that we're using binding to update the `htmlSaysContent` label.

Now let's look at the script. See Listing 21.5.

Listing 21.5   public/index.mxml #3–28

```
<mx:Script>

    import flash.external.*;

    [Bindable]
    private var htmlSaysText:String;

    public function init():void {
        if (ExternalInterface.available) {
            ExternalInterface.addCallback("htmlSays", htmlSays)
        }
    }

    public function htmlSays(s:String):void {
        htmlSaysText = s;
    }

    public function tellHtml():void {
        var s:String = tellHtmlText.text;
        if (ExternalInterface.available) {
            ExternalInterface.call("flexSays", s);
        }
    }

</mx:Script>
```

On `applicationComplete`, the `init` method is called, which registers a function
called `htmlSays` with JavaScript and tells Flex to call the function with the same name
when that function is called. It then updates the `htmlSaysText` string, which is bound
to the content.

Notice the condition for `ExternalInterface.available`. It checks to see that the
browser is supported by `ExternalInterface`.

Now, in the `tellHtml` method, we get the string from the text input and call the `flexSays` method in the JavaScript, passing the string.

This application is quite simple, but it shows the same patterns you would use even with a more complex application using `ExternalInterface`.

Flex-Ajax Bridge in Action

Now let's look at using the Flex-Ajax bridge, which makes it a little easier for HTML to get deeper into the Flex application without calling functions in between.

The sample application for the Flex-Ajax bridge is simple as well. In Flex, we have an unsuspecting panel and we'll change its the width using JavaScript. Figure 21.2 shows the application. To run it, go to http://localhost:3000/fabridge.html.

Figure 21.2   The unsuspecting panel.

First, in Flex, as you can see in Listing 21.6, things are pretty simple.

Listing 21.6   **public/fabridge.mxml**

```
<?xml version="1.0" encoding="utf-8"?>
<mx:Application xmlns:mx="http://www.adobe.com/2006/mxml" layout="vertical">

    <fab:FABridge xmlns:fab="bridge.*" />

    <mx:Panel id="unsuspectingPanel" width="200" height="200"
title="Unsuspecting Panel">

    </mx:Panel>

</mx:Application>
```

We have to include the FABridge, which is why we compile with the extra sp+= option in the Rakefile, which means "append this source to the source path." The FABridge is included with the Flex SDK.

This unsuspecting panel doesn't have any Flex methods to change its width, so how is it happening? Let's look at the HTML.

First of all, at the time of writing, there's an issue using the Flex-Ajax bridge together with SWFObject. Looking at the HTML, you may notice that it's Adobe's generated HTML that comes with Flex Builder. It creates a DOM structure, where the SWF is placed, that matches what the FABridge.js code is looking for.

The buttons are simple (see Listing 21.7).

Listing 21.7   **public/fabridge.html #109–113**

```
<div id="htmlContent" align="center">
      <input type="button" value="bigger" onClick="bigger()">
      <br />
      <input type="button" value="smaller" onClick="smaller()">
</div>
```

And the code is pretty simple too (See Listing 21.8).

Listing 21.8   **public/fabridge.html #93–106**

```
function bigger() {
      var width = getFlexApp().getUnsuspectingPanel().getWidth()
      getFlexApp().getUnsuspectingPanel().setWidth(width + 10)
}

function smaller() {
      var width = getFlexApp().getUnsuspectingPanel().getWidth()
      getFlexApp().getUnsuspectingPanel().setWidth(width - 10)
}

function getFlexApp() {
      return FABridge.flash.root();
}
```

The getFlexApp function returns a handle to the Flash application through the FABridge object created in the FABridge.js file.

Once we have that handle, we can use a convention of prefixing get or set onto any property name we want to get or set. For instance, in both bigger() and smaller(), we get access to the panel, which has an ID of unsuspectingPanel in Flex, by calling getUnsuspectingPanel on the Flex app. Then we can get and set the value of the width of that component by calling getWidth() and setWidth(). It's possible to call methods on the Flex application as well.

The Flex–Ajax bridge is really to make it easier for developers that only know Ajax to call in and make Flex do something they want it to do. To make it even easier, consider writing an interface to anything JavaScript developers would need to call, by simply pointing JavaScript variables at whatever components you needed to modify. To send instructions to the HTML wrapper from Flex, you still need to use `ExternalInterface`.

Summary

Which one should you use? Well, the Flex–Ajax bridge makes it a little easier to work the Flex app from HTML, but since the method you use is to act directly on the properties of components or variables on the application, you may want to think twice about using it for anything but simple manipulation of the Flex application through JavaScript. Of course, for simple use cases, it's easier than the `ExternalInterface`. Really, it's a judgment call based on the complexity of your application—and how much you trust the JavaScript developers working with your Flex application!

22

File Upload

Goal

You need to provide a Flex application that lets the user upload files from a hard disk. It must also upload bitmap images to a Rails application.

Solution

Use the `attachment_fu` Rails plug-in together with the `FileReference` and `URLLoader` classes provided by the Flex framework to quickly add file upload capabilities to your Flex with Rails application.

File Upload

Your application may need to let the user upload images, such as an avatar, a screen capture, an album cover, photos, or a word document. The HTTP protocol supports form-based file uploads, and every browser implements a file upload widget. So, in Rails, to create an HTML form with a file upload widget, you create a form using the form helper and set the `:multipart` parameter to `true`, and then add a file field to your form:

```
<% form_for(:attachment_metadata, :url => { :action => "create" },
:html => { :multipart => true }) do |form| %>
Find the file <%= form.file_field :uploaded_data %>
<%= submit_tag("Upload this file") %>
<% end %>
```

Each browser implements this file field slightly differently. In Safari, a Choose File button is added, and just the name of the file is displayed once you select a file (see Figure 22.1).

Figure 22.1   Safari provides a Choose File button.

In Firefox, a text field with a Browse button is rendered, as shown in Figure 22.2, and the text field contains the full path to the file once the file is selected.

Figure 22.2   Firefox provides a Browse button.

Flex also supports file uploading, but it doesn't render the file field, giving the application total control of the look and feel of how the user starts the file selection process. File uploading is, in fact, implemented by the Flash Player and can be triggered in ActionScript by using the `flash.net.FileReference` browse method, as we will show you soon. Additionally, with Flex you can select multiple files at once, thus making multiple file uploads a better user experience than is possible with its HTML form counterpart.

The HTTP protocol defines form-based file uploading to enable uploading of binary files by specifying that an HTTP request can contain multiple parts, and one or more of the parts can be in binary format and be the selected file content. Read more on the specifics in section 17.13.4, "Form content types," at www.w3.org/TR/html401/interact/forms.html and under RFC1867 at www.ietf.org/rfc/rfc1867.txt. But, in short, Rails understands these multipart requests and lets you access the file to upload via the controller `params` object. For the form we declared above, simply read the file to upload directly from the `params` as follows: `params[:uploaded_data].read`. Now, behind the scenes, Rails knows it's a file upload field as part of a multipart request, and if the file size is smaller than 10240 bytes, it creates an `ActionController::UploadedStringIO` object with the content loaded in memory. Otherwise, it creates `ActionController::UploadedTempfile` that enables it to read the content via a temporary file. But, you don't need to worry about these details.

Once your image or document is uploaded, you want to store it using Rails. That's where `attachment_fu` comes into play, because it enables you to define an active record that has the file content as an attachment. You can even configure `attachment_fu` to store the uploaded files to s3, to the local file system, or in the database.

So let's go ahead and create an example application that implements file upload. We will create the asset manager application that lets you upload documents from your file system and images from Flickr.

Creating the Rails Application and Installing attachment_fu

So let's create a Rails application:

```
$ rails rails; cd rails
```

Next let's install the `attachment_fu` plug-in:

```
./script/plugin install git://github.com/technoweenie/attachment_fu.git
```

The installation will complete by displaying the instructions on how to configure and use `attachment_fu`. Now let's generate the `asset` resource and use the generated active record and controller as starting point.

```
$ ./script/generate scaffold asset size:integer content_type:integer
filename:string height:integer width:integer parent_id:integer
thumbnail:string
$ rake db:migrate
```

You then need to specify that the asset active record has an attachment:

```
class Asset < ActiveRecord::Base
  has_attachment :storage => :file_system
end
```

The `has_attachment` declaration can take many parameters to define different aspects of your attachment, such as constraints on the file size, image size, or which storage system to use, like the file system, the database or s3. We simply set the storage to use the file system, which will create a folder in the public folder of your Rails application with the pluralized name of the active record, `assets` in our case, to store the uploaded files when we upload assets.

Now let's go change the assets controller create action and just remove the `respond_to` block since we will just use this Rails application from Flex.

```
class AssetsController < ApplicationController
  def create
    @asset = Asset.new(params[:asset])
    if @asset.save
      render(:nothing => true, :status => 200)
    else
      render(:nothing => true, :status => 500)
    end
  end
end
```

We don't change the core of this method, which is `Asset.new(params[:asset])`. The controller method doesn't seem to have any special code to handle file uploading. This is thanks to the magic of `attachment_fu`, which decorates the active record with a new `uploaded_data=(file_data)` method, which ensures that if the client application uses a file upload field named `asset[uploaded_data]`, this file is passed to the active record. The active record can then read it and store it based on the selected storage system.

You are done with the Rails part of the application. So let's start the server and move on to the Flex part of the application.

Using Flex's FileReference Class to Upload One or Several Files

To get started, let's create a new Flex application and add the flash.net namespace so we can use the `FileReference class`, which is the key to provide file uploading from Flex:

```
<mx:Application xmlns:mx="http://www.adobe.com/2006/mxml"
xmlns:net="flash.net.*" layout="vertical" >
```

We can now refer to the `net` namespace defined in the application tag, and we can instantiate any class from the flash.net package using MXML. Next, you need a FileReference instance, so let's create one using MXML, as follows:

```
<net:FileReference id="fileReference" select="selectHandler(event)"
complete="completeHandler(event)" />
```

Let's also add the following button to our minimalist Flex application to start the file selection process:

```
<mx:Button label="Upload..." click="fileReference.browse();" />
```

Now when you click on the Upload button, the code invokes the `browse` method of the file reference, which opens a file browser and lets you select a file. You can also simply double-click on a file or use the Select button. Now this doesn't directly upload the file to the server, but it invokes the `select` handler you specified on the `FileReference` instance. In our case, it is a method we named `selectHandler`. If you think about it, the Flex framework gives you full control of how to trigger the file selection process and returns control to you once you have selected the file. In your selection handler, you can now start the file upload process for the selected file:

```
private function selectHandler(event:Event):void {
  var request:URLRequest = new
URLRequest("http://localhost:3000/assets")
  var uploadDataFieldName:String = 'asset[uploaded_data]'
    fileReference.upload(request, uploadDataFieldName);
}
```

In this, we decided to directly send the file to the server. Before sending the file, your application has access via the `FileReference` instance to the filename, the size, and the creation and modification dates of the selected file. The `upload` method takes the URL of our Rails asset controller and makes a request using the HTTP `POST` method, which is exactly what we want. The only little gotcha is you must name the data field the same way `attachment_fu` expects, which we do using the second parameter to the upload method. Set it to `asset[uploaded_data]`, which will result in the file reference being passed to the Rails controller parameters. If we inspect these parameters, we'll see the following:

```
Parameters: {"Filename"=>"Photo 1.jpg", "action"=>"create",
 "Upload"=>"Submit Query", "controller"=>"assets",
 "asset"=>{"uploaded_data"=>#<File:/var/folders/3x/-Tmp-/CGI122-4>}}
```

Now the controller can just use `params[:asset][:uploaded_data]`, if needed, and if you use `attachment_fu`, just pass `params` to the `Asset.new` method. We did also set a complete handler on the `FileReference`, which we named `completeHandler`. This handler is invoked upon a successful upload and simply displays a message that the file was successfully uploaded.

Et Voila! File uploading is accomplished using Flex with Rails. But, how can I see the progress of the upload? Glad you asked. To see the upload progress, we can add the following `ProgressBar` component, which is set to `event` mode, and use the `fileReference` as source. In `event` mode, the progress bar listens to the progress events of the source, in our case, the `fileReference`, which happens to dispatch progress events during the upload process.

```
<mx:ProgressBar  mode="event" source="fileReference"/>
```

So now your application provides visual feedback on the upload progress (see Figure 22.3).

Figure 22.3   Visual feedback on the download process.

But wait. There is more. Flex provides a way to select multiple files from one folder. This can be achieved by using the `flash.net.FileReferenceList` class instead of the `FileReference` class. The `FileReferenceList` list also provides a browse method that opens a file browser similar to what we've seen before, but this time, you can select multiple files using the shift and control keys. Upon selecting multiple files, `FileReferenceList` provides a `fileList` property, which is an array of `FileReference` containing a reference to the files you selected.

The `FileReferenceList` class doesn't provide an upload method; you need to take `fileList` and programatically upload the files one by one in the same way that we uploaded the files in the examples above. When all files are uploaded, you can consider the upload complete. This is not too hard to program and can be a nice usability improvement when you want to let the user select multiple files from the same folder. That is a common use case, and instead of having to pop open a file browser for each file to upload, the users can open the file browser once, select all the files, and press the select button and they are done!

But wait. There is even more.

Using Flex URLLoader Class to Upload a PNG File

As we saw, uploading a file to a Rails server is fairly straightforward. But for many applications, Flex can create images, for example, taking a snapshot using the built-in camera, or manipulating an image, or providing a product configurator where you could build your own T-shirt, shoes, or motorcycle, and you want to send the final product to the server. In this scenario, `FileReference` is not very useful since you don't have a file, but just an image in memory, so how can we send it to the server? To upload an image directly to our Rails application from Flex, we need to build a multipart request and send the binary data of the image using that request. Flex doesn't provide a MultiPartRequest class (yet), but it allows you to send binary data using the `URLLoader`. And, creating a multipart request is not too complex. So let's try it.

For our example, use the `mx:Image` tag to download an image from Flickr to your Flex application.

```
<mx:Image id="image"
source="http://flexonrails.com/book_images/butterfly.jpg" />
```

You can then add a button that invokes a method to upload that image to your Rails application by performing the following three tasks. First, convert the image to a PNG-formatted byte array, then create a multipart request, and, finally, upload the data using the `URLLoader` class. So let's look at the conversion to PNG. Flex provides the `mx.graphics.codec.PNGEncoder` class that takes a `flash.display.BitmapData` instance and enables you to get the image's content. That content is a `flash.display.Bitmap` instance, which in turn, exposes the `bitmapData` of the image and passes that to the encode method of the encoder. The following code does the conversion just described:

```
var pngEncoder:PNGEncoder = new PNGEncoder();
var bitmap:Bitmap = image.content as Bitmap;
var bytes:ByteArray = pngEncoder.encode( bitmap.bitmapData);
```

The encoder returns a `ByteArray`, which contains the bytes of the PNG image we want to upload to the server. Next, create a multipart request that contains three parts: the file name, the image data we created above, and the form submit action. We are moving the creation of that data to the `getMultiPartRequestData` method and will show the details later. For now, let's create the request we will pass to the `URLLoader`. For the request, you need to specify the URL and set the method to `POST` to ensure that the `create` method of the assets controller is invoked. Then you need to declare the content type as being `multipart/form-data` and specify the boundary string to use between each part. The boundary can be any string that doesn't conflict with the content of each part. Finally, you set the data of the request to be the multipart form data.

```
var request: URLRequest = new
URLRequest("http://localhost:3000/assets");
request.method = URLRequestMethod.POST;
var boundary:String = '----------Ij5GI3GI3ei4GI3ei4KM7GI3KM7KM7';
request.contentType = "multipart/form-data; boundary=" + boundary;
request.data = getMultiPartRequestData(boundary, 'asset',
'picture.png', bytes);
```

Next, let's create an instance of the `URLLoader` that is hooked to our usual completion handler. Note that you can also bind a progress bar to the loader as it dispatches progress events while executing the request.

```
<net:URLLoader id="loader" complete="completeHandler(event)"
dataFormat="binary" />
<mx:ProgressBar  mode="event" source="loader"/>
```

Now, to trigger the upload, just invoke the load method of the loader and pass the multipart request you created above.

```
loader.load(request);
```

Et Voila! Your PNG file is uploaded to your Rails server in the same way the `FileReference.upload` was working. Note we moved the creation of the multipart request data to the `getMultiPartRequestData` method, so let's look at it. Each part needs to be separated by a boundary string, which is also passed to the content type declaration. I'll let you check the whole method, then we will walk through the specifics:

```
private function getMultiPartRequestData(boundary:String,
   resourceName:String, filename:String, bytes:ByteArray):ByteArray {
 var lf:String = "\r\n";
 var part1:String =  '--' + boundary + lf +
   'Content-Disposition: form-data; name="Filename"' + lf + lf +
   '{0}' + lf +
   '--' + boundary + lf +
   'Content-Disposition: form-data; name="{1}[uploaded_data]";' +
   'filename="{0}"' + lf +
   'Content-Type: application/octet-stream' + lf +lf
 var part2:String =  '--' + boundary + lf +
   'Content-Disposition: form-data; name="Upload"' + lf + lf +
   'Submit Query' + lf +
   '--' + boundary +  '--'
```

```
var result:ByteArray = new ByteArray();
result.writeMultiByte(StringUtil.substitute(part1, filename,
resourceName), "ascii");
result.writeBytes(bytes, 0, bytes.length)
result.writeMultiByte(part2, "ascii");
return result;
}
```

For our file upload to work, we need to create multipart request data as a `ByteArray` with three parts where each part will be converted to bytes. The first part defines the filename and the fieldname; notice we use the `mx.utils.StringUtil.substitute` method to inject the filename and the resource name to use for the fieldname in the `part1` string. The substitute method replaces the {0} and {1} tag with the filename and resource name.

```
result.writeMultiByte(StringUtil.substitute(part1, filename,
resourceName), "ascii");
```

The second part is the bytes from the PNG image, and we can copy them directly to the resulting byte array:

```
result.writeBytes(bytes, 0, bytes.length)
```

The last part is a string specifying an upload form submission.

```
result.writeMultiByte(part2, "ascii");
```

This `getMultiPartRequestData` method simply follows what the W3C specification describes as required to perform an upload. This multipart format may sound a little cryptic, but try it out. It works.

Summary

As you can see, file and image uploading from Flex to Rails works very well, and we hope you soon find a reason to use it in your applications.

Index